Social Theory and Later Modernities

The Turkish Experience

STUDIES IN SOCIAL AND POLITICAL THOUGHT 9

STUDIES IN SOCIAL AND POLITICAL THOUGHT
Editor: Gerard Delanty, *University of Liverpool*

This series publishes peer-reviewed scholarly books on all aspects of social and political thought. It will be of interest to scholars and advanced students working in the areas of social theory and sociology, the history of ideas, philosophy, political and legal theory, anthropological and cultural theory. Works of individual scholarship will have preference for inclusion in the series, but appropriate co- or multi-authored works and edited volumes of outstanding quality or exceptional merit will also be included. The series will also consider English translations of major works in other languages.

Challenging and intellectually innovative books are particularly welcome on the history of social and political theory; modernity and the social and human sciences; major historical or contemporary thinkers; the philosophy of the social sciences; theoretical issues on the transformation of contemporary society; social change and European societies.

It is not series policy to publish textbooks, research reports, empirical case studies, conference proceedings or books of an essayist or polemical nature.

Discourse and Knowledge: The Making of Enlightenment Sociology
Piet Strydom

Social Theory after the Holocaust
edited by Robert Fine and Charles Turner

The Moment: Time and Rupture in Modern Thought
edited by Heidrun Friese

Essaying Montaigne
John O'Neill

The Protestant Ethic Debate: Max Weber's Replies to his Critics, 1907–1910
edited by David Chalcraft and Austin Harrington

Breeding Superman: Nietzsche, Race and Eugenics in Edwardian and Interwar Britain
Dan Stone

Unhastening Science: Autonomy and Reflexivity in the Social Theory of Knowledge
Dick Pels

Global America? The Cultural Consequences of Globalization
edited by Ulrich Beck, Natan Sznaider and Rainer Winter

Social Theory and Later Modernities

The Turkish Experience

IBRAHIM KAYA

LIVERPOOL UNIVERSITY PRESS

First published 2004 by
Liverpool University Press
4 Cambridge Street
Liverpool
L69 7ZU

British Library Cataloguing-in-Publication Data
A British Library CIP Record is available

ISBN 0–85323–888-X hardback
      0–85323–898-7 paperback

Typeset in Plantin by Koinonia, Bury
Printed and bound in the European Union by
Bell & Bain Ltd, Glasgow

To the memory of my mother

Contents

Preface

Currently, a debate on varieties of modernity occupies a central place within social theory and research. Within the conceptual context of this debate, this book aims to understand the Turkish experience as a particular model of modernity. In the light of current developments in the tradition of comparative-historical sociology, this book shows that an alternative to Eurocentric social theories is a perspective that accords a central place to the concept of varieties of modernity. The starting point of the book is the possibility of the emergence of multiple modernities, with their specific interpretations of the 'imaginary significations of modernity'. In this context, a critique of perspectives that reduce the modernization of non-Western societies to 'Westernization' emerges immediately. The assumed equivalence between the West and modernity is problematized through the themes of a plurality of histories, civilizations, modernizing agents and projects of modernity.

The concept of 'later modernities' developed in this book suggests a new approach to understanding and interpreting multiple modernities. It inspires renewed attention to the current state of the social world. The term 'later modernities' refers in particular to non-Western experiences that came about as distinct models of modernity, different from the Western European experience, in the absence of colonization. In this light, the present study questions two sorts of perspective, one of which argues for globalization and the other for localization. From this point of view, this book suggests that we need a social theory beyond the thesis of the clash of civilizations and that of the end of history. History has not come to an end, nor do the civilizations clash. And a perspective of later modernities, provided in this book on the basis of an analysis of Turkish modernity, constitutes a break with theories of convergence and divergence. Neither modernization theory nor the dependency school of thought is seen as desirable for understanding multiple modernities. By understanding Fukuyama as a theorist in the tradition of modernization theory, this book shows that his thesis of the end of history is untenable. The concept of later modernities suggests that there have been multiple ways to modernity and that those multiple ways give rise to multiple consequences. These consequences do not converge anywhere, neither under the label of liberal democracy nor under that of communist society. The multiple consequences of multiple ways indicate that history is far from coming to an end. This conclusion is reached through examining the importance of the plurality of civilizations in shaping human identity and practice. However, one should not conclude that the distinctions between people are purely cultural by eliminating political, economic and ideological differences, as Huntington (1997) does. In the light of the concept of later modernities I shall show that Huntington's thesis fails. This book argues that modernity plays a part in reducing oppositions between civilizations. Civilization is important for the creation of different modernities, but modernity does not allow civilizations to remain stable. In conclusion I stress that we need a theory beyond the thesis of the end of history and that of the clash of civilizations.

The Turkish experience is a particular modernization, an analysis of which is able to clarify the argument for varieties of modernity. The Turkish experience has so far been analysed only as a case of Westernization, but by analysing both civilizational patterns and modernizing agents in Turkey, this book suggests that Turkish modernity cannot be read as a version of the Western model. This conclusion is reached through examining Turkish history in terms of a 'singularization of culture', against the view that sees Turkey as a border country between the West and Islam. It is argued that the division between West and East is, in fact, irrelevant in the case of Turkey. The Turkish experience, as a later modernity, does not express a Western model of modernity, nor does it correspond to a 'pure' Islamic East.

This book first took shape during my doctoral study in the Department of Sociology at Warwick University, England. I would like to thank Peter Wagner for his supervision; his critique and comments provided me with an excellent opportunity for revising my perspective and I benefited greatly from the works he suggested. Some of the ideas in this book have been developed and presented in several workshops and seminars. To mention some of them, I gave a talk about non-Western experiences of modernity in a seminar on Advanced Social Theory at the University of Warwick and my thanks go to those participants who provided both critique and comments. Again at the University of Warwick, I presented a paper on the relations between Islam and modernity in the workshop on the Plurality of Modernities, organized by David Toews. In

Florence, at the European University Institute, I presented a paper on later modernities twice, first in the workshop on Varieties of Modernity and secondly in a seminar on European Modernity and Beyond, both organized by Peter Wagner. I am particularly grateful to Johann Arnason, Heidrun Friese and Peter Wagner.

The Theme of Varieties of Modernity

The theme of varieties of modernity, in its new form, has come to the fore at a time when the primary interest of social sciences is no longer the transformation of societies from tradition to modernity. Rather, in recent decades, social science has dealt with a 'new' phase of modernity, termed 'postmodernity', 'late modernity', 'high modernity' or 'liquid modernity' by diverse theorists. In this development, one element has been central to the theorizing of modernity: the fact that a notion of modernity has spread around the globe so quickly. As a critique of modernity or as a perspective on a so-called 'new modernity', postmodernism led some observers to pay renewed attention to modernity's current phase.[1] The debate on varieties of modernity could be seen as a response and a contribution to new theoretical developments regarding modernity.

Recently, several works have appeared treating the 'plurality of modernities' (see Arnason, 1997, 1993; Eisenstadt, 1996; Wagner, 2000, 1999a, 1999b). This shows that current events under conditions of modernity not only give rise to arguments between the defenders of modernity and postmodernists, but also make it feasible, for some critics, to employ the concept of varieties of modernity in the exploration of the contemporary social world. The debate on varieties of modernity, as a sociology of knowledge would show, is not an intellectual product that does not seriously consider the social, but rather, a reflection on the realities of the social world.

In the first place, it might seem surprising that the theme of varieties of modernity has come to the fore at a time when the end of crucial conflicts and tensions between societies has been largely celebrated, with an insistence on the 'happy ending' of the war between the socialist and the capitalist blocs (see, for example, Fukuyama, 1992). This, however, should rather be unsurprising, because the collapse of the Eastern bloc, contrary to widely shared assumptions,

1

indicated that 'convergence' was far from being achieved. Against those who argued that the collapse of communism marked the end of conflictual relations between human societies, it revealed that societies should be seen as distinct from one another. The realities of the social world failed to support the assumption that societies were converging. Two cases are of particular importance: the Islamist movement and the case of East Asian specificity, both of which played a crucial role in the emergence of the debate on varieties of modernity.[2]

The Islamist movement emerged at a time when the new world order was being prepared. Some Western writers were of the opinion that after the collapse of communism the major conflict was to be between the West and Islam. Islamic societies not only rejected the new North American and West European convergence but, at the same time, showed that they differed from the owners of the project of a new world order. First, in social science, the reaction of Islam was taken as showing that postmodernism's observation was convincing: Islam, it was assumed, resisted modernity and the West (Ahmed, 1992; Sayyid, 1997). This observation was intended to prove postmodernism's assumption of the end of modernity, rather than trying to understand the motivations of Islamist movements in order to open a discussion as to whether Islamic societies are modern too but in different configurations. In this respect, the concept of varieties of modernity can be used to argue that the Islamist movement is far from demonstrating how modernity came to an end, but it is rather the expression of the distinguishing features of 'Islamic modernities' (see Chapters 5 and 6 below).

The theme of varieties of modernity emerges in works on Japan and, to a lesser degree, on some other East Asian cases, for example South Korea. Japan was the first non-Western country to become a highly advanced modernity. The specificity of Japan, on the one hand, and the development of some other East Asian countries, on the other, has led some scholars to pay attention to the region (Eisenstadt, 1996; Arnason, 1997). Some of the following crucial theoretical questions arise from these studies on East Asia and, in particular, on Japan: if modernity is a Western project, how did East Asia, by keeping its civilizational distinctions, produce modernities without imitating or even having much contact with the West? What are the specific elements in these countries, particularly in Japan, that brought about very advanced modernities?

Taking Islamism and East Asia into consideration gives rise to the most crucial question: can modernity not be interpreted as having variations? In other words, can it not be argued that there are distinct modernities with their own specific interpretations of 'imaginary significations of modernity'?[3] It could be said that the above questions have played a great part in the emergence of the debate on varieties of modernity on which this study is built. Thus, this book is set in the conceptual context of the current debate on varieties of modernity by aiming to understand the Turkish experience as a particular model of modernity. So far I have briefly mentioned some realities on the social ground from which the debate about varieties of modernity stems. It is now necessary to discuss what this perspective signifies in terms of theory and research.

Most of all, the perspective of varieties of modernity should, in two respects, be able to show that modernity may no longer be read as a uniform progress towards final integration. First, modernity should be viewed as a phenomenon open to definitions and interpretations and as a condition under which conflicts and tensions are constantly at stake. This observation expresses a break with mainstream modernization theory, which emphasizes that an individual society should be understood as an integrated functional system (Parsons, 1971). Once modernity is seen to be unable to unify or integrate a single society, the 'universalization' of human societies under conditions of modernity must be rejected. Thus, secondly, modernity should not be understood as progress towards universalization. Modernity cannot end conflicts and tensions between social actors in a single society, nor can it end conflicts and tensions between societies and between civilizations. Modernity should not be viewed as a unifying phenomenon. It could be shown that there are different, even conflicting, interpretations of modernity that do not permit human history to come to an end. Both the concept of the integration of individual societies and that of the 'universalization' of world societies must be rejected, in order to elaborate a concept of varieties of modernity.

This perspective constitutes a break with Eurocentric theorizing, but it should also be noted that 'it is obviously incompatible with postmodernist positions' (Arnason, 2000a: 1). Rather than viewing a radical pluralism of lifestyles and cultural worlds as an indication of the failure of 'the project of modernity', the perspective of varieties of modernity should read the plurality of cultural worlds as an indication of the possibility of different interpretations of the imaginary significations of modernity.[4] This possibility could indeed make it plausible to talk about varieties of modernity. For this argument to be developed, the perspective of varieties of modernity needs to define the themes of its analysis as explicitly as possible. In other words, in what way this perspective could overcome a Eurocentric view of modernity needs to be shown explicitly. In the following outline, some of the most basic themes will be considered.

Historical Background

A study of varieties of modernity should question the universalistic perspectives of history, most importantly by portraying the plurality of histories, for example that of feudal Europe versus that of the centralized Ottoman Empire.

In this light, it can be argued that different historical backgrounds do not necessarily converge under conditions of modernity. In brief, an analysis of varieties of modernity is necessarily a comparative-historical analysis of modernity (see Chapter 2) with a rejection of evolutionary-universalist theories of history.

The Varieties of Modernizing Agency

The plurality of modernizing agents should be taken to be an important factor in the formation of different modernities. Because of historical and contextual distinctions, the agents of modernization differ from place to place. The conflicts causing change do not occur between the same actors in all places. For example, in feudal Europe, civil conflicts gave rise to the bourgeoisie as an important agent of modernization, whereas in the imperial-patrimonial Ottoman Empire, the central conflict emerged with regard to responses to the rise of the West, which gave rise to a new elite that produced the Turkish project of modernity (see Chapters 2 and 3).

The Multiplicity of Projects of Modernity

Modernity could appear in different versions because of factors that define the views of the agents of modernization. In this respect, it is important to insist on the fact that institutional spheres of modernity could be formed in different ways. Modernity does not explicitly define or found institutional spheres automatically. It is because of this fact that Western modernity aimed at imposing capitalist economy, liberal democracy, and autonomous individuality as universal and explicitly defined, closely linked, realities. Nevertheless, modernity was not understood in the same way in other parts of the world. It is possible, for example, to examine socialist modernity as a different configuration of the institutional spheres of modernity. Thus, the institutional spheres of modernity should be used to prompt questioning, critique and interpretation, so that an observation of varieties of modernity can become plausible (see Chapters 1 and 2).

Civilization

The perspective of varieties of modernity should no doubt consider the relation of modernity to civilization. All other themes within the perspective are indeed related to civilization. For example, a most important element in defining the views of modernizing agents is the civilizational legacy on which their projects are built. Thus, the analysis of multiple modernities is also a civilizational analysis (see Chapters 2 and 3).

The theme of varieties of modernity has come to the fore at a time when the concept of the nation-state seems to have lost much of its credibility. It should not be surprising that the perspective of varieties of modernity accords a central role to civilizational analysis. In other words, civilizational analysis concentrates on units of larger dimensions and of longer duration than single societies, and therefore questions the understanding of society as a self-contained nation-state (Arnason, 2000b). Furthermore, this civilizational perspective necessarily questions the idea of civilization in the singular – a product of the eighteenth-century European intellectual climate – so it is also necessary to argue for a plurality of civilizations (see Chapter 3). In brief, the idea of multiple modernities undoubtedly needs to consider relations between modernity and civilization so as to see whether civilizational characteristics are the peculiar dynamics that shape modernities (see Chapter 2). In terms of the civilizational characteristics of modernity, two scholars are to be considered: Shmuel Eisenstadt and Johann Arnason.

Eisenstadt, a prominent authority on civilizational perspectives, reads modernity as a new civilization, which is thought to come about because of the 'revolutionary' dynamics of modernity. The modern revolutions, according to Eisenstadt (1978: 177), by means of breaking away from the past, brought about the civilization of modernity. In contrast, Arnason does not view modernity as a separate civilization in itself. Rather, for him, modernity could be described as being both more and less than a civilization (Arnason, 2000a, 1997). In terms of the dependence of modernity on civilizational legacies, in the contexts in which it is present, modernity is less than a separate civilization; while it is more than a civilization in terms of global transformations (Arnason, 2000a).

In relation to the civilizational characteristics of modernity, this book sides with Arnason's view, but with a slightly different observation: modernity is understood as a human condition rather than as a separate civilization. Modernity could be seen as a human condition in that both opportunities and discipline confront people. In other words, modernity is a human condition that provides new opportunities, such as individual liberty, but the modern condition is also a disciplining condition. But this human condition does not define how people should live their lives, and it is important here to stress that modernity is not a separate civilization. Because modernity does not create a separate civilization, civilizations are important in terms of the shape of modernity. However, civilizations are not the only distinguishing elements of modernities; there are also 'cultural worlds', which may be able to produce 'different modernities' in the same civilization (see Chapters 2 and 3).[5] It may be useful to observe that some societies might distinguish themselves as civilizations, with insistence on their own particular traits (Turkey is a relevant case). As Friese and Wagner (2000) observe, any civilizational analysis may refer to 'cultural theorizing'. The study of varieties of modernity needs a 'cultural theory of modernity'.

A distinction between civilization and culture is necessary for showing that a culture belonging to a civilizational zone may particularize itself, thus producing a different modernity. However, when defined in this way, it becomes problematic: when culture is insisted on as a value system (as in modernization theory), it becomes difficult to explore social change. We need to pay further attention to culture, and it must be stressed that without 'social actors' no culture could produce a new world or a modernity in this respect.

The perspective of multiple modernities should view culture as open-ended and understructured, an imperfectly integrated complex of interpretive patterns (Friese and Wagner, 2000). Since culture is not strictly structured, its openness to (re)interpretations makes it desirable for social actors to bring about innovation. The agency of modernization needs to be considered in each case, rather than giving all our attention to macro-level socio-historical moments, as does Arnason (1997, 1993). No doubt, cultural patterns are not reducible to individual forms of action, but at the same time the capability of actors to create new meanings and new pictures of the world must be emphasized (Castoriadis). The creativity of action should never be neglected in analysing multiple modernities. In sum, the centrality of analysis of major socio-historical moments and civilizational/cultural frameworks should not be exaggerated, nor should the creativity of action be neglected.

I have outlined four basic themes for a sociology of multiple modernities. However, it should be emphasized that these themes are not strictly separable. Rather, there are relations between them that could be clarified as follows: historical background constitutes the most general category, and civilization concerns that against which modernizing actors define their projects of modernity. It should be clear that the four basic elements for a reading of varieties of modernity are not autonomous realms, but are interrelated in ways that could be dialectical, conflictual or peaceful.

The Concept of Later Modernities

An essential goal of this book is to question ethnocentric (Western) theories of modernity. More precisely, this book aims at problematizing present-day mainstream social theory, a product of Western experience, with the theme of varieties of modernity. For this goal to be achieved, it is argued that an immediate distinction in terms of varieties of modernity remains between the West and the East. The distinction has been developed as one between Western 'original' modernity and 'later modernities'. For historical reasons, Western European modernity has been termed 'original modernity', and modernities emerging in the East, including the Russian experience, 'later modernities'.[6] This distinction accepts that modernity emerged first in Western Europe, but does not privilege Western modernity as the only model of modernity. The understanding of modernity as being identical with the West is based on the assumption that because Western Europe, with its distinctive characteristics, produced modernity, so any other modernity necessarily based itself on the existing model. The concept of later modernities breaks with this view mainly by observing contextual distinctions and a plurality of projects of modernity in which the West has not served as the model of modernity for the East. Thus, the specificity of the West should no longer matter, or, in other words, the West should be seen as just another civilization among many.

In a broad sense, 'later modernities' refers to Eastern modernities, but more explicitly it observes those modernities that emerged in the absence of colonization. In other words, later modernities are those modernities that came about on the basis of 'indigenous projects' rather than being modernized by the dominant forces of imperialist, Western modernity, as in the case of Algeria. A later modernity is a modernity that does not belong to those countries whose developments are far from being 'autonomous'.[7] And more importantly, in order to be able to speak of a later modernity, it should possess elements that should be distinct enough to problematize the Western understanding of modernity (see Chapter 2).

The distinctions between Western modernity and later modernities are examined so as to argue that it is no longer tenable to view the modernization of non-Western societies merely as 'Westernization'. Rather, it is important to observe that self-questioning and self-problematization are the basic dynamics for societies in the transformation to modernity (see Chapter 2). And these self-questionings and self-problematizations are far from being mere outcomes of the rise of the West. An analysis should consider the fact that before the rise of the West there were already some tangible conflicts in terms of interpreting the world and the self in some Eastern societies – conflicts that mark the self-transformative capacities of civilizations and societies.

In terms of the theoretical direction of the concept of later modernities, the following points should be made. The perspective of later modernities argues against the convergence thesis developed by earlier modernization theory by indicating that modernity brings about 'tension-ridden' relations rather than being the integrating force of human societies. In other words, under conditions of modernity, conflicting projects of life contest one another, for instance the liberal Western interpretation of autonomous individuality versus the Islamic insistence on community. Nor is the concept of later modernities in agreement with neo-modernization theory. The social theory of Beck, Giddens and Lash (1994) is a neo-modernization theory in that it emphasizes autonomous individuality, the contrast of modernity to tradition and the rationalization of culture (culture as an expert system). Emphasizing both new individuation and globalization, the theories of Beck, Giddens and Lash and others are indeed continuous with earlier modernization theory.

Nor is dependency theory considered to be a desirable perspective in applying to the exploration of later modernities. Emerging as a critique of modernization theory, the dependency perspective surprisingly read diverse socio-cultural formations as being one and the same (Amin, 1976). In understanding the world according to a centre–periphery dichotomy created by Western capitalism, the dependency perspective saw the West as shaping the entire world. Therefore, it is, in an important sense, a Eurocentric theoretical observation. World systems theory is also continuous with that tradition. By adding the notion of semi-periphery, it observed the world as one socio-historical system, that of the capitalist world economy (Wallerstein, 1987).

On the other hand it is important to note that this book does not side with perspectives that reduce modernity simply to the imperialist power dimensions of the West (Said, 1978). This book recognizes that Western modernity has possessed imperialist characteristics, but it also proposes that modernity is much more complicated than a mere power struggle. The interplay of different dynamics should be investigated, for example that between power and culture. Nor is a theory of civilization as unitary and self-defined taken to be important (Huntington, 1997). The latter perspective sees civilizations, as unitary and self-defined, causing conflicts that leave no room for peaceful relations between civilizations.

A perspective incorporating the notion of later modernities does not aim to argue that multiple modernities are necessarily antagonistic. Although one of the goals of this book is to argue that in order for a society to represent a distinct version of modernity a 'different' interpretation of modernity is unavoidable, there is still a way of showing that since these societies exist as part of the same human condition – larger than a separate civilization – they also share some basic characteristics. Here, I wish to state that the modern condition, which provides opportunity but also disciplines human beings, may not be viewed as subject only to civilizational contexts, but in itself changes civilizational characteristics. It is important in this respect to note that this book argues neither for globalization nor for localization.

Convergence and divergence need to be considered not as necessarily antagonistic but rather as dialectical partners in the formation of modern histories. Neither is the one achieved nor does the other establish itself as the rule of human nature. Neither universalism nor particularism may be seen as providing the full condition of human life. From the beginning, human practice and identity have always followed 'local' patterns. In this respect, it is unavoidable to submit to the truth: world interpretations and cultural worlds are subject to a radical pluralism. In other words, in this world, in different places, human beings have built different socio-cultural worlds with no project able to assimilate the differences between the world interpretations. However, human beings are always aware that all other human beings belong to the same species. There have always been commonalities among human cultures regardless of how distinct they are.

The concept of later modernities does not understand the existence of different modernities as an indication that there is more conflict among modern societies than in previous ages. In contrast, it is held that modernity, as an actor between civilizations, has a strong capability to reduce oppositions between societies and between civilizations. However, the concept of globalization is rejected, precisely because it is understood as the diffusion of Western civilization. In fact, for the achievement of a 'universal' world, the recognition of 'different' modernities is an unavoidable condition. Globalization will not be achieved on the basis of a specific world-interpretation, but would have to set procedural foundations, which do not read the world as an integrated unity. By this I mean that a global world would need a mentality that would recognize all societies as equal but not as unified on the basis of a specific civilization, namely the Western desire to unify the world around its own values.

The Specificity of Turkey

Turkey has often been assumed to be a bridge between the West and the East, more specifically a bridge between the Islamic East and the Christian West. This already observes a particularity about Turkey's 'civilizational patterns'. Some have seen Turkey as having the capacity to bring Islamic East and Christian West together in order to reach a consensus in ending historical conflicts (see Berkes, 1976). However, to assume that Turkey might play such a role is problematic, in that Turkey has never aimed to achieve full membership either of the Islamic East or of the West. As history shows, the Turks did move culturally towards the West, while never leaving Anatolia, Islamic since Turkish conquest. And thus it has been assumed that, in modern times, Turkey could move further towards the West, and hence that a non-Western 'identity' could be Westernized (see, for example, Eren, 1963).

It should not be surprising then that Turkey has recently been regarded, in contradictory terms, as an image of the East in the West and as an image of the

West in the East (Stokes, 1994). This perspective aims to show us that as a contradictory image of significance and power Turkey is a 'European Islam' on the one hand, and a 'modernizing context' in the Middle East, on the other. Despite the many apparent reasons to regard Turkey as presenting the West in the East and the East in the West, the reality should be opened to discussion. The Islamic East found by Westerners in Turkey does not correspond to a 'pure' Islamic East; and the West found by Easterners in Turkey may not typify the actual West. This is to say that the division between West and East is, in fact, contested in the case of Turkey.

It is, first, in this respect that Turkey presents an interesting case for a civilizational perspective. One cannot grasp the meaning of Turkish modernity by observing Islamic civilization as the context from which Turkish modernity stems.[8] Nor can one investigate the Turkish experience by analysing its connections with Western civilization as the determining force. Rather, the 'singularization' of culture requires interpretation. In referring to the singularization of culture, I mean to stress that views that aim at understanding the Turkish experience by using a West–East division as the basis of their analyses necessarily fail because Turkish modernity may be seen as a case in which the opposition between West and East is not determinative. Turkey's position may be understood by observing the fact that Turkish culture singularizes itself. In the formation of the Turkish world in Anatolia, Islamic civilization played a very important part, as indeed did the West. However, what is necessary is to examine the capability of a single culture in terms of its 'openness' to the 'outside world' and in terms of its success in coping with the 'outside world'. Borrowings from other cultures, however, should not lead one to conclude that the culture under investigation is not 'authentic' or 'distinct'. On the contrary, it is possible to show that this sort of culture could display a distinct experience due to its assimilation of borrowings.

No doubt precisely because of this feature, Turkey is often observed as neither becoming truly Western, nor easily locatable in Islamic context. The second important feature of Turkey regarding the theme of varieties of modernity is the interpretations of the experience. The crucial question should not be whether Turkey could become a Western society. The starting point of previous works on understanding the Turkish experience, therefore, needs to be problematized. Kemalism has been emphasized, by both critics and supporters, as aiming to Westernize Turkish society. It is hardly relevant to ask whether a society already considered as belonging to the West was Westernized or not. This sort of question could be posed in the context of an Eastern country, such as India, that did not have close relations or connections with the West before the beginning of modernization. Although the West has played a part in the formation of 'Turkish identity' for much longer than is commonly assumed, Turkish modernity needs further interpretation, because it does not express a Western modernity. It is thus a basic argument of this book that it is important to explore the Turkish experience as a different form of modernization rather than viewing it merely as a case of Westernization. Certainly, to an extent Westernization plays a role, but this is not abnormal for a society that long ago made its entry into the West. Nonetheless, it is not Westernization that makes Turkey a specific case.

Thirdly, it has often been stressed that Turkey is the first modern Muslim country and that it provides a model of modernity for other Islamic societies. In this respect, a most crucial point in terms of the centrality of the Turkish experience to the theme of varieties of modernity may be demonstrated. It has been argued by many observers that Islam does not separate the worldly and the divine orders and that, therefore, the way to modernity is undermined (Gellner, 1992). Islam is known not to separate religious and political authority and it is therefore assumed that Islam does not permit a republic or a democracy to emerge (Watt, 1988). Islam is also viewed as a communitarian model that does not credit 'individuation', one of the distinguishing elements of modernity. The Turkish experience, however, does not prove these observations.

In analysing the relations between Islam and modernity it is essential that both are seen, not as clearly defined and fixed entities, but as open to interpretation. Not only are there different modernities, but there are also different Islams. Turkey in this respect presents a very interesting case that casts doubt over the view of Islam as incompatible with modernity. Contrary to those observers who stress the unified nature of Islam (see, for example, Ahmed, 1992), the Turkish experience indicates that there is more than one Islam. Thus, it is urgent to pose questions to those observers who regard 'Islamism' as a rejection of modernity.

Fourthly, the Turkish project of modernity, Kemalism, needs to be reviewed in order to understand whether it merely replicates European Enlightenment. It is in this respect that the Turkish experience deserves attention as part of an analysis of modernity as existing in different versions. An interpretation of Kemalist modernity shows that there is not just one project of modernity, but many. Emerging from an imperial state system, which was in no way feudal, the proponents of Kemalism did not look for agents of Western modernity on whom to model themselves; rather, the actors were already at hand for modernizing Turkey. Kemalism was built according to a specific historical-cultural legacy. Its protagonists did not have the same notion of modernity as did Westerners. Not only the historical background but also the individual actors who formed Kemalism imagined a modernity that was different from the Western model. It is clear that Kemalism needs to be interpreted as a different project of modernity.

So far, I have briefly outlined the specificity of Turkey in relation to the debate on varieties of modernity: civilizational particularity, the Westernization–modernization argument, the Islam–modernity debate, and the existence of a different project of modernity. I shall now identify what I specifically aim to examine in order to understand Turkish modernity as a different model.

In mainstream social theories, modern society is viewed as a self-contained society, the nation-state (see, for example, Giddens, 1985). The transition from 'local' characteristics of human practice to wider network relations and the transition from the imperial state tradition and from small, regional polities to nation-states are assumed to mark the beginning of the modern epoch. However, this study, though accepting the centrality of the nationalization process to the modern experience, reads modern society as not completely breaking with civilizational legacies and does not take the nation-state to mean a harmonious collectivity.

Recently, it has been argued that national boundaries and the centrality of the nation-state are being undermined by the forces of globalization and localization. Turkey seems to present an interesting case in that, on the one hand, it seeks to achieve full membership of the European Union while, on the other hand, inside its borders a problem shakes its integrity: that of the Kurdish question. These situations need an interpretation that considers civilizational and cultural characteristics and that observes the question of 'ethnicity'. Thus, the nationalizing process and its aftermath in the Turkish experience are analysed by considering the themes of civilization, culture and ethnicity (see Chapter 3).

The redefinition of collective identity and its symbols could be equated with a social revolution (Eisenstadt, 1978). This has a special place in the Turkish case. Not only is the 'invention' of the nation important for the present purposes, it is also important to note distinctive characteristics of one nation-building process among others. Turkish modernity shows, for example, that it is not necessary to privilege previous history and traditions in the nationalizing process, but rather that history could be used 'negatively'.[9] Or, for example, there do not always exist imperial institutions for political and economic development, as assumed by Arnason (1998, 1997). Rather, the Turkish experience presents a unique pattern of transition from an imperial state system to a non-imperial one. The case of Turkey is, for example, quite different from that of Japan, which became an imperial centre in East Asia where it had played a marginal part before (Arnason, 1997). A different picture of nation, nation-state and civilization is observed, showing how the concept of nation could be differently interpreted (see Chapter 3).

Integrating and differentiating forces must be analysed in relation to the specific configuration of a later modernity. The social world comprises three main spheres: polity, economy and culture. It must be stressed that these spheres do not necessarily determine one another, nor does one of them shape the entire social world. This makes the concept of the plurality of modernities plausible; for example, the industrial economy does not require a standard, universal culture. There is every reason for social actors in different contexts to form these spheres in different ways. Hence the Turkish experience involves its own specific configuration of state, economy and society (see Chapter 4). For example, efforts to impose social integration were much less successful in Turkey than in Japan.

Legitimizing aspects of the integrative forces and the self-interpretation of differentiating forces are examined to show that the Turkish experience paints a specific picture of the tensions between liberty and discipline. Interpreting some elements as either integrative or differential forces has led, paradoxically, to both discipline and liberty: Islam was an integrating element of society for the 1980 military coup, while the attempts at Islamizing society caused new conflicts between different parts of the same society. The relations between the state and society and between the state and the economy need to be considered as key indicators for a different configuration of modernity. It is, therefore, argued that in the Turkish case the differentiation and integration of the state, society and economy deserve special attention; for example, the modern state and the capitalist economy are much more closely integrated in the Turkish experience than in the West (see Chapter 4).

In terms of the current debate on Islam's relations with modernity, Turkey presents a particularly interesting case. This is so for two reasons. First, with its particular project of modernity – Kemalism – Turkey has often been noted as a model of modernity for the Islamic world. Secondly, however, the Iranian Islamic revolution posed a serious question of whether Kemalism had failed because Iran had, to a large extent, chosen the Turkish way of modernization as its model for development. By analysing modernity and Islam in Turkey, this book argues that in terms of relations between Islam and modernity, a different interpretation is needed (see Chapter 5).

So long as critics continue to operate with 'idealized' versions of Islam and modernity, concrete historical experiences cannot be explored. Previous work on the relations between Islam and modernity tends to display a sense of Islam as being either incompatible or fully compatible with Western modernity. But it must be considered that neither Islam nor modernity can be shown to be a fixed and unitary way of living. Thus, by analysing modernity and Islam as projects open to interpretation, this book questions modernist, postmodernist and traditionalist perspectives on Islam.

Gender relations play an important part in shaping the entire social world, and it is in modern history that the place of women in society has become a crucial debate, giving rise to some disputes over goals in modern history. More perhaps than in any other social setting, it is in Islamic societies that the question of women's role in society occupies a special place in relation to understandings of the 'good life'. A distinguishing characteristic of Turkish modernity can be analysed by considering the 'female question' (see Chapter 6). Some of the most crucial tensions between Kemalist modernity and Islam relate to women's liberation and the Turkish experience expresses this characteristic explicitly. By examining the central place of this issue in the Turkish experience I show how both Kemalism and Islamism, as opposed projects, have seen women as key actors for the achievement of their ambitions. The analysis of Islamist veiled women is taken to serve as a cornerstone both for understanding Kemalism's distinction among other projects of modernity, and for understanding how the question of women's role in society has reasserted itself in the current phase of Turkish modernity. The chapter also serves to show that the Islamist movement should not be understood as a rejection of modernity. The two basic goals in analysing Islamist women are, first, to show that different modernities display different characteristics because of differences in historical background, and secondly that Islamism deserves attention beyond being viewed simply as fundamentalism (see Chapter 6).

The lessons to be learned from the Turkish experience serve as theoretical conclusions to the theme of varieties of modernity (see Chapter 7). In other words, the main findings of this analysis of a 'later modernity' point to the usefulness of a concept of varieties of modernity. However, a conceptual analysis of modernity needs to be completed before attempting to investigate the crucial distinguishing points of later modernities and the specificity of Turkey. Therefore, I begin with an analysis of modernity as a 'field of tensions' (Chapter 1). Once an argument is made for the plurality of modernities, a view of modernity as 'open' needs to be developed. To this end, I shall analyse modernity as a field of tensions that cannot be assumed to be a singular entity or an a priori project of the good life. In analysing modernity, we must observe the process of differentiation, but, contrary to the claims of modernization theory, this differentiation does not end with (final) integration. Since the concept of modernity is open to interpretation, the project of modernity cannot be completed once and for all. The 'openness' of modernity is unavoidable, although we need to ask how far it is open. The consequences of openness require a new understanding of modernity's current phase.

CHAPTER 1

Modernity as a Field of Tensions

In current debates on modernity, theoretical and practical issues predominantly centred on questions about modernity's lifetime are increasingly prominent. In recent social theory, in particular, the central concern, in relation to the current phase of modernity, seems to be whether modernity is 'exhausted', or an 'unfinished project'. Modernity is theorized as either dead or incomplete. Despite the oppositions between these two theoretical perspectives, both sides have understood modernity as a coherent whole.[1] The central point that apparently drives these two theoretical perspectives is the view of modernity as coherent.

Modernity is explained as representing, over the last two centuries or so, a single, uniform, coherent world (see Kolb, 1986). It is for this reason that modernity can be conceptualized either as reaching its end or as an incomplete project. These are the conclusions to which 'postmodernism' and 'modernism' have thus far arrived. In other words, reading modernity as a coherent whole has led some observers, on the one hand, to conclude that modernity is a dead end, while, on the other hand, others reconstruct modernity as the incomplete project of Enlightenment.

It is no accident that the debate between Habermas and Lyotard has become a vantage point for observing the tensions between the two central theoretical perspectives on modernity in recent years. These two central theoretical perspectives, namely postmodernism and the defence of Enlightenment modernity – perhaps better termed 'the defence of modernism' – agree as to the coherence of modernity, despite their different understandings of this coherence. It is because of this assumed coherence of modernity that both perspectives have attracted supporters. In other words, it is easier to argue for or against modernity when modernity is viewed as a coherent whole. Once modernity is defined as a totality – rational, ethical and so on – it becomes impossible to think about

15

any alternative perspective beyond its rejection or defence. If modernity is thought of, for example, as a totalizing logic on the basis of instrumental rationality, one would have to view it as a dark age, causing the Holocaust, Hiroshima, Chernobyl, and so on. This is so because if an epoch is fundamentally unifying, and unified, there cannot be any way of talking about it other than marking it as a destroying or dehumanizing epoch. But, on the other hand, if modernity is read as an emancipating project, one would have to celebrate it as the bright age, bringing about liberty, universality, social security, and so on.

From the above considerations, one could readily argue that modernity is a double-edged phenomenon. In fact, both dark and bright 'stories' have taken place in modern history. Certainly the Holocaust, ethnic cleansing and other such atrocities occurred, but so did 'development'. A Japanese person who lost his loved ones in Hiroshima might view modernity as a collapsing, dehumanizing epoch. A Turk, whose national history (up to the emergence of the Turkish republic) was marked by nothing else than war-making, might understand modernity as a humanizing epoch. Does this reveal that modernity is a double-edged phenomenon? Not quite. Viewing modernity as a double-edged phenomenon would also imply holding a coherent vision of life. In other words, dividing modernity into its dark and bright sides could easily lead some to conclude that modernity is a totalizing epoch, with the 'dark' aspect viewed as a by-product of the 'bright' aspect or vice versa.

Rather than seeing modernity as a coherent whole or even as a double-edged phenomenon, we should understand it as multiple: 'Our horizons are multiple, and that multiplicity is not itself a collection or a system appearing within some last unified horizon' (Kolb, 1986: 241). Kolb does a wonderful job of showing that, beyond Hegel and Heidegger, there are other ways of understanding modernity. In other words, one does not necessarily need to be an adherent of the Enlightenment, nor does one need to be a priest in order to judge modernity from a Christian point of view. To the observers of modernity as a coherent whole, it may be said that 'many of the cultural, political, and scientific forces in our lives move in competing and often inconsistent directions' (Yack, 1997: 130–31).

It is possible, using the concept of multiplicity, to argue that neither is it possible to complete the project of modernity once and for all, nor does modernity come to an end. Indeed the current conditions under which we live are modern, that is, modernity is the only world we have (see Berman, 1983). This could be demonstrated, for example, by the computerization of society: in contrast to Lyotard's view, the computer could be seen as characteristically modern, in that it possesses an extraordinary capacity for information storage. But, on the other hand, current conditions also point to the impossibility of completing 'the project of modernity' once and for all. This could be demonstrated, for example, with reference to the unfeasibility of 'communicative action' producing 'consensus': in contrast to Habermas's theory, there is no convincing reason why communicative reason should be able to resolve the problems of 'divided modernity'.

To talk about multiplicity is to say that modernity is a field of tensions (Arnason). It is a field of tensions, because it is open to interpretation. In other words, because modernity is open to interpretation, tensions are constantly at stake. There is no single, agreed idea of modernity, but there is space that provides opportunities to interpret 'imaginary significations of modernity' in different ways. And this space is 'culture', or 'language', or 'history', whose importance is no less than that of 'power' or 'rationality': 'There is too much culture, language, and history we find ourselves always already within, and we do not have the one necessary logical sequence to make things transparent to our gaze' (Kolb, 1986: 267).

To make this argument plausible, the openness of modernity to interpretation must be discussed. In other words, if it can be shown that modernity can exist in different versions, the idea of modernity as a coherent whole will fall. In the next section, the openness of modernity will be argued for by means of two questions. First, what is it that makes modernity a 'field of tensions'? I shall argue that it is modernity that makes it possible for radically plural world-interpretations to express themselves openly. And it is for this reason that the field on which human beings live necessarily becomes a field of tensions. More precisely, because conflicting views of life find shelter under the conditions of modernity, tension-filled relations between human beings become unavoidable.

The second question I shall ask is: how far is modernity open? I want to show that arguing for the openness of modernity does not mean that modernity has no distinguishing characteristics. First, the openness is itself a distinct feature of modernity. Traditional world-interpretations would not be able to bear that sort of openness. This is why it is argued that the modern age is the bloodiest in history. Secondly, the argument should show the limitations of modernity's openness. In other words, what is possible and what is not possible in the interpretation of modernity must be clearly shown; for example, whether ethnocentrism is (or is not) modern.

In the third section, an argument in terms of the contemporary phases of modernity will be proposed, reminding us of the consequences of modernity's openness. These consequences create new possibilities for the further opening of modernity. Certainly, changes in the recent history of modernity are precisely due to its openness and these changes give rise to new theories of modernity. Finally, it will be shown that modernity's openness to interpretation makes necessary a concept of the plurality of modernities. In other words, I shall argue that modernity is alive, but that 'the project of modernity' cannot be completed once and for all.

The Openness of Modernity

The perspectives that see modernity as a coherent whole need to be questioned. It has been assumed that modernity as a programme of the Enlightenment has shaped our lives.[2] In other words, modernity is 'conceived as a closed monolith, incapable of being shaped or changed by modern men' (Berman, 1983: 24). It seems that modernity is viewed as being an external force to human beings' lives. That is, whatever has occurred is supposed to be the outcome of modernity as an external force. The way in which a historical age has come to be understood as a singular, fundamental phenomenon is certainly striking. However, modernity could be regarded as an open-ended civilizational horizon, under the conditions of which human beings have the freedom to develop their own life-perspectives. This shows that modernity cannot be defined as a fixed way of life. However, modernist and postmodernist theories alike have supposed modernity to be an explicitly defined way of life. Here we shall consider totalizing perspectives of modernity using an alternative argument, showing that modernity is an open, rather than a closed, way of life.

Totalizing theories of modernity stem from the belief that modernity is driven by unilinear progress, absolute truths, the rational planning of ideal social orders and the standardization of knowledge and production (Harvey, 1990). This constitutes a grand narrative of the 'hidden reality' of modernity, which emerges because modernity could in no way be understood as a unifying phenomenon on the basis of any single, fundamental feature. To begin with, the multiplicity of the cultural-political programme of modernity should be stated. Given the fact that the concept of modernity is strongly linked to the belief in the shapeability of the social on the basis of totalizing reason, plurality and a diversity of ideas and practices in current history makes many observers curious as to whether modernity has exhausted itself. More precisely, modernity is theorized as the strong belief in the ability of society to create an orderly world. Therefore, current modernity is viewed as coming to an end due to its failure to end disorder (Bauman, 1992). However, as Eisenstadt (1999: 67) has argued, the 'multiplicity of the modern cultural and political program attest[s] to the fact that modernity was continually perceived, within wide sectors of societies, as being [an] "endless trial"'.[3] This shows that, from the very start, multiplicity has been situated in modernity. As well as the totalizing tendency, there has also always been the other side that emphasized multiple ways of life, the pluralistic view of modernity. Totalistic perspectives denied the legitimacy of different interests, different conceptions of the good life and the common good, and emphasized the totalistic reconstruction of society through political action. In contrast, the pluralistic view saw a plurality of interests and different conceptions of the good life as being legitimate (Eisenstadt, 1999). In this respect, it is also important to note that both the totalistic and the pluralistic views included variations. For example, national socialism, liberalism, fascism, Leninism, Kemalism or Islamism cannot be viewed as pieces of the same programme of modernity. On the contrary, they are radically different answers to the question of how a (good?) modernity should be formed. This suggests that danger and opportunity do not come about as a result of just one conception of modernity; there are multiple conceptions of modernity.

Tensions between reason-centred totalizing views and pluralistic conceptions of culture have always been at stake in human history.[4] In modernity, these tensions have become radicalized. Tensions over the place of reason in human life, the construction of nature and society and individual autonomy reach their high point under conditions of modernity. These tensions could, in brief, be categorized as the tension between liberty and discipline (Wagner, 1994). In other words, attempts are made on the one hand to synthesize different rationalities and values on the basis of the totalizing concept of instrumental rationality, while, on the other hand, it is modernity that provides the opportunities for different ways of life to be lived. However, to view modernity as a tension between liberty and discipline might seem to prove that modernity has two central features around which all other features and experiences could be unified. In saying that the tensions could be categorized as those between liberty and discipline, I certainly do not mean that all the different programmes of modernity (socialism, liberalism, Islamism and so on) are merely tiny pieces of the same grand narrative. In contrast, I do think that both liberty and discipline have variations that cannot be reduced to one another.

From the above argument it can be seen that multiplicity is rooted in the cultural programme of modernity. Eisenstadt (1999) shows that the search for an ideal social order, political theories of modernity, the accountability of rulers, and traditions of representation and representative institutions, have occupied central places in the programme of modernity and are derived from different sources: axial civilizations, feudal Europe, antiquity and beyond. Tension is rooted in modernity: since different, even conflicting, perspectives are brought together in the programme of modernity, tensions are unavoidable. For example, while representative institutions refer to plurality – local cultures, different interests and so on – the rediscovery of ancient Greek philosophy could be taken to refer to a belief in an absolute truth. Or, for example, the belief, derived from axial civilizations, in the possibility of reforming the social may not fit coherently with the accountability of rulers. Therefore, the openness of modernity derives in one important way from the fact that modernity is unable to unify irreconcilable perspectives; rather, multiple 'centres' of power, culture and rationality find their homes within modernity, and this in turn maintains modernity as an 'endless trial'. Since modernity is conceived of as a goal of political action, it is important to examine this.

Since, in the political programme of modernity, the rights to freedom of speech, to membership of associations, to protest against existing socio-political orders and to participate in social movements are basically granted, multiplicity in ways of life cannot be eliminated. Although oppression is sometimes a by-product of the modernizing process, multiplicity is an inevitable consequence of modernity. Autocratic, totalitarian methods of reaching modernity have certainly included dehumanizing processes but, nevertheless, because even these totalizing methods included the possibility of variation, modern human beings could not be forced to be identical. To illustrate this case, we can consider one of the goals of modernizing projects: creating a 'reading public' (Anderson, 1991). This was paradoxical: once a reading public emerges, it becomes impossible to master this public in any fundamental way. This reading public could criticize, question and, most importantly, alter existing orders. As a contemporary case, Islamism could only be considered possible under conditions of modernity, because the 'reading public' came about in Islamic societies as a consequence of modernization: it is only as a result of the education provided by modernity that current Islamists are able to question existing social orders on the basis of a specific interpretation of Islam. If Islamists had not been educated by modernity, it would not have been possible for them to reach the sources of Islam, Koran and Sunna, in order to construct a political project. This can be taken as an important example, showing that modernizing attempts, no matter how totalizing, were unable to eradicate multiplicity. The recent computerization of society is in fact an extension of the realm of the reading public, rather than a successor to it, and does not therefore imply the end of modernity.

However, arguing for multiplicity in the modern experience does not imply that modernity is the equivalent of a peaceful democracy. In the modern experience, there have always been clashes between different sectors of society. That is to say that since it has been possible for diverse people to interpret modernity in different ways, the world has witnessed the bloodiest clashes between people. In some societies, in some periods, the brutality of the state has caused uprisings and, in other societies, civil wars have broken out. This, however, is not to argue that modernity can only cause disaster. What could be argued is that, under the conditions of modernity, human beings have more possibilities of destroying one another as well as of reaching understanding. Modernity cannot be reduced to brutality because it is within modernity that it is possible to fight against brutality. Under the conditions of modernity, human beings have opportunities to defend their cultures, gods, moralities and so on. If it is modernity that makes oppression possible, it is also modernity that makes it possible for people to fight back.

The tensions and clashes in modernity exist because it is in modernity that there is a multiplicity of centres of power, culture and rationality. Tensions have been attributed, by critics with different perspectives, to various dualist divisions – between state and society, between the bourgeoisie and the proletariat, between the elite and the people. However, regarding tensions, conflicts and clashes, the importance of *multiple* centres should be considered. There is an irreducible pluralism in civil society, in the bourgeoisie, in the working class and in the state. To illustrate this case, I shall now briefly take some socialist perspectives into account. It cannot be argued that, as an alternative social order to capitalism, there is a standard, agreed, socialist perspective on society. In fact, there is a radical plurality within socialist critique of liberal modernity. Is 'socialism' Leninism, or Maoism; is it the perspective of Enver Hoxha or that of Stalin? Is it possible to merge Althusserian Marxism with the Marx of Gramsci? Or is it right to see the Chinese model as identical to the Soviet one? These questions show that there is no one centre that could universally represent the socialist perspective. The working class cannot be seen as a coherent whole. It is therefore impossible to regard the working class as a universal subject that would bring about universal revolution. Equally, there is radical pluralism within capitalism. As we shall see, for example, the Turkish interpretation of capitalist economy cannot easily be seen as a mere version of Western capitalism.

Another way of seeing modernity as open to interpretation is to recognize that different spheres of human activity cannot define one another, nor can one of them shape the entire social world. Modernity, in other words, can be imagined and projected in different versions based on the elements that define the views of modernizing agents. Human spheres do not define one another automatically (for example, industrial economy does not require a universal culture). In other words, modernity itself does not found institutional spheres in one fundamental way. The openness to interpretation, importantly, lies in the fact that economy, polity and culture remain radically open to discussion and dispute. This could be taken as a basic reason why, in modern societies, the dispute over the socio-political system never ends in consensus. As Bernard Yack (1997) shows us, socio-economic and cultural practices do not fit coherently together, and viewing modernity as a coherent whole, in this respect, is a type of fetishism: 'The fetishism of modernities is a "social myth" that unifies many-sided social processes and phenomena into a single grand objective' (Yack, 1997: 6). Precisely for this reason, liberal Western modernity aimed at imposing the capitalist economy, the nation-state and autonomous individuality as universal, explicitly defined, and closed realities. But one could examine socialist modernity, for example, as a different configuration of the institutional spheres of modernity. It is important here to stress that there is no single space that is essential to our lifeworld, because no single realm or activity could completely define our relations to the world.

However, arguing for the openness of modernity does not mean that modernity does not possess unique features. On the contrary, because modernity is unique in human history, it is open to different definitions – in other words, the uniqueness of modernity is due to its openness. But this openness derives mainly from two basic features of modernity: rational mastery and individual autonomy. It might be objected that totalizing theories of modernity are also based on the understanding that modernity is about rationalization and individuation. It is true that totalizing theories of modernity have been dependent on the cultural and political programme of 'original modernity', and that this programme's goals could be summarized as the achievement of mastery and autonomy. First, as Turner (1992: 13) notes, 'the most popular totalizing theory of modernity rests upon a distinction between religion and science, understood as not sets of social practices but as rival, societal ordering principles'. In other words, modernity is often assumed to be the emancipation of reason from revelation (see Kolakowski, 1990), discrediting religious argument in favour of rational analysis. This understanding was to give rise to totalizing perspectives on modernity that claimed that 'being modern is being rationalized' (Shils, 1981: 290). Following this, one could believe that modernity leaves no space for ways of relating to being other than rationality (Heidegger, 1977).

Secondly, the principle of individual autonomy is another source for totalizing theories of modernity. The individual is thought to attain his or her self-consciousness, identity and autonomy by separating himself or herself from nature, God, society and history (Berger, 1977). In other words, 'modern man' needs to be a self-determining subject (Marcuse, 1941). And for this to be achieved, it is necessary to possess the power of reason. Therefore, identity formation is understood as a process of actualizing the potentialities of an individual on the basis of reason – and this is a totalizing process. However, while observing autonomization and rationalization to be central processes in modernity, there is still a way of showing that modernity is not a totality or a totalizing project. Autonomy and mastery are interpreted differently by different subjects, which marks modernity as a field of multiplicity. The point here is that the openness of modernity must nonetheless include the aims of mastery and autonomy. That is, in order to talk about modernity, rationalization and autonomization are processes that must unavoidably be considered.

Looking at rational mastery and individual autonomy, we must always consider the fact that these two imaginary significations could have radically different meanings to diverse people in the world. The question that has to be answered in this respect is this: how is it possible to interpret 'rationality' and 'liberty' in different ways? It must be stated that modernity is possible in different configurations, because imaginary significations are to do with 'cultural worlds' which cannot be unified on the basis of rationality. So, if different ways of relating to the world cannot be unified through rationality, rationality has to be related to these cultural worlds in new and different ways. In other words, 'traditions' relate themselves to the world in new ways with the advent of rationalization. Since there are different cultures, there are different rationalities too. What then must be said is that, in the experience of modernity, rationality and culture or Enlightenment and romanticism cannot and should not be contrasted. Rather, it needs to be observed that both culture and rationality are important partners in modern experiences. Thus, the scope for interpreting rationality and liberty in different ways is determined by the cultural world. In this respect, it is necessary to note that the space for interpretation of modernity could be explained by a view that takes civilization, culture, history and creativity seriously. Emphasizing the importance of civilization and/or culture also means considering historical background. That is, history is a powerful factor that provides some possibilities for human action and, since the historical backgrounds of societies are different, those possibilities are diverse. For example, a Turk may find some possible answers to present-day problems by considering Turkish history, but these answers may not relate to the problems of another society because of the different history of that society. Finally, omitting to consider creativity of action would render modernity simply a product of tradition. However, modernity is a new phenomenon that cannot be fully viewed as an expression of previous history. Hence, a dialectical reading is needed in understanding the possibility of different interpretations of the imaginary significations of modernity, namely mastery and autonomy.

The plurality of ideas and practices is an unavoidable outcome of the possibility of interpreting autonomy and mastery in different ways. In some recent social theory, the plurality within the current phase of modernity is seen as implying the end of modernity. We shall see, however, that the plurality of ideas and practices in the current phase of modernity should be seen as a consequence of the openness of modernity rather than as an indication of its end.

The Consequences of Openness

The current stage of modernity seems to be full of contradictions, full of dualities, full of tensions. For example, on the one hand, globalization is promulgated by many observers as the most powerful force in our lives (Beck, 1992; Giddens, 1991). Yet the emergence of 'new communities', on the other hand, is seen as celebrating the right to be different (Delanty, 1999). The 'end of history' thesis seems to have convinced some, on the one hand, yet religious, nationalist and ethnic movements show the unfeasibility of the very same thesis, on the other. This multi-faceted recent era could be seen as a reflection of modernity, in which tensions, contradictions and dualities express themselves more openly than in previous eras.

It is because of the existence of multiplicity in the experience of modernity that distinct, irreconcilable, conflicting lifeworlds have been competing. This, however, does not imply a break with modernity, because any one of these lifeworlds is strongly tied to the basic characteristics of modernity. More precisely, since the actions of inhabitants of different lifeworlds take place under the same conditions that have provided spaces in which their voices can be heard, it becomes difficult, if not impossible, to go beyond modernity. In his critique of modernity Alain Touraine (1995: 92) wrote that 'because modernity is a critical rather than a constructive notion ... a critique of modernity must be hypermodern'. Modernity is not unified and includes multiplicity. Therefore, it is neither necessary nor possible to work outside modernity. In other words, if totality is far removed from modernity, it is possible to work within modernity. This is what has been happening, rather than modernity being broken down. In what follows, I shall consider some of the most important events of the current era to illustrate that we live under conditions of modernity.

In sociological terms, it is important to look at the position of 'the social' under current conditions. Tribes – emotional communities – seem to be replacing 'mass' society, seen as a devil by Adorno and Horkheimer (1988). This current situation causes pessimistic perspectives rather than optimistic ones. It is seen that unlimited relativism makes it very difficult, if not impossible, for people to live together. This assumption is based on the belief that the emergence of new communities means the celebration of the right of 'difference' against 'universalism'. In other words, the 'universal subject' is assumed to have collapsed (Delanty, 1999). However, it is necessary to ask whether a universal subject really emerged and lived previously. For example, it was considered until recently that the Enlightenment brought about universal subjects.

Apart from the rise of relativism, there is another occurrence that seems to be very important: classical social theory's society – the self-contained society of the nation-state – is in question (Giddens, 1985). Globalization is thought to be undermining self-contained societies. This idea has indeed been responded to by social theories. Recently, there has been a growth in literature on globalization. It could be argued that this literature succeeds earlier modernization theory by viewing the current phase of modernity as a Western success (Giddens, 1991). In other words, globalization is held to be the diffusion of Western civilization. Thus, we notice that in analysing the current stage of the social world these two perspectives, namely coherent and divergent visions of life, seem to point to a contradiction. If there is a rise in importance of local cultures but at the same time a move towards globalization, then it would not be right to call recent processes either the victory of the convergence thesis, proposed by modernization theories, or the reversal of 'society' by small communities. Rather, if there are many-sided processes in the current stage of modernity, this could be understood as a consequence of the openness of modernity.

An important characteristic of the current social world is the irreducible plurality of cultural worlds and world-interpretations. This is indeed an outcome of the modern experience, precisely because only multiplicity, situated in the heart of modernity, could have brought about that sort of plurality. From the beginning there have been plural world-interpretations in modernity, but recently this plurality has revealed itself more clearly, particularly by means of new telecommunication technologies. Since modernity is not unified or totalized, it has been possible for diverse worldviews to work within modernity. It may precisely be said that a most powerful argument against postmodernism is that, since modernity is an open rather than a closed way of life and since it is multiple rather than monolithic, it is neither necessary nor possible to work outside modernity. In other words, since 'critique' is situated within modernity, attempts at changing life should not be viewed as attempts to end modernity.

Since postmodernism has understood modernity as a totalizing epoch grounded on rationality, a diversity of ideas and practices is taken to mean that a new social condition begins: the postmodern condition (Lyotard, 1984). Therefore, the irreducible plurality of ideas and practices has been linked to the meaning of postmodernity (Bauman, 1992). The increase of plurality in ideas and practices, however, could be analysed as referring to the extension of modernity or the increasing openness of modernity. By this I mean that the number of social actors does increase; we can no longer hope to see a centre in society capable of shaping the entirety of social relations. This means that the recent era of modernity reveals more clearly that modernity has never been a world with an ordering, shaping centre. Rather, it has been open to disputes over the common good or the good life. The current conditions indicate that the conceptions of modernity of social elites are now subject to questioning more than ever before, because new modern actors from all corners of society demonstrate what they understand by modernity. Modernity is in the streets more than ever before, now that modernity no longer refers only to the programme of the Enlightenment. This situation is due to the recent increase of possibilities and choices open to human beings. What should be emphasized is that modernity is on endless trial, because no centre provides the content for social life (Kolakowski, 1990). If modernity is viewed as a reversal of substantive rationality (Weber), being driven rather by formal rationality, then it could be argued that modernity has an inherent capacity for multiplicity because the content of social life is to be created by the diverse actions of diverse people. In other words, because modernity does not define how social life should be experienced, it is the work of people to create their own life perspectives. It must be clear that modern society is not a coherent whole, but rather a conflicting diversity of world-interpretations indicating the radical pluralism of cultural worlds. This is to say that the creation of life perspectives is not free from cultural worlds and meanings. Therefore, Weberian pessimism could be overcome, in that substantive rationality which gives meaning to life is not replaced by a formal, instrumental rationality governed purely by the goal of 'efficiency'.

What is more astonishing in some current social theories is that the distinctive features of non-Western cultures are seen as indicators of the beginning of postmodernity (Delanty, 1999; Gülalp, 1998; Smart, 1990). However, the recognition of the openness of modernity to interpretation not only enables us to understand how the plurality of ideas and practices increases in Western modernity, but also, importantly, results in increasing attention being paid to the perspective of varieties of modernity on which this study is built.

The discussion so far must indicate that there can be no completable project of modernity once and for all. The multiplicity of histories and of ways of life, the plurality of people's relations to the world, show that a universal conception of modernity cannot be argued for convincingly. People who are diverse are not convinced by theories aiming to show the feasibility of attempts to complete the 'project of modernity' once and for all. An American would not like a European's conception of history; a Japanese person would not agree with the view that reduces modernity to a Western project; a Russian would not support the 'end of history' thesis because of its overly Western orientation. To find a way to analyse the current conditions of life, we must adopt a theoretical perspective that could show us the plausibility of the concept of varieties of modernity.

First of all, in order to analyse current conditions of modernity, and in particular to analyse *multiple* modernities, it is necessary to show that there is

26

no equivalence between the West and modernity. If we look at social theories of modernity, it is noticeable that they are mostly attempts at providing an explanation of the 'uniqueness' of the West. From Hegel to Marx, and from Weber to Habermas, a central concern has been to achieve an explanation of how capitalism – 'modernity' – emerged 'only' in the West.[5] In its process of identity formation, the West seemed exceptional to these theorists, and it was this 'exceptionality' that, for them, made modernity identical with the West.

Since the making of the modern epoch first took place in the West, until very recently there was no serious questioning of the purported superiority of the West. The modern political revolutions – American and French – and the Industrial Revolution emerged in the West. Since then it has been assumed that modernity is equivalent to the West, enabling a distinction between the (superior) West and the (inferior) rest. What then became a common view of the West developed by Westerners, but also agreed on by many Easterners, is that the West presents a particular way of life of advanced civilization when compared with the 'rest' (see Hall and Gieben [eds.], 1992). It is unsurprising, then, that Heller wrote that 'modernity, the creation of Europe, itself created Europe' (Heller and Feher, 1991: 146). Hence, modernity must be Eurocentric. Thus 'the project of modernity' could be understood as nothing other than the expression of European identity formation.

By arguing for the unique place of rationality in European civilization, then, Weber (1958) was also arguing for the exceptionality of the West, grounded in its universalizing logic. Therefore, the distinction between modernity and tradition was shown to be the distinction between the West and the rest.[6] First, the idea of civilization in the singular (see Arnason, 2000a) needed to be developed in order to mark the West as 'civilized' against the 'uncivilized' rest. This was certainly motivated by nothing other than the aim of achieving a self-identity for the West. However, it was this 'other-descriptive' identity form-ation that gave rise to Eurocentric social theories of modernity. In brief, modernity emerged as an outcome of a specific civilization; therefore, if the 'rest' wanted to join modern life, they would have to Westernize first. Thus, the West not only represented a particular way of life – democratic, civilized and so on – but it also had the historical mission of 'universalizing' human societies.

In truth, however, modernity, like any other epoch, should not be identified with a particular geography, civilization or ethnicity.[7] The theme of varieties of modernity provides most important opportunities for showing this clearly. In the next chapter, I shall argue that the assumptions of modernity as equivalent to the West must be problematized so as to show the tenability of the concept of varieties of modernity. I shall argue that the modernization of non-Western societies cannot be viewed merely as Westernization or Europeanization. The concept of 'later modernities' will be introduced in order to show that existing social theory, a product of Western experience, is not adequate to analyse non-Western experiences of modernity.

CHAPTER 2

Social Theory and Later Modernities

Most social theorists of modernity have been Westerners, precisely because social theory is a product of the Western experience of modernity. Despite the fact that diversity has undoubtedly played a constitutive part in the formation of human history, the convergence thesis has gained a prominent place in social theory, because of the claims for Western modernity as the 'universalizing phenomenon' of human societies.[1] For the same reason, modernity has been associated with the advent of 'Reason', bringing human beings to believe that it is possible for different cultures to live harmoniously together. Viewing modernity as identical with Reason gave rise to entirely Western-based ethnocentric social theorizings.[2] For example, Weber's (1958) analysis of the uniqueness of the West influenced many later social theorizings. A key element of modernity, rationality, was seen as unique to the West; therefore, what seemed to be at stake was the weakness of the East in giving shape to history.

However, rather than producing simple convergence, Western modernity also led to the radicalization of dualities, oppositions and differences. In order both to support its own self-image and to legitimize its imperialist ambition, the West constructed the East as 'uncivilized' (Said, 1994).[3] Western modernity saw colonization as a crucial method for shaping the world in its own image. By means of colonization, in the eyes of Western imperialists, civilization would be brought to Eastern countries, while, in fact, this imperialism was distancing the West further from the East. In stark contrast to Western hope, a different reality was to emerge: some societies were not manageable along the lines of Western modernity. Self-defensive liberation movements came about as reactions to Western rupture: Western modernity challenged its others in the name of civilization, but this challenge created reactions that resulted in different modernities.

We can therefore understand the rise of the West as a double-edged pheno-menon. On the one hand, the West killed some of the particular traits of the countries it colonized but, on the other hand, the rise of the West played a part in the radicalization of some Eastern self-questioning and the problematization of Eastern countries' worldviews, despite the claim of dependency theory (which emerged as a reaction against modernization theory) that the rise of the West had a totally negative effect on 'underdeveloped' countries (see Amin, 1976). I consider that there were already some tangible, conflictual develop-ments making way for new and different understandings of the world in some Eastern countries before Western modernity challenged them. However, it is important to see Western modernity's contribution in terms of a 'radicalization of dualities', which was a basic precondition for inventive modernizations. Thus, the crucial point is that Eastern modernizations cannot simply be understood as Westernization, precisely because self-questioning in the East did not allow actors of modernization to imitate the Western model of modernity, even though the rise of the West played a part in the radicalization of this self-questioning. Indeed, since social diversity is a precondition of human actions bringing about social change, the emergence of modernities in the East was unavoidably different.

Against the convergence thesis, then, it can be argued that the challenge of Western modernity radicalized oppositions and differences. Different modern-ities came into being partly in order to counterbalance the West. Japanese modernity, for example, has received some attention from Western scholars (Arnason, 1997; Eisenstadt, 1996), since it has been able to compete with the West in terms of economic power relations. But the Russian experience was an 'extreme other' or an opposite modernity which created the long period of the Cold War (Arnason, 1993). However, these different experiences of modernity have not been conceptually considered. Current social theory needs to be problematized because it is to a great extent invalid for the analyses of these different modernities. It should be seen that there are imaginative processes within other experiences of modernity beyond the imitation of Western modernity.

Modernization theory, emerging in the 1940s (and re-emerging in the 1990s), conceptualized modernization as both a Westernizing and a homo-genizing process: modernization makes societies more like one another; in other words, the world becomes a global village (Roxborough, 1979). However, since modernization theory derived its theoretical basis from Western European and North American experiences, it was unable to explore unique historical cases (see Nisbet, 1969). Since modernization theorists saw modernity and tradition as antithetical, their perception was that there was always something wrong in the East.[4] The imitation of the Western model of the social world was seen as the only possible means by which the East could join the 'good life'. This theory proved unable to understand the East.[5] In the 1990s, however, this perspective reasserted itself, this time in terms of 'reflexive modernization', 'globalization', the 'consequences of modernity' and so on. The language, however, is the same: 'modernity is a western project' (Giddens, 1991: 174); 'models of modernization have been western models' (Turner, 1999: 4); 'the end of history [is] the universalization of western liberal democracy as the final form of human government' (Fukuyama, 1989: 4). These views inescapably fail, because they argue for a convergence thesis while divergence poses itself as an unavoidable consideration. A perspective that identifies a plurality of modernities is therefore more tenable than one based on concepts such as globalization or Westernization.

In terms of an argument for varieties of modernity, an urgent distinction remains between the West and the East. This should be conceptualized as the distinction between the 'original' Western model and 'later modernities'. The concept of later modernities reflects historical difference: since they are *later* modernities, they cannot be the same as earlier versions. In other words, later modernities are different interpretations of the world. Historically different beginnings bring about different modernities, and different contexts do not permit modernizing states simply to imitate the Western model of modernity. As an alternative to Western modernity, there is not one later modernity, but multiple later modernities; for example, those of Russia, China, Turkey and Japan. Although they share some basic features, for example the fact that reactions against Western domination played a significant part in their emergence, their specific contexts meant that they differed from one another too. For example, all these experiences saw the strong state as the main agent of modernization, but their interpretations of the good life differed.

Because of these contextual differences, current (Western) social theory is inadequate to analyse later modernities. How, for example, can we explain why, in the Turkish experience, liberating women was a most important project of the transition to modernity? In the Western context, the 'female question' was situated within an already existing modernity, whereas women were regarded in Turkey as particularly important agents in the *formation* of a modern society.[6]

Proposing the concept of later modernities requires answering two unavoidable questions. First, what makes these modernities different? This question should be answered by seeing historical background, cultural context, modernizing actors and projects of modernity as central elements. In analysing later modernities, first of all, the specificities of historical and cultural context must be taken to be particularly important elements. How human beings understand themselves and how they relate themselves to the world are points that should be analysed in conceptualizing modernities. Collectivities shaped by their own norms, values and rules do not interpret modernity in the same way as Westerners do: historically different contexts cannot come to be one and the same. This is a response to globalization theory: for instance, in Giddens' terms, the radicalization of modernity means the globalization of modernity (Giddens, 1991). This perspective simply re-emphasizes the convergence thesis, which, as we shall see, is inadequate. Secondly, the specificities of modernizing actors and their projects should be taken into account, since no civilization or history can give rise to modernity without creative social actors and their projects. It must be emphasized that the relations of modernizing actors to the historical backgrounds and civilizations of their respective societies may be conflictual or peaceful, but are necessarily dialectical. For example, a project of modernity in an Islamic society could be defined by actors in opposition to Islamic civilization. However, over time, this project of modernity enters into dialectical relations with Islamic civilization, which might change some of the central features of the actors' perspectives – as, indeed, the project could alter some of the central features of Islamic civilization. Both the cultural context and the specific modernizing projects will produce modernities in Islamic societies that differ from the Western model of modernity.

The second question is this: do different modernities simply mean that different parts of the world stand against one another more than ever before? This question should be answered by emphasizing the relation of modernity to civilization. Modernity alters some of the basic conditions of civilizations and thus it is able to play a part in reducing the opposition between civilizations. In this respect, it is important to look at the relations between 'modernity', 'tradition' and civilization. 'Tradition' does not refer to any specific civilization, but to a human condition existing across many different civilizations. Likewise, in modern times, multiple civilizations continue to exist and modernity is an actor between them. By means of this second question, I also aim to show that, contrary to Jean Baudrillard's proposal, the 'nihilistic' worldview is not appropriate.

The Challenge of Western Modernity and Responses To It

In one way, modernity is an antagonism-creating force; the 'radicalization of dualities' is a crucial business of modernity. For example, the tension between social classes dramatically increased in nineteenth-century modernity and this could be seen as a first, powerful indication of modernity as a many-sided phenomenon. A significant amount of attention was paid to this antagonism, particularly by Marx. However, modernity was creating another antagonism outside its own birthplace: the challenge of the West to the rest of the globe.

Until the emergence of modernity, there was no remarkable distance between Western Europe and other geographical locations. There was no criterion for placing the West above other places. Technologically, no geography had a distinct position that was 'unreachable'. Some technological differences between places could be found, but there was no geographical 'rupture' in modernity's sense. By radicalizing the dichotomy between nature and humanity, modernity forged a great distance between the West and other geographical places: Western Europe seemed to be the unreachable geography of the time.

Western modernity was bringing about tensional dichotomies. First, human beings' war against nature was radicalized by the advent of science-oriented technology. Secondly, a growing antagonism between the bourgeoisie and the proletariat developed. As a consequence of these developments, Western modernity gave rise to two opposing groups of countries: industrialized metropolitan and non-industrialized colonial and semi-colonial countries. Within the modern experience, military power played a crucial part, although this has rarely been considered in socio-historical analyses.[7] For Western militaries, advanced technology provided easier access to other parts of the world: it was by means of war that Western modernity began to challenge other civilizations. Thus, colonization entered the history of modernity as a violently divisive process.

The East, the old world, was confronted by the powerfully destructive forces of the modern West. Western military power was not easily overcome and so old powers were forced under the rule of Western domination. Western imperialism aided the further development of Western countries, which thereby became ever more distanced from the East. Western modernity shook the East; Eastern cultures began to lose a sense of their own history and identity, and this situation led to their becoming split and conflict-ridden (see, for example, Sheyegan, 1991). But, in turn, this splitting was to awaken the East.

Modernity radicalized an essential contradiction between civilizational places and, in particular, between the East and the West. It shook Eastern civilizations, aiming to recreate them as stabilized entities. Already existing disputes were radicalized by the challenge of Western modernity; for example, the tension between civilian bureaucracy and the *ulema* (Islamic scholars) in the Ottoman Empire became more noticeable when Western modernity challenged the Empire.

Modernity has been understood as a universal system by most Western observers. The emergence of modernity is seen as a radical break with history, with Reason at its core. Since Reason is claimed to be completely independent from the cultural world, modernity has been seen as a universal project; the keys to modernity are universalistic norms. Enlightenment-centred theorizing proposes that modern society is constructed by equal citizens; that is, individuals who liberate themselves from serfdom by means of rationalization and freely form a collectivity. In this representation of modern society, there is no room for cultural difference, and it is precisely for this reason that modernity is taken to be universal. When human beings achieve autonomy in the world and mastery over the world, and when these free and rational individuals form a society, this collectivity can no longer be taken to be 'particular'. Thus, it comes as no surprise that modernization theory did not wish to deal with unique experiences.[8] Clearly, this perspective pushes historicizing and contextualizing out of the analysis of modernity. This is why modernization was regarded as a process of the global diffusion of Western civilization (Offe, 1987).

Crucially, however, the Western challenge helped agents in 'backward' countries to radicalize their self-questioning. A historic force, the rise of the West, helped 'backward' countries to create a search for a self-transformative capacity. In relatively powerful countries, in particular, radicalized self-questionings began when Western modernity problematized indigenous understandings of the world. This must be called a dialectical power of modernity: it was due to these self-questionings that other modernities came to enter history. The Ottoman Empire is an appropriate starting point for analysis of this process.

The decline and subsequent collapse of the Ottoman Empire can be understood in relation to the emergence of modernity in the West. However, modernization of the Turkish world also began during the same era because the Empire took stock of Western modernity's achievements and advantages. Until the challenge of Western modernity, the Ottomans did not have a serious problem in terms of their identity; in their minds they were the masters of the world; the Empire represented advanced civilization. The Ottoman Empire was indeed a powerful empire, which even threatened the heart of Christian Europe, twice capturing Vienna. It was the Empire's status as a centre of power that led to a sense of superiority over 'others'. In the Middle Ages, the poor and 'backward' societies of Western Europe were the pupils of the Islamic world, whose centre was the Ottoman Empire, in medicine, mathematics, chemistry, astronomy and philosophy. Therefore, Europe of the time had almost nothing to offer to the far more advanced Ottomans. However, the centre of power shifted to Western Europe with the emergence of modernity. During the eighteenth and nineteenth centuries, the Ottoman state – both the civilian and the military elites – was obsessed with one question: how to save itself. A world power was shaken and this shaken power was, for the first time, forced to consider its shortcomings. It is no surprise that the self-questioning began within the military, which was the central force within the Ottoman state. Although reforming the military did not enable the Ottomans to 'catch up' with the West, it was the first step towards radical institutional change.

The rise of the West posed unforeseen questions to the Ottomans: should the West be recognized as a power? Were the Ottomans themselves no longer capable of governing the world? These questions could best be thought of as a search for a new definition of the Ottoman Empire. It is no surprise that Islamism and Westernism, as well as Turanism to an extent, came to be important paradigms in the nineteenth century. Historians have largely argued that Westernism was a progressive ideology, while Islamism was reactionary (see Lewis, 1996). However, it must be held that both of these agendas were concerned with the redefinition of the Empire; both of them came about as responses to Western modernity's challenge. So long as the Empire was perceived to be Islamic, there could be no question as to whether it functioned according to Islamic rules. However, when things went wrong, Islamic actors argued that what was needed was a 'true' Islam; it was hoped that Islamism would keep the Ottomans apart from the West. It was difficult to maintain this argument, however, because Islamists also agreed with Westernists that the Empire was in a backward position. Islamists proposed that 'authenticity' could be maintained while, at the same time, a modern infrastructure could be created. This would be a difficult task; modernity is not likely to be fully based on the 'origins' of a country or culture. Westernists also went too far; they found Islam to be an element that was blocking development. They even came to regard the Western domination over the East as inescapable reality, and did not give sufficient importance to autonomous development. This was problematic because the creation of a powerful modernity requires significant autonomous development.

Western modernity, then, forced the rest of the world to become modern. Once modernity confronted the Islamic East, there were two choices for Islam: either to submit to the rule of modern countries or to fight against Western modernity with the aim of creating its own modernity. Against observers who argued that it was possible to reject modernization, it must be said that, either way, Eastern countries had to become modern. Those countries (such as India) that were colonized could not, as a consequence, escape from the conditions of modernity; others, such as Turkey, achieved modernity without coming under the rule of Western imperialism. But there were only two options: either autonomous modernization, or modernization by foreign domination. A self-defensive movement was the only way to resist the hegemony of the West and this way necessarily opened up a road to modernity. In order to analyse potential examples of later modernities, then, we need to consider whether the country in question succeeded in autonomous development or whether the modernization process was characterized by foreign domination. To explore this situation we need a civilizational perspective.

Japan, a powerful modernity, Russia, an 'extreme other', and Turkey, provider of a model of modernity for Islamic countries, could be taken as three important cases in this regard. None of these countries can be easily defined in terms of its civilizational context. Japan, in Arnason's (1997) analysis, could not be subsumed under Chinese civilization but rather included elements from different civilizations, and it was this context that facilitated modernizing processes in the development of Japan. Turks were neither exactly members of Islamic civilization nor of Western civilization. They were included in the East in the eyes of Westerners, whereas for Easterners they represented the West. This could explain why it was easier for Kemalists in Turkey than for agents in other Arabic countries to develop a project of modernity. Again, Russians struggled to choose between being Easterners and Westerners; they could be taken as being neither proper Occidentals nor Orientals.[9] It is when civilization cannot be clearly defined that it becomes more possible to bring about innovation. If a country is taken as a full member of, for example, Islamic 'tradition', 'development' could be difficult because it would need to be compatible with that tradition. It is also important that these three countries achieved modernization without coming under the rule of Western domination. Perhaps it is the case that these cultures neither present strong resistance to innovation nor could be assimilated.

To resist colonization by the West, then, it was necessary for Eastern countries to develop their own modernities. It is important to recognize that different interpretations of modernity are always possible due to cultural differences, even though the idea of modernity is imported from the West. Even if we acknowledge that modernizing agents in the East are influenced by Western ideas, it must be recognized that their specific historical contexts did not allow them to interpret modernity in the same way that Westerners did. Astonishingly, however, when differences in later modernities recently began to be noticed, some observers were ready to call these experiences 'postmodern' (see, for example, Smart, 1990; Gülalp, 1998). Countries such as Japan have been seen as being capable of combining tradition and modernity to a greater extent than the West and, for this reason, observers see later modernities as postmodern (see Delanty, 1999: 97). In fact, these countries have always retained their differences from Western modernity, but because they are only now being recognzied by Western theorists, they are called postmodern.

Self-defensive modernizations thus brought about 'different' later modernities. Culture needs to be considered as a decisive element in creating space for different interpretations of the dual imaginary signification of 'mastery' and 'autonomy'. It must be argued that there is no clearly defined, standard modern culture. If there were, it would have to be accepted that modernization precisely means the global diffusion of Western civilization. But this is not the case. Modernity does not reflect a separate civilization (Friese and Wagner, 2000; Arnason, 1997) and thus cultural-civilizational contexts provide some spaces for interpreting rationalization and individuation. Furthermore, it must be considered that autonomization and rationalization can never be taken as unique to the European Enlightenment: ideas of autonomy and mastery can be found in other civilizations. It is due to this fact that different elements in later modernities have played decisive parts. Buddhism, for example, had a place in the modernizing experience in Japan, while in other Buddhist traditions religion did not contribute to the modernization process as such. In the case of Turkey, Islam played a unique role in the emergence of modernity, though tensions were high. Again, the 'unquestionable' nature of the state in the Turkish and Russian traditions caused, in Turkey, a politically projected experience of modernity and, in Russia, the experience of state-socialism. Therefore, against modernization theory and the world-systems perspective, I would insist that particular forms of modernization rely on particular civilizational and historical contexts and on the possibility of different interpretations of mastery and autonomy.[10] In brief, it could be argued that social practices appear to be shaped by meanings and beliefs as much as by rationality and/or by power.

My argument here might appear to be putting too much emphasis on divergence. To show that this is not case, I shall consider whether the existence of later modernities suggests that different parts of the world cannot communicate at all. The Western thesis (that modernity is universal) created its antithesis (later modernities) and, dialectically, a relative synthesis seems to be occurring: the West and the East have begun to come closer. The power of modernity needs to be seen: culture is important for the creation of different modernities but, in turn, modernity does not allow cultures to remain unchanged. We shall see in the next section that culture can no longer be seen as 'authentic' and that it cannot be seen as an integrative sphere of modern society. Nor should culture be taken to be simply shared values, because otherwise it would be synonymous with social structure.

Modernity as an Actor between Civilizations

Since modernity is not a separate civilization (Arnason, 1997), but rather a human condition, different civilizations share some of its basic elements – modernity is to some extent globalized. Distinct human identities and practices can still be remarked, but modernity does not permit societies to maintain fully their traditional cultural values. Although there is every reason for societies to form different modernities, one condition remains: modernity cannot be simply a product of a particular culture. Once a society modernizes, it becomes difficult to retain its previous cultural context. This is because modernity is not compatible with stability; in modernity, culture is no longer stable and homogeneous. Culture therefore cannot be viewed as an integrating sphere of modern society. There needs to be a dialectical reading of this cultural agenda: a specific culture creates a specific modernity, but this culture is no longer homogeneous; rather there are different interpretations of the world within a single collectivity.

East and West being different historical phenomena, each refuses to be subsumed by the other. However, they encounter each other because it is no longer possible for either to remain locked in its traditional contexts. When cultures enter modernity – albeit *different* modernities – their traditional cultures are altered. A rupture occurs in each modern experience and, therefore, it becomes difficult for any culture to maintain its uniqueness, despite the fact that there is also a cultural continuity in each case that makes modernities different from one another. It is precisely due to this dialectical occurrence that a dichotomy has recently arisen in social writings, that of localization and globalization.

Within modernizing periods, the ambitions of actors of modernization and contextual realities clash. Modernizing state elites have proposed a development that uses advanced modernities as a model, but the ultimate goal is not to catch up with the West; it is, rather, to bring about a more developed version of modernity. In this respect, state elites have the opportunity to learn from an already experienced modernity, that of the West. However, when a state aims to follow that model it encounters a historical/contextual resistance to it. In other words, the historical/civilizational context makes it almost impossible for non-Western countries to imitate the Western model. Elites encounter their own socio-historical ground. This is why later modernities are all different, but it is also the case that modernizing society undermines cultural uniqueness to a considerable extent. In brief, history is an important factor in interpreting the meaning of modernity, and 'history' here represents the civilization against which modernizing actors define their projects. Therefore, a project of modernity is subject to a civilizational context, but the project is also able to alter some central features of that civilization.

Later modernities can be analysed as based on state-centred political projects, in the first place. The Japanese Meiji state, the Leninist Soviet state and the Kemalist Turkish state, as major agencies of change, made strenuous efforts to create more powerful modernities than the Western one. While aiming to bring about development, these states learned from the West; however, they had to oppose it, for two reasons. First, if they did not stand against the West, they would become dependent on it. Secondly, to move people towards development, a dichotomy was assumed to be necessary: modernity, in this respect, is about the radicalization of an insider–outsider duality. Uniqueness, therefore, became a very important concept in later modernities; for example, the Turks were taken to be the creators of civilization in Anatolia. In the process of modernization, the 'original' characteristics of the nation need to be emphasized by state elites, who generally invent them. However, this indicates the reality that, to a considerable extent, modernization undermines uniqueness.

In terms of the loss of 'traditional culture' in later experiences of modernity, the formation of a society or a nation is a central process that must be considered. Nationalizing or standardizing practices and identities have several purposes. Gellner (1964) claimed that nationalization and modernization need each other, especially for creating the networks required by industrialization. Although this view seems true for the Western experience, it cannot be held to be the case for later modernities. When the nation-building processes began in later experiences, industrialization or industrial economies were not present. The nation was not built because the industrial economy required it, but because collective action towards industrialization was an immediate need.

For the autonomy of the country, state elites imagined that the collectivity should know its own creations and traditions. This 'imaginary' was needed to create the nation on behalf of which the remaking of the social world was thought to be possible. Here we can apply Anderson's (1991) concept of 'imagined communities' to define the goal of state elites in later modernizing societies. In later experiences, it is not at all the case that the nation is a community that tends to produce a state of its own, or that a modern society requires integration and that this is to be found in the idea of nation. In stark contrast, the state creates the nation for the sake of autonomy against colonizing Western modernity. Collective action is needed for this ambition to be achieved, and the collective actors should think in terms of national development. To bring about this imagined community, actors of modernization must invent 'traditions' that are either revised versions of existing ones or completely new. The aim is to create a modern society, as a 'bounded collectivity', on the basis of 'political' projects. A nation is created by means of a nationalist ideology, which requires the alteration or even loss of unique local cultures.

Breaking away from older structures of the lifeworld is achieved by means of the standardization of practices and identities. Local cultures – ethnic or religious – are destroyed by the power of the new framework for integrating society, the nation-state. A common language and 'high' culture are imposed on the entire population by means of nationwide mass education. This process is supported by urbanization as a product of industrialization. Gellner's distinction between low and high cultures provides a useful perspective here (Gellner, 1983). Already existing distinctions between the high culture of the state elite and the low culture of the rest of the population are radicalized with the aim of socializing low culture into high culture. In this respect, the notion of the 'invention of tradition' is particularly helpful for understanding how the authenticity of culture is destroyed. Urban or high culture is therefore imposed on the community. This process is exemplified by the following two cases.

1. Industrialization and Islamic civilization. The development of an industrial economy requires female labour. When women begin to become visible in the economic sphere, it can no longer be easily held that men have the right to marry more than one woman. The dependence of women on men in traditional Islam is altered by means of the participation of women in the economy. And when gender relations are altered in an Islamic society, the wider social world cannot remain unchanged, because women's participation in the public realm was unfamiliar in traditional societies. Established rules, values and norms therefore face a challenge: with the emergence of different understandings, culture becomes increasingly heterogeneous and less coherent. For example, in the Islamic East introducing a car to the wedding ceremony could lead to two opposing views on the relation of people to the world. The car could be resisted as the carrier of the bride because it might be the first step towards changing all the rituals; alternatively, the car might be seen to represent the power of the groom by carrying the bride and making things easier. When the car becomes popular, as is presently the case, praying is no longer possible during the bride's journey as it was when the journey was made by camel. Once practices are altered, it may also be the case that identities may become destabilized.

2. Citizenship and Islam. Popular political participation is central to modernizing periods and this has the power to alter existing orientations. For example, in an Islamic context, people's relation to the world changes: people become citizens of a nation-state rather than subjects of the caliphate. This diminishes the power of sheikhs and opens up opportunities for 'individuation'. The ambiguous achievement of modernity, in this respect, is that, on the one hand, the rise of civil society is witnessed and, on the other hand, individual freedom is celebrated. Both of these processes change culture; local 'uniqueness' is removed and connections between people become thin, so that this collectivity can no longer take its old form.

Modern technology and political structures, then, may be introduced as purely functional and convenient, in line with older values, but they may well turn out to change socio-cultural relations. In traditional ages shared norms and values played a central role in holding people together, but when modernity advances, homogeneous culture is destroyed and a political body, the nation-state, replaces culture as the integrative sphere of society. The nation-state, unlike culture, assumes a global power leading to increased interrelations between civilizations.[11] In modernity, even solutions to internal problems do not appear to be achieved without the state's capacity to play a role at the global level.

To put it more explicitly, modernity cannot easily be ignored by any culture. The dynamics of modern elements seem uncontrollable in terms of their influence on cultures. There is no cultural boundary that is not touched by modernity. Therefore, 'authenticity' is not the right word to use in the definition of cultures. In this respect, we must pay attention to a voice that argues that 'modernity has been and will continue to be resisted by many cultures' (Mestrovic, 1998: 156). Here, resistance against the West is wrongly taken to be synonymous with the rejection of modernity. Some anti-Western movements have arisen in the East because, culturally, the West is not seen as being compatible with the East. In this respect, Western imperialism is the reason why militant movements shake the structures of some Islamic countries, for example. Islamism has been seen by some observers as a rejection of modernity or even as postmodernity (Ahmed, 1992). A careful examination, however, shows that Islamism is, rather, a part of modernity (see Chapters 6 and 7). Islamism reflects the reality that culture plays a pivotal part in socio-political life, but it does not reject modernity despite questioning the West.

At this stage, I must make clear that my argument for the concept of later modernities shares neither the assumptions of the postmodernist critique of modernity, nor those of Huntington's (1997) version of civilizational theory, which sees civilizations as necessarily locked in conflict. The modernity/ postmodernity debate seems to exist around the same problematic. Against Enlightenment-centred theorizing, postmodern theorizing sees it as impossible to eradicate cultural diversities by 'rationality'. Postmodernism also sees culture and rationality as incompatible – not surprisingly, because postmodernism is also an intellectual product of a certain stage of the Western experience of modernity. By contrasting non-Western cultures to modernity, postmodernist scholars take cultural diversities as indications that modernity is over (Gülalp, 1998). But cultural distinctions should not lead one to conclude that modernity is a dead end, because these distinctions indicate that there are varieties of modernity. Regarding the pessimistic view of civilizational interrelations, what has been said in this section about culture must be kept in mind: within the modern experience, cultures can no longer be seen as stable entities. In the search for an 'imagined community', modernization destroys the origins of a culture, which loses its capacity to function as an integrative sphere of the collectivity.

However, if modernity undermines and marginalizes civilizations, how can there still be an insistence on varieties of modernity? It is not only possible, but also necessary, to argue for varieties of modernity, precisely because a dialectic is at work. As an actor between civilizations, modernity is capable of reducing some of the oppositions, but there is a limit to this ability. Transformations of cultural worlds always have varieties. The East is no longer the old East due to modernization, but nor is the East the West. Societies are not at the stage some call globalization. Modernity's alteration of cultures does not necessarily mean that these cultures are Westernized. Rather, different cultural worlds evolve in different directions. Thus, the relation between universalism and particularism constitutes a basic tension in modern experiences. Traditions are being lost as part of the price of modernity, but there is always space for societies to interpret modernity in their own ways. Modernity does not provide fixed ways of doing things, but provides the conditions for interpretation. Thus, modernity's properties are adapted to different civilizational/cultural frameworks. Distinct models of modernity are possible because no absolute break from the history of a culture is ever achieved, and because the interpretations of modernity by modernizing actors in the East are not copies of the Western understanding of modernity.

The tension, within experiences of modernity, between universalism and particularism leads some observers to interpret the current era as one of globalization, and others to interpret it as one of localization. But these paradigms are inadequate; what is needed is a detailed analysis of the specificities of later modernities. I shall attempt to construct a model for analysing later modernities using historical sociology (see Abrams, 1982) as a method by which contemporary societies can be explored. By using historical investigation a sociologist is not only exploring past times; he or she can also show how societies change and why there are distinctions between present societies. From this starting point it should be clear that historical sociology is necessarily a comparative sociology. This is so in two respects. First, the present is compared with the past in order to understand both change and continuity. Secondly, the unit of analysis is historically compared with other experiences to see both the distinctive and the shared characteristics of present societies.

A comparative historical sociology, in analysing a later modernity, must emphasize two concepts: continuity and discontinuity. This perspective will help us to understand both the differences between contemporary societies and what they have in common. I propose that the history and creativity of modernizing actors are two specific elements to be considered in order to answer two questions: how do later modernities emerge and why are they different? We should not view modernity as a complete break with the past, nor should we ignore the centrality of 'creativity of action'.[12] Modernity is not entirely the product of tradition, but nor is it entirely the product of the creativity of actors. That is to say that previous structures cannot be viewed as contexts that bring about modernities in the sense of evolution; but, at the same time, without considering the historical background, which provides possibilities for the direction of human actions, modernity cannot be fully explored. Therefore, the historical context is a central element in the creation of different, later, modernities, but modernity is not something that comes about without creative actors. Human actions are shaped by given historical possibilities, and human life unfolds within the historical process of societies, but we must not neglect 'freedom of action'. (Historical) institutions shape human actions, which, however, in turn (re)create and change these institutions. Thus, historical sociology must take into account both social setting and action, which create and contain each other; both the history and the creative power of modernizing actors must be considered.

The Historical Background of Turkish Modernity

Turkish modernity has often been seen merely as a product of Kemalism (Kislali, 1997; Kongar, 1985). This view understands modernity as a discontinuity, a radical shift from the past. On this basis, modernization is viewed simply as Westernization, on the assumption that there was no alternative. Because the West is viewed as an advanced civilization and because the characteristics of the West were different from those of Turkish society at the time, many have argued that advanced civilization could be attained by imitating the West (see Berkes, 1976). This necessarily implies a radical break with previous Turkish history. This is not only the view of many social scientists in Turkey, but was also considered desirable by the early Kemalists themselves. However, it is impossible to escape a history when some of its central features persist, even if it is politically interpreted as dead. Thus, without analysing historical continuity it is impossible to discuss present-day Turkish society.

It is possible to claim that the idea of modernity was imported from the West. However, Turkish society had also imported Islam. Should we then argue that the Turks have always been ready to imitate inventions from around the world? The answer is both yes and no. A historical investigation indicates that the Turks imported both the idea of Islam and that of modernity, but added their own characteristics to them. Both Islam and modernity have been reinterpreted and, therefore, they have become 'Turkified'.

If one sees the Turkish republic as the true beginning of Turkish modernity, one necessarily needs to consider the Ottoman Empire. This is so because the history preceding the republic could point to the discontinuities of Turkish modernity. Is Turkish modernity merely a product of Kemalist actors? When we look at the central characteristics of the Ottoman Empire, we find that it is difficult to argue for the Turkish republic as a radically new phenomenon. A brief overview of the Ottoman Empire will suffice to show that historical background did play an important part in the formation of Turkish modernity, and thus that the latter cannot be seen as purely a product of Kemalism.

The central question is the following: was the Ottoman Empire a 'static' world that did not permit the 'dynamic' modern world to emerge? Founded in 1299, the Empire played an important role in the formation of some modern states in the nineteenth and twentieth centuries, including Greece and Turkey. However, observers mainly concentrate on the features of the Empire that are viewed as unable to prepare the way for modernity (Mardin, 1994). This is grounded in a focus on the era preceding modernity in the West. Thus, feudalism is supposed to be the only context from which modernity stemmed (Mahçupyan, 1997). Since the Ottoman Empire was not a feudal state-society, critics argue that it could not have produced modernity (understood as a uniform phenomenon); therefore, it is wrongly assumed that the only way to modernize the Turkish world was to Westernize it.

Because of this non-feudal historical background, the emergence of modernity was to be different in the Turkish context than in Western Europe. There were no autonomous structures and actors in the sense of European feudalism, but this does not mean that there was no agent of modernity in the Ottoman Empire. In the Empire, domination was not determined by socio-economic criteria, but by the polity and the military. Thus, the bourgeoisie was not to be a decisive force in the modernizing process, but it was not the only possible force that could create modernity. Rather, the intelligentsia, made up of military and civilian actors, was to be the decisive dynamic that would remain in power and that also survived in Kemalism. Therefore, the Ottoman Empire did not aim to keep its traditional position, but aimed at modernizing itself, while nevertheless retaining some historical continuity. The collapse of the Empire was not due to its 'traditionalist' response to the rise of modernity in the West, as many observers have argued (Berkes, 1976); rather, the Empire came to an end partly because modernization, in the Turkish world, required its death. I am not arguing that modernity necessarily implies that an empire dissolve itself, but more specifically that the death of the Ottoman Empire paved the way for the formation of Turkish modernity. Turkish modernity, or rather the Turkish project of modernity – Kemalism – was partly a consequence of the responses of the Ottoman Empire to the rise of the West.

The beginning of Turkish modernity could be marked by the date 1839 when the *tanzimat* ('regulations') era began. In the nineteenth century, the rise of the West prompted some radical questions in the Ottoman Empire. The Ottoman intelligentsia attempted to understand the superiority of the West. This search created new ideas among the new intellectuals known as the Young Ottomans, such as Namik Kemal. These ideas produced a number of reforms, which were to prepare the way for the emergence of Kemalism. In 1876, the Young Ottomans achieved the establishment of the first constitutional regime, with the first written modern constitution in Turkey. In this *tanzimat* era (1839–78) secularism was an important subject of intellectual discussion, and this was the background for Kemalist secularism. For the first time in the Turkish world, a parliament was formed to oversee the economic activities of the state, work out a synthesis of *sharia* (Islamic) law and secular laws, and change the laws that were assumed to be against the interests of the state. The last task – to protect the state – was to be a prominent feature of Kemalism in the 1930s. These reforms were driven by the intelligentsia, and the Turkish republic's central actors were to come from the same group.

In 1878, the *tanzimat* era ended when the Sultan Abdülhamit dissolved the parliament. But this act was to give rise to new developments based on the ideas of a new group, the Young Turks. In 1908, the Young Turks, many of whom were from the military, acted against the sultan and succeeded in establishing the second constitutional regime. The first modern political party in Turkey, Ittihat Terakki, was formed (the Kemalist party, the Republican People's Party, was thus not the first modern party). The year 1908 was a very crucial time: it provided some answers to the problems of Turkish society, but, in later years, these answers would themselves create new problems. The fact that the establishment of the constitutional regime was achieved by a military coup was to be frequently echoed in the history of the Turkish republic.

Without creative actors, modernity cannot be produced from within any culture or civilization. The Turkish project of modernity, then, should be understood as a consequence of the Ottoman Empire but also to an important extent as a new phenomenon created by new actors. This is therefore an argument that rejects structuralist and evolutionist perspectives but nonetheless emphasizes the centrality of history in the formation of modernity. Now briefly Kemalism shall be introduced. Faced with the rise of the West, the Ottoman Empire had a limited number of possible responses. If we look at the final century of the Empire, we can see that there were three alternative responses to Western modernity. *Rejectionism* was a traditionalist response by a group of the *ulema* which assumed that it was possible to reject modernization. *Reformism* was developed by the Ottoman reformers against the traditionalist response, and argued for the possibility of both 'development' and 'authenticity'. Finally, against both rejectionist and reformist perspectives the *revolutionist* option proposed the remaking of the social world.

Kemalism was a radical form of the third option. Looking at both Ottoman decay and Western development, the Kemalists saw no solution other than 'radicalizing dualities' in Turkish society. Successfully bringing about revolution requires that the proposed revolutionary project be seen as meeting the needs of dissatisfied or disoriented people (Skocpol, 1979). The Kemalist project of revolution therefore had to problematize majority consensus on the existing system. Thus the 'radicalization of dualities', which was necessary to this problematization, emerged as specific to the history of Turkish modernity. In the course of the Kemalist revolution, two other factors were also important: international pressure and a vulnerable old system. The First World War destroyed the imperial system of the Ottoman Empire and the sultanate was vulnerable.[13] Therefore, it is not surprising that Kemalism appeared as a project for emancipating Turks. In brief, the autonomy of the Turks was the first ambitious goal of the Kemalist revolution.

The Kemalist revolution's first aim was to replace one imagined community, the Islamic *umma*, with another, the Turkish nation whose ultimate goal was to create autonomous modernity. In their efforts to achieve this autonomous modernity, the Kemalists went to great lengths. Modernity was, in the first place, taken to be a universal civilization which, according to the Kemalists, could be achieved by a high degree of rationalization of the social world. This was a dual perspective. In the post-First World War era, the first successful movement against Western imperialism was the Kemalist movement, which provided a model of liberation for colonized countries. Kemalism's war was nothing if not a war against Western hegemony and for the autonomy of the Turks. However, the view of modernity as a universal civilization created a contradiction within Kemalism, that of autonomy versus universality; the latter would assimilate the former if it were achieved.

In the Turkish experience of modernity, the tension-ridden relations between Enlightenment rationality, on the one hand, and Romantic critiques of and reactions against this, on the other hand, have played an essential role. This may remind us of the German experience. However, this tension could be considered to exist in all experiences of modernity, though in very different contexts. Romanticism should never be taken as a rejection of modernity, but rather as an important part of the experience of modernity (Friese and Wagner, 2000). Similarly, against the argument that present-day cultural differences show that modernity has come to an end, we need to bear in mind the necessarily dialectical and tension-ridden nature of modernity. This situation is clearly shown when we consider the question of nation, which reveals that both Enlightenment and Romanticism play a part in the transition to modernity. In the next chapter, the nationalization process in the Turkish context will be examined. I shall argue that civilization and culture must be discussed in analysing nation-building, and that the question of ethnicity must also be included in the analysis.

CHAPTER 3

Ethnicity, Nation and Civilization

In the experience of Turkish modernity, 'nationalization' obviously occupies a prominent part. This is why the Turkish transition to modernity has often been seen merely as a transition from the Islamic Empire to the Turkish nation-state. With reference to this transformation, the Turkish experience has often been called unique, because of the perceived incompatibility of Islam with the idea of 'nation'. The creation of a nation-state in a predominantly Islamic society is a major reason why Kemalism is seen as providing a model of modernity for Muslim societies.

The Turkish experience of modernity has thus been seen as dominated by the foundation of the Turkish nation-state (Kongar, 1985); in other words, the nation has been viewed as an end rather than as a means. To show that the nationalist principle of Kemalist modernity was a means to other ends, the nationalizing process and its aftermath need to be analysed. To put it more explicitly, the nation is generally seen as the dominant social configuration of modern times (Gellner, 1983; Giddens, 1985, 1991) and, thus, it seems necessary to explore the move towards a nationalized collectivity in Anatolia.

Some observers see the nationalization process as being obviously related to the ethnicity of the community (Smith, 1986; Gutierrez, 1997). This perspective reads nation as an expression of an earlier sense of ethnocentrism. Nationalization has also been stressed, by some observers, as having connections with an idea of 'civilization' that came into existence with the emergence of modernity (Gellner, 1964; Elias, 1994 [1982]). That is, modernization was seen to mean 'civilization'; it is observed that civilization does not refer to a pre-existing category, but is only something to be reached, the goal of the process of 'becoming civilized'. In the Turkish experience, this understanding of civilization was taken to be the case without being critically observed. Then, *kültür* or *hars* was seen as peculiar to the Turks, while *medeniyet* or *uygarlik* was emphasized as common to the whole of humanity. Therefore, it seems clear that *kültür* places essential stress on nationality, while *uygarlik* may be common to all human beings. From this observation, it becomes obvious that a study of nationalization should take ethnicity and civilization into account.

In analysing the Turkish experience, the nationalizing process of Anatolia must be looked at from a viewpoint that considers the relations of nation to ethnicity, culture, civilization and modernity. This will also enable us to see whether the Turkish experience requires a reading other than that of Western-ization. Using a comparative perspective the culture and civilization of the Turks, both before and after the creation of the nation-state, must be analysed in order to see whether nationalization has the capacity to change cultural and civilizational orientations. I shall begin with a conceptual analysis of the rela-tions between 'ethnicity' and 'nation' and between 'culture' and 'civilization'.

The Relations between Ethnicity, Nation, Culture and Civilization

Ethnicity and Nation

As mentioned earlier, one perspective emphasizes the 'ethnic' element as a tangible ingredient in the formation of nations. In the light of the current literature on nationalism, we see that this perspective is gaining ground (see, for instance, Wicker, 1997; Guibernau and Rex [eds.], 1997). In particular, social movements that claim to be based on ethnicity seem to provide the basis for the growing adherence to this perspective. The collapse of the Soviet Union and of Yugoslavia, in particular, leading to the emergence of new nation-states based on 'ethnicity', on the one hand, and to some ethnocentric movements within the borders of some nation-states, on the other, seem to prove the role of ethnicity in providing a basis for communal self-assertion. In Turkey, the Kurdish question seems to represent a parallel. I shall briefly discuss whether this perspective on nation-formation is tenable.

Mann (1993: 215) claimed that a nation is 'a community affirming its distinct ethnic identity and history and claiming its own state'. Smith (1986) emphasized the importance of subjective factors in the formation of a nation by arguing that, in the form of ethnocentrism, collective memory plays a central part in the reproduction of a 'self' over centuries. More recently, Gutierrez (1997: 164) argued that 'the renewal of ethnicity is less a result of external forces than a self-discovery'. These observations could be viewed as privileging 'ethnic oneness' and homogeneity within the nation. Ethnicity, without critical observation, is taken as a given historical reality. In other words, powerful memories of the 'ethnic past' are seen to determine the formation of a nation: 'ethnie have emerged and re-emerged at different periods in several continents and culture-areas right up to the modern era; and that ethnicity has remained as a socio-cultural "model" for human organization and communication' (Smith, 1986: 168). This observation inevitably shows the nation as in existence within history long before modernity emerged. It was this assumption that led to the debate on nationalism between Ernest Gellner and Anthony Smith. The former, as is well known, saw no possibility of the existence of nations in pre-modern times (Gellner, 1964, 1983), while the latter objected to the idea of 'nation' as a modern social configuration and accorded a central place to ethnicity in the analysis of 'nation' (Smith, 1971, 1986, 1998). Before considering the Gellnerian – modernist – perspective on the concept of nation, let me discuss the ethnocentric perspective associated with Smith's work.

'Ethnic oneness' is a chimerical idea. Even in prehistoric times an ethnically pure community did not exist: there have always been processes (marriages, migrations, assimilations, capturing of women, wars) that have led to intermingling among peoples. More crucially, ethnic purity has never existed because social traits are not transmitted through biological inheritance but only through education. As Gökalp (1959: 135) considers: 'Man does not bring with him language, religion, aesthetic feeling, political, legal or economic institutions. All these he acquires later, from society and through education.' We could argue that Smith's idea of the ethnocentric nation is not tenable in a historical perspective. The conditions of pre-modern ages did not allow for the possibility of forming a nation: for example, in the Turkish case, the lack of communication between people in the south-eastern region and people in the Aegean region of Anatolia would prevent them coming together to form a nation.

However, when ethnicity is understood in terms of the *feeling* of belonging to a cultural group, it becomes plausible that it plays a central role in nation-formation. Recently, some critics have come to admit that biological or genetic difference alone does not constitute an ethnic group but that common customs are also an important factor (Guibernau and Rex [eds.], 1997). In other words, common traditions, shared ways of life and the memory of the common past are viewed as defining the meaning of ethnicity. It must be acknowledged that objectively it is impossible to argue for a pure ethnicity, but this does not matter much because the crucial point is the myth through which individuals attribute ethnic unity. An 'ethnic group' can therefore be defined as a group that considers itself as (and is sometimes regarded by others as) a culturally distinctive unity. Nevertheless, for the argument on nationalization, notions of ethnic purity or even of ethnicity itself should not be overemphasized. In the emergence of the nation, several other elements are equally important.

Gellner (1964: 168) wrote the following: 'Nationalism is not the awaking of nations to self-consciousness: it invents nations where they do not exist'. He thus sees the nation as a purely modern phenomenon, detached from the past (Gellner, 1983). Therefore, in Gellner, the first explicit contrast with the ethnocentric view of the nation is that the nation does not necessarily refer in any way to an ethnic past. On the contrary, the nation is a framework, an instrument of modernization. There is thus a direct relation between industrialization and nationalization. This perspective primarily refers to the notion that the nation epitomizes the culture of modernity. The nation, in other words, as a modern phenomenon, which cannot be traced back to pre-modern times, is a construct of people as a necessary response to 'objective' processes of economic, social and political conditions of an emerging modernity. In terms of social configuration, the emergence of the nation marks the discontinuity of modernity – modernity does not rely on any principle that existed in previous ages in terms of community type. In this perspective, the important aspect is the unrelatedness of nation to ethnicity. An ethnic group is not seen as tending to produce a state of its own; on the contrary, the emergence of the nation is preconditioned by the presence of the state, which is seen as the main force in the formation of the nation (Gellner, 1983). It is clear that, on this view, 'ethnicity' has almost no part to play in the emergence of the nation. Rather, the nationalist ideology of the state elite produces the nation to meet the needs of modernization. The emphasis is on a common language, mass education, 'high culture', and communication within a high level of division of labour, possible only under the conditions of modernity.

This Gellnerian perspective on the concept of nation is also problematic, although it is more plausible than the ethnocentric view. Gellner describes the nation as a product of modernizing periods, but fails to explore how this process was achieved. It is not difficult to see how, by means of mass education, urbanization, a high level of communication and political participation, a 'high culture' can be imposed on a society. However, the question of how these processes alone could eradicate former lifeworld practices and identities remains unanswered. It must be seen that without subjective interpretation by the people, the emergence of the nation would not be possible. In this regard, two critics may be considered: Anderson and Hobsbawm.

Anderson (1991 [1983]: 6) wrote that the nation is 'an *imagined* political community – and imagined as both inherently limited and sovereign. It is *imagined* because the members of even the smallest nation will never know most of their fellow-members, meet them, or even hear of them, yet in the minds of each lives the image of their communion'. Hobsbawm (1990) shows that national traditions are 'invented traditions'. What is particularly important in these views is that the nation is seen as a 'creation' or 'invention' and that not only its objective conditions but, importantly, people's image of the nation need to be focused on. Therefore, following this understanding, the static view of the nation from an ethnocentric perspective and the lack of an 'imaginary' in a Gellnerian perspective may be overcome. The nation is neither an expression of a formerly existing ethnocentrism, nor can it be seen as a product of objective processes.

What then is a nation? As Gellner has shown us, the nation is definitely a modern phenomenon but, in its emergence, an 'imaginary' played a major part. In these terms, it becomes possible to see that nationalist ideology could also use 'ethnicity' as the basis for its argument. Nevertheless, ethnicity itself does not define the meaning of the nation; on the contrary, ethnicity is itself 'invented' or 'created'. Thus, there are two possible types of nationalist movement: one tries to actualize the past of an 'ethnic' group and privilege it, while the other argues that it is not ethnicity, blood, or race but common history and a belief in a common future that define what a nation is. There are therefore two possible kinds of nation-building project: civic and ethnocentric models. Both use an imaginary, but the latter also invents an ethnicity. We can say that a nation is a product of a nationalist ideology that is necessarily creative and based on an imaginary.

It is surprising that observers do not seem to recognize the unavoidable relationship between the idea of nation and a particular 'imaginary signifier of modernity' – the idea of autonomy or self-determination. The constitution of a nation is driven by this imaginary signification: a people in a certain land imagines itself as having autonomy in the world, distance from 'others'. By means of this understanding we can analyse two processes as central to the emergence of a nation: the disintegration of larger social formations, such as empires, and the standardization of practices and identities in a clearly defined land as the 'country' of a specific people. In the standardization process, mass education is particularly important in the sense that it creates a 'reading public' (Anderson) that is open to influence, so that people begin to imagine themselves as living within a nation, an 'imagined community'. The concept of nation is therefore closely related to the imaginary signification of autonomy of a people and its country, and this 'autonomy' could only be achieved by means of modernization: the economic and political processes of modernization are necessary conditions for the autonomy of a country.

This process of nationalization, however, could not take place without a 'radicalization of dualities' – the power of 'the project of modernity'. There are two dualities at stake here: the problematization of locality in the country, and the dichotomization of the 'particular' and the 'universal': the insider/outsider problematic. It is therefore no surprise that nationalization is often criticized as destroying the 'authenticity' of local cultures and as dividing the earth into warring nation-states. Since the nation is a self-expression of a people it is obviously related to civilization and culture, which are the bases for the self-definition or the self-expression of a people.

Civilization and Culture

'Civilization' could refer to various things: to a society's level of technology, to its social customs and manners, to the development of scientific knowledge, to religious ideas and customs (Elias, 1994 [1982]). One could use this observation to argue that there is almost nothing in human life that could not be considered as civilized or uncivilized depending on the criteria used. Yet this view would necessarily force us to admit that, from the beginning, civilization has been tangible in human life. However, this is not the case: the history of civilization starts with the beginning of settled life or, in an Islamic interpretation, civilization starts with the emergence of Medina as the Islamic city. While this understanding refers to the fact that human beings have been civilized for a long time, the emergence of modernity created new thinking on the meaning of civilization. Scientific knowledge, science-oriented technology and a secular polity are seen as the markers of civilization. This is nothing other than the expression of the self-consciousness of the West. But it is this definition of civilization that has circulated around the world and continues to be dominant.

We could argue that, in fact, the concept of civilization has always related to societies' own self-definitions: a society identifies itself as 'civilized'. For example, Uygur Turks, who lived in Central Asia long before Islam emerged, saw themselves as *uygar*, 'civilized' (from the contemporary Turkish word for civilization, *uygarlik*). However, we encounter a problem when we compare different civilizations. Which groups of people would a particular civilization include? For example, could Islamic civilization include Greece? It is important here to stress that civilization is not a universal phenomenon; it also divides people, and a plurality of civilizations is inevitable. Nevertheless, the theorizing of civilization as identical with Western modernity is still powerfully present, as can be illustrated by the example of Francis Fukuyama.

The collapse of communism led Fukuyama to conclude that history had come to an end (Fukuyama, 1992). Fukuyama recognized that the clash of ideas has been an important factor in shaping human history and that in the twentieth century capitalism and communism have been understood as the two clashing ideas shaping the world. With the collapse of communism in the early 1990s, Fukuyama was quick to see the liberal democracy of the West as

53

the victor. Since communism and capitalism are seen as the only two clashing ideas and since communism lost the war 'forever', liberalism is understood to be the last order and 'liberal man' as the 'last man'; history is thus over. However, Fukuyama does not take account of civilizational distinctions, which do not allow for the end of history. For the thesis of the end of history to be credible, there should no longer be any conflict between civilizations. However, in reality the world still witnesses communal and social international struggles and these are quite often due to civilizational distinctions.

However, considering civilization as classifying peoples and as causing struggles leaves a problem. For example, if it is admitted that there is an Islamic civilization, does this generalize or universalize all Muslim societies? In other words, could an Islamic civilization overcome differences between particular Muslim societies?

Elias's (1944 [1982]) well-known study of the civilizing process shows the concepts of 'civilization' and 'culture' to be respectively associated with two worldviews: the French and the German. It may be argued that 'later modernities' – with Germany understood as belonging to this category – saw themselves in terms of *Kultur* while 'original modernities', such as the French and the English, interpreted themselves as civilizations and, thus, applicable to all peoples. It could follow that this was why original modernity aimed at shaping the whole world in its own image, while the interpretations of later modernities were specific, particular to themselves. This observation could and should be used to understand the current era of the social world, but it does pose another question: does original modernity refer only to civilization and later modernities only to culture? In fact, it is not surprising that original modernity uses the concepts of civilization and culture synonymously; culture and civilization are taken to be one and the same phenomenon. I shall now briefly consider a contemporary perspective on civilization, Huntington's thesis, to show that culture and civilization are still taken to be synonymous.

Huntington's response to the post-Cold War era differs from that of Fukuyama. He developed a theory of the 'clash of civilizations' (Huntington, 1997). Huntington's observation of 'differences' led him to claim that the rest of humanity did not accept the Western world as 'superior' because of civilizational incompatibilities. First, one should be critical of Huntington's neglect of 'culture'. Within one civilizational zone, Huntington does not see distinctions between particular societies. He underestimates ethnic, linguistic and even religious differences. However, it must be observed that conflicts do not only exist between civilizations; conflicts between cultures belonging to the same civilization must also be considered. A good example is the distinct interpretations of the world by Shia Muslims and by Sunni Muslims despite the fact that, civilizationally, they are alike. Thus, there are civilizations that include multiple cultural worlds. How then might we define culture?

It is useful to start by saying that culture is the distinguishing element of human beings: symbolic representation is unique to humans. There is no doubt that culture is the learned aspect of human society. The history of culture is the history of a struggle to give meaning to everything. When, for example, the power of nature was considered unacceptable, it was imagined that there must be a higher category governing that powerful nature: God was created. But culture's war did not stop there: it had created God whom it was also to kill. Therefore, culture is what is remarkable about human creative achievement. If, however, we define culture simply as the creative achievements of humankind, we may be inclined to understand it as universal, when in fact it is not. Culture refers to the intellectual and moral characteristics of particular societies – to their practices and customs, commonly held beliefs, values, norms and so on.

It was perhaps structural-functionalism that tried hardest to accommodate ideas of culture in social theorizing about modern society. Talcott Parsons saw three interrelated systems: the social, the personal and the cultural (Parsons, 1951). However, since Parsons' theory focuses on the problem of the social order, culture is inevitably reduced to being the legitimizing sphere of the social. Culture is subordinated to the social and, necessarily, it is theorized simply as shared values. In brief, culture is heavily determined by institutional factors according to this perspective. If we criticize Marx for being too materialist, we should also criticize Parsons for seeing the social as to a large extent independent of culture. Culture should never be reduced to the sustaining of social relations but, rather, the power of culture to produce and reproduce the social (Weber) should be recognized. Thus, it is important that Weber (1958) understood the Protestant ethic not just as legitimizing capitalist market relations but, essentially, as providing a way of being moral and rational.

Secondly, it should be stressed that culture is not simply a reflection of material conditions. Culture is not easily considered as a superstructure coming out of the economic base. In Marxism, one does not need to look at 'meaning', but should understand the material elements that 'meaning' reflects. As is now quite clear, however, not only economic interests but also issues of cultural identity play an important role in human life. We should, of course, recognize Gramsci's theorizing as to the importance of culture in Marxist tradition. Gramsci (1971: 323–35) theorizes culture as part of the process of domination. The ideological domination of society by 'organic intellectuals' is called 'cultural hegemony'. While this is important as an attempt to introduce the concept of culture to Marxist theory, most orthodox Marxists do not acknowledge that culture also has the power to challenge, criticize or control authority.

Culture should never be seen as clearly defined, or as a fixed way of doing things, otherwise culture would be 'objective' and, thus, would not be open to change by the will of social actors. Culture is an open-ended interpretive space. It is always open to reinterpretation and to different interpretations. Under changing conditions, culture could be homogenizing but yet diverging, hegemonizing but yet resisting. By this I mean that culture is not at all static but, in contrast, plays a vital role in the interactions of social actors with existing structures; culture is central to attempts to bring about change. From this, we can grasp the meaning of culture: it is the self-interpretation of society. If we take culture as being 'collective learning' because its elements of tradition and reason are collective, it refers then to the self-construction of society. However, social realities are at times in conflict with cultural goals and it is here that social actors find a space in culture to review and reinterpret it in order to make innovations. Otherwise, one might (as critics often do) take culture as determining human action, thereby closing off the possibility of social change, itself the substance of social science. And culture is particularly open to reinterpretations within modernity.

The idea of cultural autonomy in 'the project of modernity' refers to two basic ambitions: the emancipation of cultural knowledge from tradition, God, and political authority and culture's mastery over nature. Although these ambitions are questionable, and have often been criticized, they provided a sort of autonomy for culture. The separation of three realms of culture – morality, science and art – gives space to social actors to interpret themselves and the world in new and different ways. Although this is problematic, since fragmentation leads to painful conflict, it also opens up space for a plurality of worldviews. For example, before modernity, Islamic people were not free to express what they understood from Islam because of the total political authority of Islamic regimes and the people's corresponding lack of autonomy. Today, however, under conditions of modernity we witness the emergence of Islamic actors who demonstrate their understandings of Islam and of the world.

Finally, we must focus on culture's relation to civilization. Gökalp (1959) observed that culture is national, while civilization is international: that is, there is only one contemporary civilization, that of modernity. However, while civilizations are international in the sense that they typically include groups of countries, there are distinct civilizations in modern times just as there were previously. Within a civilizational zone, in modern times, there are nation-states that – at least ideally – posses national cultures. 'Civilization' refers to the total 'cultural area' which indicates some common features of the self-interpretations of the relevant societies. In other words, there are multiple cultures that belong to the same civilization. There will be some basic commonalities between these cultures, but also differences: a nation could present itself as a member of a civilization while also claiming to be culturally specific, and in its constitution ethnicity might be an important element. In brief, ethnicity, nation, culture and civilization all refer to the self-interpretation and representation of peoples. I now want to examine the Turkish experience in terms of the nationalization process by keeping ethnicity, culture and civilization as key concepts of the argument.

The Invention of the Turkish Nation and its Aftermath

Defining the Turks in a Civilizational Perspective

The Turkish world, in Anatolia, could be described as a cultural area belonging to the Ural-Altai group in terms of language and to Islam in terms of religion. However, in terms of civilization, it is always problematic to know where to place the Turks. We need to look at the nineteenth-century intellectual climate in the Ottoman Empire. Some were sure that the Turks constituted a separate civilization, which included all Turks from the Balkans to China, and that their ideal country was called Turan. For other observers, there was no doubt that the Turks were members of the Islamic civilization; since they became Muslims, their way of life was completely determined by Islamic principles. However, a surprising observation was also to emerge: the claim that Turks belonged to Western civilization.[1] None of these perspectives could be refuted easily; each of them constitutes part of the truth. One could conclude that the Turks are a people without originality; they have always borrowed from, and been easily influenced by, other civilizations. However, the Turks have never been *entirely* assimilated into any one civilization. It is important to ask, therefore, whether there is a factor peculiar to the Turks that has prevented them from becoming completely 'Islamic', 'Western' or even 'Turkish'.

We can begin with the fact that the Turks have always lived alongside 'other' groups of people. The Turks were nomadic people who never settled down in a definite place until they reached Central Asia from the Far East. In Central Asia, particularly in Turkestan, the Turks established a 'civilized' territory for themselves, before Islam emerged. We see from archaeological findings that the people living in that region called themselves Turks. Some, especially Kemalists, have seen this period as the bright era for 'Turkish civilization'. For example, Gökalp (1959) saw that era as the golden age when Turks created their own civilization without borrowings from outside. Some argue, however, that when Islam emerged the Turks found it desirable to take it as a model of life and that Islam 'civilized' them. Although, as historical studies show (Aydin, 1994), the Turks did not accept Islam easily, they did eventually become Muslim, which is one of the elements that distinguishes Turkish identity from its Christian neighbours. Becoming Muslim did not, however, mean that the Turks forgot their existing culture. Among Muslim societies, the Turkish one differed from the very beginning with its institutions and way of life.

It can be argued that, rather than Turkish culture becoming completely assimilated by Islam, the Turks 'assimilated' Islam in making it compatible with their way of life, which already included elements not completely of Turkish origin. I want to give two brief examples. First, unlike the Arabs, the Turks had man-made laws, *kanun,* which were not dictated by Islamic *sharia* law. This was why the Ottoman Empire formed itself on two different kinds of law, *örfi* and *serii*. Islam did not undermine the sultanate; in contrast, the state was able to use Islam as a legitimizing element. The state did not rely on the origins of Islam and this could be considered as a reason why the Ottoman Empire was 'developmental' in comparison with other Islamic states. This is an important historical background to the nationalizing process of Anatolia, the Kemalist move away from the Islamic community. Secondly, some people in Turkey follow Alevilik, an alternative reading of Islam, although claimed by some to be a branch of Shia Islam. Alevilik could, in fact, be compared to Protestantism in terms of its openness to innovation. Its followers do not practise Islamic rules as they are explicitly defined in the Koran, but interpret the Koran as permitting Muslims to go further in finding 'perfection'. This could be seen as a move towards secularization. Among many cases, the two examples mentioned above should make it clear that Kemalism did not just happen to come about in Turkish society; rather, the socio-historical ground for that sort of project of modernity already existed in the Turkish context. It should be clear that the Turkish world in Anatolia was not completely located within 'Islamic civilization' even before the start of modernization. In the later stages of the Ottoman Empire, new experiences led the Turks to meet another civilizational zone and, thus, they moved towards the West.

When the Turks conquered Anatolia in the eleventh century, they met there a diverse pattern of tradition. This often escapes notice but it provided an important source for Turkish identity in Anatolia. While Greek hegemony was replaced, indigenous cultures did not disappear (see, for example, Lewis, 1961). The indigenous cultures influenced Turkish culture as much as did Islam or Europe. For instance, in Anatolian villages, the houses and mosques are quite different from those of Syria and Iraq; or, again, Turkish music is popular in contrast to Arabic or Persian classical music. During the Ottoman era, the Turks lived with European peoples and with Jews: in the Balkans with Serbs, Romanians, Albanians, Bulgarians and so on, and in Anatolia, particularly, with the Greeks. The Ottoman Empire had the largest Jewish community in the world. Some of the borrowings from these peoples were remarkable. For instance, the fez was borrowed from the Greeks, but because it was banned by Kemalism it has been claimed as 'originally Islamic' by Islamists. The Ottoman Empire, in brief, was a 'Western' state in comparison to Eastern states of the time. These historical trends gave rise to three conflicting ideologies in terms of Turkish identity in the nineteenth century: Islamism, Turkism (considered in the following section) and Westernism. How and why Turkish national identity emerged can be understood by considering the power of the Turkish language.

The Turkish language, although it was undermined by the ruling class of the Ottoman Empire (who developed their own language incorporating aspects of Turkish, Persian and Arabic), never lost its ability to assimilate borrowed foreign words. There are many Arabic and Persian, as well as European, words in Turkish. However, these words are not used in their original forms. For example, the Arabic *nerduba* became *merdiven* and *ghirbal* became *kalbur*. From European languages, 'Europe' became *Avrupa*, 'cigarette' became *sigara*, and so on. Reading the Turkish language's power of resistance against foreign words could also reveal some clues with regard to the civilizational adherence of Turks. In some periods, when it was impossible to replace European words with original Turkish words, the Turkish language used either Arabic, for scientific terminology, or Persian, for general vocabulary. But in other periods, especially in modern times, the Turkish language eliminated Arabic and Persian words and, if it was difficult to replace them with original Turkish words, used European words (Gökalp, 1959). One could argue that because Europe is now a centre of history, the Turkish language is more influenced by European languages. However, during the period when Arabic or Persian words were used to replace European words, the Turkish world was far more powerful than the Arabic and Persian worlds. Rather, when the Turkish world in Anatolia finds itself culturally threatened by one of these civilizational zones, it resists assimilation by refusing the use of words from that zone.

In brief, until the twentieth century the Turkish world in Anatolia could be viewed as a threefold world in terms of civilizational zones. Ziya Gökalp argued in 1914 that the three dominant movements, Turkism, Islamism and modernism, showed that the elements that the Turks took from the three civilizations were still not assimilated and remained in conflict with one another. For him, this was due to the fact that 'Turkish culture [was] not identical with the civilization of the Turks' (Gökalp, 1959: 179). His solution was to 'nationalize'

Turkey with the aim of bringing about modernity. We shall consider in the next section whether nationalization did have the power to make Turkish culture and the civilization of the Turks compatible, and whether Turkey is now expressing a 'healthy' *kültür* and *uygarlik*.

The Nationalization Process

In terms of the development of Turkish national identity, three competing views were at stake: Islamism, Turkism and Westernism. None of them achieved its objectives, but it was Turkism that paved the way for the Kemalist perspective. It is important to note the central characteristics of Turanism – pan-Turkism – in order to see both its continuities and its discontinuities with Kemalism.

Turanism could best be viewed as an outcome of the decaying Ottoman Empire. Turanism should be seen as an attempt to continue with the imperial tradition: the unification of all Turkish people from the Balkans to China was promulgated and the proposed country of this 'imagined community' was named Turan. This could be construed as a pure manifestation of 'ethno-nationalism', and any observation of ethnic nationalism has to consider the impact of people of the same ethnicity from the outside. It could be shown that 'Turkism' in the Ottoman Empire referred to the unity of the Turks in the Empire but, at the same time, pan-Turkism was being developed by the Outside Turks. The late nineteenth and the early twentieth century witnessed the rise of pan-Turkism, especially because Turkic groups in Russia, particularly Tartars, were expressing a will for the unification of all Turkic people under the same political body. Yusuf Akçura, an important leader of pan-Turkism, should be focused on here.

A dedicated pan-Turkist throughout his life, Yusuf Akçura, Tartar in origin, emigrated to Turkey from Russia. He viewed the world of the Turks as one indivisible unity based on evident signs of both cultural ties, especially language, and material bonds – race and blood (Akçura, 1978). In Akçura's 1928 book *Turk Dili* the term 'Turk' referred to all those of Turkic origin – the Tartars, the Azeris, the Kirghiz, and others – and they all constituted the Turkish nation. This perspective made a great impact on Turkist intellectuals in the Ottoman Empire. There was also an external factor in the development of Turanism: Russian brutality in Central Asia in the 1860s, and Bulgarian brutality against Turks in the newly established Bulgarian state. Perhaps the most important factor in the development of pan-Turkism was the study of Turkology in Europe. By reading some Turkologists, such as Leon Cahun, some Young Turks began to be proud of their Turkish origins, rather than of Ottoman and Islamic roots (see Berkes, 1976). Thus, in the early twentieth century, a Turkist version of nationalism was becoming a force in the intellectual climate of the Empire.

In the 1910s, Turkism had already advanced itself through journals – especially *Türk Yurdu* and *Halka Dogru* – and crystallized into an organization: *Türk Ocagi* (Heart of the Turks), founded in 1911. Ziya Gökalp, known as the Grand Master of Turkism, was a member of that organization. More than any other ideologue, it was Gökalp, of Kurdish origin, who had a major impact on the Kemalist view of the nation. However, we should note the changes over time in Gökalp's view of the Turkish nation. He first emerged as a defender of the Turan, but later he came to see Turan as a 'utopia'. For Gökalp, a huge 'imagined community' such as Turan was not an easily realizable ambition, although he conceded that in the future it might be possible. But what was achievable, for Gökalp, was to build a Turkish nation in the motherland, Anatolia and Rumelia. The first problem Gökalp faced was the Islamic definition of collectivity as 'universal'. For Gökalp, Islam could not be excluded from the formation of the Turkish nation, and for this reason his studies could, in a way, be described as an attempt to synthesize Turkishness with Islam. But he was also aware that, in terms of achieving modernity, religion needs to be made a matter of personal conviction. And since modernity referred to Western civilization in Gökalp's reading, he dedicated more attention to the synthesis of Turkish-Islamic identity with the West. He argued that there was a hidden Turkey which was not completely Arabic-Islamic, but specifically Turkish, with its own language and traditions, the sum of which is called *hars*, or culture. Thus, Gökalp's later views were to influence Kemalism: Turkish culture should be privileged, Turkish history and traditions should be traced back to a pre-Islamic era. Kemalism, however, would go further than this in relation to the nationalizing process.

The Kemalist view of the Turkish nation was formed as a response to the decaying Ottoman Empire. The Ottomanists had proposed 'Ottomanness' as a citizenship and identity, but this did not achieve a positive response from ethnic groups including the Greeks, the Bulgarians and even the Arabs and the Serbs. Kemalism broke with imperial ambition by declaring a Turkish nation in a certain delimited territory: Anatolia. Defining the territory, therefore, was the first task. Kemalism also broke with Turkism in that the Kemalist definition of the Turkish nation derived not from 'ethnic oneness' but, in contrast, from a common history and a belief in a common future. Thirdly, to Kemalists, nationalization meant the necessary process of bringing about a 'civilized Anatolia'. Therefore, what had to be done was to 'disembed' people in order to 're-embed' them in the form of the Turkish nation. However, this process was not at all an easy one.

Kemalism, I suggest, must be understood as a 'territorial' ideology, which requires us to acknowledge the unavoidable link between autonomy and modernity. I would also argue that Kemalism's main concern was to create a 'true republic'. Unlike observers who see nationalism as an ideology of the rising middle classes (see Mahçupyan, 1997), I would argue that nothing less than republicanism was the most powerful ideological factor behind the nationalization process. In other words, the self-determination of a people within a clearly defined boundary was necessary for the construction of a republic. A republic, by its very nature, needs to see people as 'equal' and 'free'. This ideal could be achieved through 'development', and nationalization was seen as a prerequisite for that ambition to be achieved. Therefore, we need to read nationalization, in the eyes of Mustafa Kemal, as 'democratization'. For Kemalism, only by means of nationalization could the 'public' emerge and the 'republic' function from then on.

For a nationalizing movement, the first tool to use, either negatively or positively, is history. Kemalism began by using 'negative history'. The preceding era, that of the Ottoman Empire, was condemned as a dark age for the Turks. It can be seen here that republicanism was the main principle used by Kemalism in its attacks on Ottomanism. The Ottoman Empire was criticized as a despotic empire, understood as a painful experience, especially for the Turks. It could be argued that in imperial state-societies the founding ethnic element suffers from its own dominance, precisely because its ruling class becomes cosmopolitan and remains above the masses. Kemalism, especially according to Gökalp's teachings, criticized the Ottoman governing class as being cosmopolitan and imperialist, putting its own class interests above 'national' interests (see Gökalp, 1959). Thus, according to the Kemalists, the ruler was the cosmopolitan Ottoman and the ruled the Turkish subject. It is certainly true that during the period of the Empire, the governing class indeed saw the Turks as peasants, lending justification to the Kemalists' exclusion of the Empire from 'true Turkish history'. However, it must be stated that, while Kemalism apparently undermined Ottoman history, the Kemalist republic nonetheless took many features from the Ottoman Empire.

Rather than the 'high culture' of the sultanate, the 'people' were privileged in Kemalism. Although this could be called the first step towards the republic, this republic needed patriots who, when necessary, could give their lives for the country. But history shows that, under despotic rule, no patriotic sentiment can emerge in a country. Hence it is not surprising that when the Greeks invaded Western Anatolia in 1919 there was at first almost no collective patriotic movement against the invasion. Mustafa Kemal Atatürk, the founder of the modern Turkish state, achieved the awakening of Anatolians to 'reality' and won the first victory against Western modernity in the East. Therefore, the Greek invasion of Western Anatolia could be seen as the first important event in helping national consciousness to emerge among the Anatolian masses. The Turkish war of independence, between 1919 and 1922, must be viewed as the first important step towards a national society. For the first time Anatolia was owned by its people as a homeland. From east to west and from north to south, this country was now 'the people's', a step towards the republic. However, a republic cannot remain just a people's consciousness of its homeland; what is needed is the emergence of people to participate in a public sphere, to criticize and question. This in turn could only be brought about by nationalization, according to Kemalism.

Problems emerge when a modernizing state begins to see its people as 'uneducated', 'too traditional', 'unskilled' and so on. Kemalism's first question, therefore, was how to nationalize Anatolia in the sense of moving away from tradition towards modernity, a transition thought to be achievable by nationwide education, industrialization, urbanization and 'civilization'. Thus, one cannot analyse the nationalization of Anatolia without considering the 'civilizing process'. It is in this respect that Kemalism's second reading of history emerges, one that privileges pre-Islamic Turkish history. According to the Kemalists, the Turks had always contributed to world civilization, but they had lost this ability during, and because of, the Ottoman Empire.

Kemalism aimed at civilizing people with the tool of the nationalizing process. This process did not aim at completely Westernizing Turkey, as many claimed. However, a further problematic needs to be seen too: with the teachings of Gökalp, Kemalism saw no problem in combining being Turkish with aiming to become a member of Western civilization. Gökalp had taught that religion cannot constitute a civilization: there is no Islamic or Christian civilization, but there are Western and Eastern civilizations and, since Turkish culture was not alien to Western civilization, the aim must be to achieve Western civilization while keeping Turkish culture 'unique' (Gökalp, 1959).

The Kemalist ideology, then, could be summarized as follows: adopting 'modern' civilization, stressing Turkish culture and making Islam a matter of personal conviction. At this stage, Kemalist nationalism should be clearly defined. As Suna Kili (1980: 386) argued, 'Kemalist nationalism is not racist and it is not a persecuting nationalism. According to Kemalist ideology one's Turkishness is not determined by one's race or religion but by the degree [to which] a person associates himself with the ideals and goals of the Turkish republic and through commitment to Turkey's independence and modernization.' Thus, first, Kemalist nationalism is not 'imperialist' in the sense that the idea of the nation is not invoked to justify the invasion of other nations. Secondly, Kemalist nationalism is, in principle, not an ethnic nationalism. Thirdly, Kemalist nationalism is inseparable from republicanism. I shall now consider the central strategies adopted by the Kemalists as part of the project of nationalizing Anatolia.

The Ban on Tarikats

The Islamic *umma* was an 'imagined community' in the sense that members of that community never met and never knew one another. And this 'imagined community' had to be replaced by another, that of the Turkish nation. Kemalists, however, knew well that in the Ottoman Empire, the village and *mahalle* were the real communities that provided people with a communal identity. In order to break with this legacy, Kemalists found the ban on *tarikats*, local religious communities, important for several reasons. *Tarikats* represented an obstacle to nationalization because they divided and classified people. Each *tarikat* had its own life philosophy, leader and community with which members identified themselves. Thus, the division of people of the same religion into *tarikats* needed to be dissolved and replaced by the imagined community of Turkishness. By banning *tarikats* Kemalists aimed at achieving de-localization and secularization.

The Turkish History Thesis

An important intellectual concomitant to the project of nationalization was the Turkish history thesis, which emerged in the 1930s. The thesis holds that the Turks had already developed a settled civilization in Central Asia, in what today is called Turkistan, before the advent of Islam. This established civilization, however, as Aydin (1994) has demonstrated, was exposed to three centuries of the Arab objective (ultimately, largely successful) of turning the Turks into Muslims. By leading an outright nationalization of Turkish society, Kemalism aimed at reversing this process. It thus exacerbated the opposition to Islam, since the latter could not support the idea of Turkish nationalism as it could Arabic nationalism due to its assumption of some broad congruence between the Arabic and the Islamic worlds. Thus, Kemalism in the 1930s invented a history which showed Hittites and Sumerians as being Turkish. By imagining Turkish history as a bright history, Kemalism aimed to show the Anatolian masses that being a member of an imagined Turkish community was worthwhile: being confident and feeling *uygar* (civilized) were needed for moving society towards modernity. We should not read this as racism; the Kemalists knew that Hittites and Sumerians were not of Turkish origin, but claiming the history of Anatolia as Turkish history was designed to support the development of the Turkish nation. It is for this reason that the first important banks of the Turkish republic were named Etibank and Sumerbank. This reading of history, in fact, gave Kemalism the opportunity of overcoming both pan-

Turkism, which would not name Sumerians as Turks, and Islamism, to which the idea of the Turkish nation was alien. Another important factor in the formation of the Turkish history thesis was the invisibility of the Turks in official Ottoman history, In the official Ottoman education programmes and books there was no Turkish history, but only Ottoman and Muslim history. While the Arabs, Kurds and Albanians were mentioned respectfully, the Turks were never included in history books. Hence, the Turkish history thesis can also be read as a reaction-formation. For the nationalization of a collectivity, an 'idealized antiquity' is perhaps required. When Kemalism proclaimed that the Turks had to bring about a powerful modernity, a background was needed to show that the Turks had already provided a bright antiquity. So, to create modernity in the future first requires the creation of a golden age in the past.

Language Reform

More than any other factor, language reform played the greatest role in the process of nationalization. Without the creation of a 'reading public' nation-formation would be much more difficult. Two goals seem to have been prioritized by Kemalism in its language reform. First, language needed to be more nationalized; Arabic and Persian words were to a great extent eliminated from the Turkish language by the creation of new words. Second, making the Turkish language easy to read and write was desirable; hence the Latin alphabet replaced Arabic script. It can be seen in both of these aims that the actual ambition was to break with the Arabic influence on Turkish, in the same way that the Soviet Union changed the Turkic people's alphabet in Central Asia to curb the influence of Anatolian Turkish. In a very short time, the new alphabet was adopted both in schools – which were then made compulsory – and in the military. The level of literacy increased from then on. But a further effort was needed to make the Anatolian people understand how important and beautiful their language was: this was the Sun language theory, according to which all Ural-Altai languages were based on the Turkish language. The Turks thus owned the Ural-Altai language family group, which included Hungarian, Turkish and Finnish, rather than being a mere member of it. For the academic study of the Turkish history thesis and the Sun language theory, a faculty was formed at Ankara University: Dil-Tarih-Cografya Fakültesi, the Faculty of Language-History-Geography. Neither the Turkish history thesis nor the Sun language theory lasted long, but they provided a source of legitimization for ultra-nationalists wishing to claim a connection between Kemalism and their own ideology.

Education Reform

For Kemalists, the 'civilized Turkish nation' could only come about by means of education. Without changing people's minds or, rather, without liberating people from tradition, nothing could be achieved, according to Mustafa Kemal, who claimed: 'Teachers, the new generation will be your creation'. This could be interpreted to show that Kemalism did not aim to institutionalize a system of social and political life. Individual actors were being insisted on as more important than the system: not a new educational system but teachers were seen as vital for the creation of new generations. And Kemalist actors worked on education with important projects. First, everyone in the country had to know at least how to read and write, and for this to be achieved primary education was made compulsory. But the actual aim was to break traditional, communal ties that were blocking nationalization and 'civilization'. Therefore, university education was a priority for Kemalism. However, nothing could be more important than 'enlightening' the village. Village institutions were founded to train teachers, who would then teach in the villages. This was an educational model unprecedented in world history. Ties of locality were being broken by teachers who were agents of nationalization, but a further aim was to achieve a sort of universality. Village institutions were a basic educational opportunity for the peasantry, with several goals. A most important goal was to enlighten individuals in order for them to know their own world rather than simply obeying the rules of the sheikhs and the local leaders. The aim was to shift social power so that, rather than depending on kinship or religious leadership, power could be transferred to the people themselves. Here we can see a difference from the Western model: under Kemalism, people could become highly educated 'subjects' in the place where they were born rather than having to move to cities for educational purposes, so that urbanization may not have been understood as a social process necessary to modernization. Naturally, village institutions were 'enlightening' agents that could not be approved by counter-revolutionaries. Village institutions were not turning out 'nationalized' youth but were creating communists, according to opposing groups such as the notables, the sheikhs, the commercial bourgeoisie and the 'new nationalists'. This clearly shows that the Kemalists' view of nationalism was quite different from that of the latter groups, whose versions of nationalism emphasized Islam and traditional norms and values.

We could see Kemalism as characterized by an openness to the outside world, aimed at breaking away from imperial tradition, ending war-oriented foreign policy – according to Kemal's saying: 'peace in the country, peace in the world' – and giving priority to the republic. However, Kemalism faced a challenge from militant nationalism which, in turn, aimed to show that 'real' nationalism had to be based on traditional cultural codes, especially those of Islam. So perhaps Gökalp (1959: 76) was completely wrong when he stated the following: 'A true internationality based on science is taking the place of the internationality based on religion. The participation of Japan, on the one hand, and of Turkey, on the other, in western civilization is giving a secular character to European internationality.' I think it is important to insist that a nationalism that aimed at bringing civilization, in the case of Kemalism, was countered by another nationalism that saw its own institutionalization as the ultimate goal. The imagined community of the Turkish nation was seen by Kemalists as an important instrument for reaching the 'enlightened' era but, for another nationalist group, the ultimate goal was Turkish nationalism itself, particularly in terms of its opposition to other nations. It is important to consider the anti-Kemalist view of the nation in order to illustrate that, in modernizing periods, human spheres are radically open to interpretation. Here, 'nation' and 'nationalism' meant different things to different sectors of the same society.

Beginning around 1946, eight years after Kemal's death, a counter-movement – including the CHP, Kemal's party – first closed village institutions and replaced them with *imam-hatip* schools, thus bringing back a dualistic (secular and religious) education system. The first thing to be exploited by the anti-Kemalist movement was Islam, whose adherents were ready to raise their objectives. The Kemalists' opponents knew that they could gain support by invoking Islam against 'Western' modernity. However, this counter-group could no longer ignore 'Turkishness'. Without linking Islam to Turkishness, militant nationalism could not be a powerful ideology. In the Turkish context, then, one understanding of the modern nation was challenged by another totalistic attempt at reconstructing society, fundamentally on the basis of militant nationalism. We will deal briefly with this totalistic project in the next section while discussing the Kurdish question.

The Kurdish Question

Since 1984, Turkey has been struggling to solve a problem that some call an 'ethnic problem', while to most it is one of terrorism: the Kurdish question. This problem has caused tremendous destruction: according to official records, thirty thousand people have lost their lives. It might seem that since the Kurdish leader Abdullah Öcalan is now in the hands of the state, there is no longer a Kurdish problem.[2] However, closer observation shows that the problem is not yet over. There is, of course, no doubt that the PKK (the Kurdistan

Workers' Party) is no longer as powerful as it was before. A battle was won by the state, not just because the leader of the movement, Öcalan, was captured, but because the PKK had already been losing its power since its establishment. This relates to the fact that, in Turkey, the Kurds are in no way united. Because of this, many observers, especially external observers, do not understand the problem well (see, for example, Chaliand, 1994).

There has been a group of Kurds, represented by the PKK and, to an extent, by HADEP (the People's Democracy Party), whose aim seems to be to achieve a Kurdish nation-state. This group has never achieved a position as the representative of all Kurds living in Turkey and has remained a separatist, minority group. If it is true that 20 per cent of the population in Turkey is Kurdish,[3] and if the PKK has the support of all this population, it seems unlikely that the state would have been able to hold out against the PKK. In other words, not all Kurds wish to see a separate Kurdish state. The problem, therefore, needs to be clearly analysed rather than presupposing it to be an ethnic problem.

The Turkish state does not recognize minority groups within Turkey. Rather, 'equality' is the priority: each citizen is provided with constitutional rights and freedoms. In Turkey there are many other ethnic groups – Laz, Albanians, Arabs, Cerkez, and so on – and no problem with them has emerged so far. Then why with the Kurds? One might argue that since other ethnic groups have their own nation-states outside Turkey, they do not need to fight for them, whereas the Kurds, constituting a nation, have the right to fight for self-determination. But this argument would have to indicate, historically, that the Turkish nation-state invaded Kurdish areas and assimilated Kurds in the name of the Turkish nation. History does not prove this.[4] Within the Ottoman Empire, assuming that it was 'originally Turkish', there was the 'Muslim millet' in Anatolia, whose occupants were mainly Turks and Kurds. When the Empire disintegrated, Turkey replaced it in the 'motherland of Turks', and this new state was founded on the basis of constitutional citizenship rather than on ethnicity by assuming convergence with the population of Anatolia. Therefore, it seems impossible to validate the Kurdish claim on these grounds. However, this does not mean neglecting a living problem. The question should rather be: were the Kemalists completely wrong to assume that Turks and Kurds could live together?

In turn, this could be analysed by asking another question: is Kurdism an ethnocentric movement? In other words, have Kurds made the self-discovery that they want to be apart? We can observe that there are two sorts of ethnic movement: first, ethno-nationalism, the political demands of stateless ethnic groups seeking to achieve sovereignty and self-rule; secondly, movements that demand cultural and linguistic recognition within the boundaries of a nation-state. In the case of the Kurds in Turkey, both of these movements exist.

The PKK can be viewed as a separatist political organization. Öcalan, while a student at Ankara University, started his political career in a socialist student union, but he was quick to be disappointed: he saw in Turkish leftism a 'social fascism' towards Kurds. He tried to hold meetings and conferences about Kurdish liberation in Ankara University but he was neither followed nor supported by other Kurdish students. He found the solution in going back to his village in Urfa, where the PKK was founded in 1978 (see Mumcu, 1998). He planned a liberation war with guerrillas, and the first bloody clashes began in 1984. At that time, the state's position was that since there were only a handful of bandits, the state did not need to take them seriously.[5] However, the PKK was to shock both the state and, more importantly, society: by 1993 three thousand armed men and many teachers in the region had already been killed by the PKK. Nevertheless, it was becoming apparent that nothing could be achieved against the Turkish state and society by guerrilla war, not because of the state's strategic advantage or powerful military, but because the Kurds themselves were no happier than the Turks with the PKK. This reality was to lead a separatist, Kerim Yildiz, to understand the situation and to say that 'if the Turkish state asked the Kurds to form a separate state, they would refuse' (quoted in Poulton, 1997: 243). Thus, separation was a dream, not because it was impossible to divide Turkey – though it would have been a terribly bloody process – but because many Kurds did not agree with doing so.

Another movement appears more realistic: the demand for cultural recognition. However, the problems within this movement were no less significant. Like France, Turkey cannot recognize 'difference', precisely because the recognition of difference by a republic would mean an attempt to overcome the republic itself.[6] The situation could be viewed as follows: some, but not all, Kurds want the state to grant them 'minority rights', but, in response, the state is unable to see them as a 'minority', because they are equal citizens inasmuch as Turks or Albanians are; they may be different culturally – and this was recognized – but this cannot give them rights as a 'minority'. It cannot be denied that in Turkey every citizen is a first-class citizen. Kurds can be found in all spheres of the economy, polity, culture, education and so on. The question, I think, must be whether the Kurds want to be 'different' and, therefore, demand to be a 'minority'. For instance, it might be that the Kurds want the freedom to be 'different' because they find the conception of 'equality' problematic, perhaps because 'equality' might be thought of as meaning 'assimilation'. Indeed, at times, militant nationalism in the Turkish state imposed 'equality' as a rule for the achievement of disciplinization. In other words, the attempts to create society as a coherent whole played a part in the emergence of the Kurdish question (see Chapter 5). However, one should ask another question: do the Kurds aim to achieve independence for the sake of 'Kurdish identity'? The answer must necessarily be that Kurds want to be different for the sake of 'ideals', or identity. But a further question poses itself: how do the Kurds live?

By this question I mean the following: in Turkish modernity Kurds seem to play a part no less important than that played by Turks. In other words, the question of who is profiting the most from 'Turkey' is not an easy one. Kislali (1997) provides an example. A Kurd who fights for education to be provided by the state in Kurdish does not seem to live up to his ideals; when he was asked whether he would send his children to the Kurdish school or to the Turkish one, he answered without any doubt, saying: 'Definitely to the Turkish school and when they graduate from university, I would like to send them to an English university for post-graduate education' (Kislali, 1997: 121). Language is seen to be important for having a 'good life' but a Kurdish identity is not emphasized. On the one hand, it could be argued that the Kurds demand minority rights, because they understand the conception of equality that the state has proposed since the early 1970s as being assimilative. On the other hand, the problem does not seem clearly to be one of identity at all: some of the richest sectors in Turkey are formed by Kurds who do not see a problem in living together with Turks. What must be considered are the differences *among* Kurds as well as those between Kurds and Turks.

There are clearly differences between the Kurds in the metropolitan cities of Istanbul, Ankara, Izmir, Bursa and Adana, and the Kurds in the south-eastern region of Turkey. 'Natural' assimilation, not only of Kurds, has taken place in the metropolises. In the case of Istanbul, it is difficult to find any convincing evidence of the 'difference' of the Kurds: when asked about Kurdish characteristics that distinguish them from the Turks, the Kurds mention cultural characteristics that they in fact share with the Turks. We have to conclude that somebody is Kurdish by virtue of believing himself or herself to be Kurdish, referring to himself or herself as Kurdish and acting in 'Kurdish' ways (see Poulton, 1997). In fact, the Kurds in the metropolises largely do not participate in 'separatist' movements.

A detailed poll about Istanbulians can provide important information. Of Istanbul's population, 13.3 per cent have Kurdish roots but only 3.9 per cent consider themselves to be Kurds, while 3.7 per cent see themselves as Turks although their parents were Kurdish. Of the Kurds in Istanbul 90 per cent strictly oppose the idea of Kurdish independence.[7] According to another poll, only 9.1 per cent of Kurds see Hep, the forerunner to HADEP, as representing the Kurds.[8] But perhaps more important is the fact that the Kurdish party,

HADEP, which won over all previous Kurdish parties, scored only 4.2 per cent of votes in the 1995 elections: if the Kurdish population is around 20 per cent of the total population, 4.2 per cent cannot represent the majority of Kurds. A political sociologist, Dogu Ergil, interviewed 1200 Kurds and only 13 per cent wanted to see a separate Kurdish state (see TOBB, 1995). To understand why a small number of Kurds are not willing to live as part of Turkey, we must consider the incompatibility of Kurds in the south-eastern region with Turks.

So far the following question has not been seriously considered: do the Kurds in the south-eastern region of Turkey have distinctive characteristics? I would argue that they do. They came from a different world system from that of the Turks – a type of feudalism. The Turks, in their history, never lived within a feudal system, while the Kurds still live according to a version of it. The second difference concerns religious understanding: while the Kurdish population in the region is mostly Safi, a Sunni school, the Turks never followed this kind of Islam: the majority of Turks are Sunni too, but of the Hanefi school. An actual difference must also be found in terms of the relations with the central political authority. A sort of feudalism that has remained alive in the south-east makes it clear that the Kurds in the region interpret the world in a crucially different way from the Turks in Anatolia. Turkish modernization could not completely succeed in altering the socio-political structure of the south-east. Since the Kemalist project was formed by a consideration of the 'general' characteristics of the Anatolian people, the modernizers had failed to realize that Kurdish regions would need further attempts and programmes to reach modernization. The problem, in fact, must be traced back to the Ottoman Empire, which did not master the region, but left it to be governed by local religious leaders, *apiret reisi*. The Turkish population was directly connected to the central political authority, because the Turks did not have local leaderships that could function between the people and the state; hence, in the transition to modernity, no revolt against the state emerged in Turkish lands. However, since the Kurds had always been governed by local landlords, when modernizing nationalism came to the fore, there were revolts against it in the south-east, such as the Seikh Sait revolt.

Religious differences are also crucially important. The plurality of Islam in the Turkish lands has been remarkable. The Kurdish population has adhered to the Safi branch of Sunnism, a relatively orthodox form of Islam, while the Turkish population has embraced different or even conflicting, although co-existing, conceptions of Islam. According to the Safi school of Sunnism, life must be led according to explicit Islamic rules, while the Hanefi school of Sunnism is more open to revision. This can be seen, for example, if we consider the place of women in the public sphere. In the south-east, women have been more controlled by men, and strong moral laws define how women must live their lives, while in the Turkish regions, the place of women in the public domain is almost equal to the place of men. The relation of the *asiret* (local clans formed by kinship ties) to democracy should be seen as a very important factor in terms of the persistence of distinctions between the Turks and the Kurds in modern times. In the Kurdish areas, most people support a political party that is found to be suitable by the leader of the *asiret*, rather than making political decisions individually. Although the region is ostensibly part of a democracy, the decisions are in fact made by the patriarchal authority without the participation of the 'people', and the possibility of disputes among the people in the region can be easily opposed by an idealized homogeneous culture. The lack of secularization and individuation in the Kurdish areas thus seems incompatible with the way of life in the western part of Turkey. But does this simply mean that the different groups have the right to be apart? Should we simply adopt a laissez-faire relativism? If it is argued that every culture has the right to operate on the basis of its specific belief, then we have to consider the options for enabling Kurds and Turks to live side by side.

In the rise of the Kurdish question, radical Turkish nationalism must be regarded as an important factor. As mentioned above, the nationalization process was open to interpretation and to disputes. Against the civic nationalism of Kemalism, a militant ethnocentric view of nationalism emerged and crystallized in the early 1960s in the political organization of the MHP, the nationalist action party. According to this totalistic perspective, Turkish society had to be reconstructed on the basis of the values held by the Turks. In an ethnically plural geographical space such as Anatolia, this sort of fascist ideology will inevitably encounter strong opposition. Until the 1970s, this militant nationalism never became powerful and, until the late 1990s, it never received important support from larger sectors of Turkish society. In the 1970s, however, ideological polarization led to intervention by the military, which sided with the militant nationalists, hoping that 'cultural values' could hold Turkish society together as a coherent whole. This nationalist attempt at totalizing Turkish society on the basis of a 'Turkish-Islamic synthesis' was to give rise to further polarization.

The 1971 military coup aimed to discipline the population of Turkey, which had enjoyed the liberty provided by the 1961 constitution. The 1968 student movement was blamed for the youth not being educated according to the principles of Turkism and Islamism; a new disciplining regime, grounded on nationalist principles, was seen to be necessary. This disciplining created a new radicalization of oppositions between nationalist militants and leftists. This, however, caused another, even more stringent, military coup in 1980. The

Kurdish question was one reason for this. However, the disciplining attempts of the state were not directed only against Kurdish identity, but also led to high tensions between Turkish society and the state. Thus, this problem cannot be analysed clearly without considering the relations between society and state. The economy also needs to be considered because it is an area that has the capacity to create tensions and clashes. Therefore, in the next chapter, we shall examine the relations between the state, society and the economy. We shall see that these relations can be configured in various ways, supporting the thesis of varieties of modernity.

CHAPTER 4

State, Society and Economy: Tensions between Liberty and Discipline

The rise of the 'social sphere' can be taken as a major turning point in the emergence of modernity. From polity to household, a realm of human activity understood as the 'social' began to emerge in the late eighteenth century alongside the development of modernity. The rise of 'society' as a new type of collectivity was, in fact, focused on by some eighteenth-century thinkers. As Wagner (1999a: 216) considers: 'In some late eighteenth-century theories, "civil society" came to be seen as a phenomenon that was different from the state but different from the individual households as well. And it is here that the story of "society" as a scientific object starts.'

We cannot discuss the rise of society without considering changing features in the state system. The socialization of individuals in a larger context, such as society, needs a 'civilizing state'. The management of an entire population from a single base is a prominent factor in the standardization of practices and identities. That is to say, modernity in one important way increases the dependence of people on others (Arendt, 1958). And in this process, the modern, centralizing state possesses a crucial power. Additionally, economic development requires the integration of local communities on the basis of a centre and thus the state needs to be a highly centralized power in order to manage this integrated population. Rationality comes to be seen as a characteristic of the state, since a social body is thought to be governed by a state that does not operate by means of kinship, emotions and friendship. These are, therefore, excluded from the socio-political sphere.

It is because of the relative autonomy of the state that, in social analyses, 'civil society' was invented as a entity distinct from the state (see Gellner, 1995; Hall, 1995). The state appeared to be a neutral sphere over society, not favouring a particular group or class. Being responsible for all members of society meant being a power that could be exercised over an entire population in order to bring about 'civilized' human beings. In other words, Hegel's state, the modern state, used Reason to reconcile antagonisms in society and it thus understood itself as the enlightening agent of humanity. This observation brought about two understandings, one of which assumed the state to be an autonomous sphere, while the other saw the state as an instrument in the service of a powerful social class (for elitist and class theories of the state, see Mann, 1993). To mention two important classical theorists, Marx (1959) argued that the state was the instrument of the ruling class, but saw a relative autonomy and domination of the state over civil society in some experiences. And Weber (1968) emphasized the modern state as a crucial determinant of capitalism. In fact, we can see the state neither as a completely autonomous sphere nor as merely the tool of the dominant social class. The state may be interpreted as the main political institution, whose legitimacy is directly based on the art of reconciling the contradictions in society for the sake of its continuity. Therefore, there must be a dialectical relation of society to the state: for example, had the state not regarded itself as a civilizing agent, 'civil society' might not have emerged.

At the same time, in the emergence of modernity, the economy was being transformed, so that it came to the fore as a driving force in the development of 'civilization'. This change required the socialization of labour: that is, in stark contrast to the principle of individual liberty seen as central to 'the project of modernity', basic developments were achieved by collective labour. As a result, work could no longer be understood purely in terms of maintaining the family; it was also for the sake of society. That is, work became socialized. Within the modern experience, the economy became even more essential than the activity of governing (Arendt, 1958). The polity can even, to an extent, be seen as a sort of economy. 'Development' is a basic tenet of modernity and it reflects itself first in the economic improvement of human life: the economy is the unavoidable medicine of both state and society in modernity. When economy and polity come to be seen as distinct entities in social science, another sphere emerges as an object of scientific study: society. However, it must be understood that a clear separation never occurred.[1] For instance, some understand family to be a sphere within the social realm, excluding the economy as system (see Habermas, 1987), whereas others see the economy as a constitutive activity of civil society, while excluding the family as belonging to the private domain (see Giner, 1995).

In discussing the relations between these three institutions, it must be clear that none of them is autonomous. Rather, the state and society play pivotal parts in shaping each other, while the economy is a powerful realm in the creation of tensions between state and society, as well as between different sectors of society. In revolutionary cases, in the emergence of modernity, these relations are much more fraught than in other cases; a comparison between France and England, for instance, would show this difference. Here we are concerned with these relations in the context of a radical social transformation: the Turkish experience. A weak society versus a strong state is generally held to be the starting point for analyses of the Turkish case (Mahçupyan, 1997; Insel, 1995). The Kemalist state has largely been viewed as aiming to create a 'Western' society by maintaining a high level of state autonomy and even brutality (see Çakir and Cinemre [eds.], 1991). However, it needs to be seen that Kemalism was a historical product as well as one of the new actors of modernity, and that it was the successful answer to an old Ottoman question: how could the modern Turkish state be formed? The Kemalist answer was that without the rise of a strong society and a strong economy, the state in modern times could easily be ravaged.

To understand the Turkish experience in terms of the relations between state, economy and society, I propose an analysis of the radicalization of oppositions, dualities and dichotomies. In the history of the Turks, tensions were present and the project of modernity in Anatolia had to radicalize the oppositions by holding in a central place the 'imaginary significations' of the idea of modernity. In this respect, the Kemalist state must be understood as the container of modernity so as to radicalize dualities: religion versus science, individuality versus community, rationality versus culture, nature versus humanity, development versus underdevelopment, and so on. Therefore, the radicalization of dualities could be taken to be one of the characteristics of the history of Turkish modernity. I shall now analyse the roles of state, society and economy in the Turkish experience, and shall examine the relations between them in terms of the tension between liberty and discipline.

The Kemalist State

The Ottoman Empire struggled to catch up with Western modernity. During the nineteenth century, modernizing reforms dominated the Empire. The Empire did not, however, achieve its ambitions, particularly because it lacked a 'society' and an 'economy' in the modern sense. The Ottoman intelligentsia did not realize that a modern state would need a society on behalf of which the state could bring about actual reforms. In other words, the modern state could not be achieved without a firm connection between the state and society. The Ottoman Empire usually cut relations with people outside the sultanate because the autonomy of the sultan was always an ultimate ambition. In other words, the people would have been a threat to the despotic sultanate if they were not excluded from the centre. The central state mechanism dominated the entire population of the Empire; conquering this centre was therefore necessary for the people to achieve any power.

Thus, the Empire's decay and collapse was importantly due to its repressive attitudes towards its subjects. New emerging forces in communities were suppressed, because those forces might have competed with the state, which regarded itself as the central power of any activity. Association between different communities was not allowed; the division of labour was restricted on the basis of ethnic-religious communities. Because the state announced itself as the centre of power, any potential force in the collectivity was seen as opposition to the state.

The Turks were excluded from central power, especially since 1453, when Istanbul was conquered. More crucially, due to the division of labour on the basis of ethno-religious communities (known as the *millet* system), Turks were not permitted to deal with 'commerce', which was the work of Jewish and Christian communities (Çavdar, 1970). The Turks were confined to farming and were forced to provide soldiers for the Empire. This was an intelligent division of labour on the part of the Empire because it neutralized any possible threat from the core subjects of this Turko-Islamic Empire: the Turks were unable to access power, nor were they able to deal with work necessary for the emergence of a strong society, such as commerce. Since the sultanate was the unquestionable power, all agricultural products were owned by the state. Thus, the Ottoman state regarded itself as the centre of all activity: if societal centres had emerged, the state would have assigned itself to compete with these powers, even by the use of physical force.

It was because of this characteristic that when Western modernity hit the Empire, both economically and ideologically, it found no power to fight against weakness in the collectivity. The French Revolution, with its idea of nation, ravaged the Empire because it was easier, due to the *millet* system, to establish separate states for different ethnic communities. The Empire immediately began reforming the army and the civilian bureaucracy, but it did not pay attention to the fact that a powerful social sphere, with a developing economy, was needed for the re-establishment of a powerful state. The Empire began to attempt this kind of reform only in the 1910s, when it had been left with only its core subjects, the Turks. However, it was too late, because the Western world was already reshaped on the basis of nation-states which were searching for more colonies; the Empire found itself enmeshed in the First World War.

The question facing the Ottoman intelligentsia was this: how can a modern state be built? In order to counterbalance the West, a modern state was needed. However, the Ottomans believed that the answer lay in reforming the army and bureaucracy, without seeing the importance of the rise of society and of economic development. A project could have been developed by the state in order to found a network within society for developing the forces of production. In many respects, without the rise of society over local communities it is difficult to build a powerful country in modern times. For example, in order for an efficient economy to work, the country needs to be centralized. Or, for instance, in order to encourage people towards 'development', the state must implement national education. This was to be observed in the Turkish project of modernity, Kemalism, in the 1920s. However, the attempts of the Ottoman Empire to catch up with Western modernity were not a mere failure; they provided a means of self-critique that played a very important part in Kemalism. The Ottoman reforms, mostly of the military, did not achieve modernity but, at the same time, they played a part in the development of the Turkish project of modernity. The successful answer that the Kemalists found to the question of how to establish a modern state distinguished them from the Ottomans, and Kemalism emerged as a new phenomenon in the Turkish world.

A modern state could well be founded by a political elite, but this state might be quickly weakened if a social base were not built for it. The Kemalists were aware of this fact. Although it was a difficult task in the 1920s, the Kemalists announced in the 1921 constitution that the people were sovereign without condition or restriction. This announcement already supposed that Turkish society was strong enough not to be oppressed by external forces. It did not, however, affect people's ways of life immediately, precisely because the Anatolian masses were not aware that the state could be an arena for people's interests and ideals; rather, they were accustomed to the view that people could only be subjects of the state. Therefore, the rise of Turkish society was to come about later.

Great emphasis was placed by the Kemalists on the idea of the *autonomy* of the new Turkish nation – autonomy being, as we saw earlier, a key 'imaginary signification' of modernity. Autonomous collectivity, however, was conceived as emerging on the basis of revolutionary political action. The Kemalist project saw no solution to problems other than 'developing' the Turks. Development was seen as the precondition for achieving autonomy for Turkish society in terms of its relations with other societies. This view was unprecedented in Turkish history: the previous state was not one of autonomy for Turks but, for the sake of the continuity of the sultanate, it was a multi-ethnic and multi-religious empire.

According to Kemalism, the Turks had to be able to form a self-sufficient collectivity that would not let itself be colonized. In other words, Turkish society should recognize its own significations and creations and should manage itself. A first priority of Kemalism was that of anti-imperialism which required the Anatolian masses to constitute the 'Turkish nation'. The self-determination of nations was a basic and vital process in the opinion of Mustafa Kemal: thus, the first principle in the political programme of Kemalism was nationalism, the requirement that the Anatolian people constitute 'the Turkish nation'. Anti-imperialism was also an essential principle of the Kemalist project of modernity: that is, according to Kemalism, not only a defence of national autonomy, but also other nations' rights to self-determination must be recognized. This feature sharply distinguishes Kemalism both from the Ottomans and from other projects of modernity. According to Kemalism, a modern state is autonomous in two senses: it should not allow itself to be colonized, nor should it colonize other nations. Therefore, according to Kemalism, imperialist countries are not modern.

Kemalism was also a form of republicanism, because the autonomy of Turkish society was thought to be achievable only on the basis of the autonomization of reason. A central belief of modernity can be seen to be at stake here: the belief in collective mastery over external forces. Republicanism was the expression of the will of the Turks to escape from external forces, which also meant the redefinition of the place of God in human life. According to Kemalism, the Turks believed uncritically in the caliph as the ambassador of Allah. The republican state, in stark contrast, claimed to be based on human reason with the aim of securing human happiness in this world. Kemalist political philosophy took the republic to be the most desirable political system because human beings were thought to be capable of governing themselves. In other words, for Kemalism, rational manageability had to be achieved.

Thus, another basic principle of the new political establishment was secularism. Since, according to Kemalist thinking, the Turks had to be liberated from external forces, mystical orders had to be destroyed. Individuation, another key imaginary signifier of modernity, was important here: Kemalism worked on the assumption that people wanted to see themselves as in control of their own development, and as having no reason to fear external forces. The 'humanization' of knowledge and action was understood by Kemalism as a precondition for moving towards a desirable life. Escaping from the Islamic *ulema* required knowledge of the world and this knowledge had to be secular. This precisely marked a radicalization of the duality between sheikhs and the people for the sake of Enlightenment. That is, there was already a tangible duality between the sheikhs and the people, and this duality was radicalized on the basis of strict secularism with the aim of moving secular forces towards modernity.

Achieving a break with mystical orders was thought to imply populism. In the Kemalists' view, this could be achieved on the basis of two principles: tolerance and equality. In this respect, the basic ambition of Kemalism was to rearrange relations between state and collectivity. The Ottoman Empire had created a centre–periphery dichotomy between the sultanate and the people. Kemalism aimed to break with this legacy using populism: the state depended on the people for its legitimacy. The essential aim was to create a society that was not divided by class; all people must be equal before the law. Of course, the paradox of a populist ideology is that there must be space for the people to criticize existing political orders, so that 'Enlightenment' itself would have to depend on the views of the people rather than on those of the political elite.[2]

Because the Kemalists perceived Turkey, in the 1920s, as lagging far behind the Western world, they argued that the Turkish republic could not be content with gradual evolutionary progress, but that, in contrast, the process of modernization had to be speeded up by revolutionary measures. This opened the Turkish project of modernity to interpretation and redefinition. Once revolution is not only allowed but made a central feature in the lives of the people, further revolts and movements cannot be avoided: if change is legitimate, then further change cannot be blocked.

In the transition to modernity a powerful agent is needed. In this respect, Kemalism's first attempts could be called imitative; a liberal model, to some extent, was accepted. However, Kemalists quickly became very critical of the liberal model with which Turkish modernity had been created in the 1930s when the Kemalist view of political and economic development was produced: the state was regarded as the agent of the transition to modernity. Kemalism can therefore be seen as a statist movement. However, understanding the Kemalist state as the main agent in the emergence of Turkish modernity should not lead us to underestimate the role of social actors, such as teachers, lawyers, and notably women, who were benefiting from the 'new world'.

To a considerable extent the Kemalist revolution could be seen as a new phenomenon in world history. In the 1930s, a leftist Kemalist intellectual stated that 'Turkey is engaged in an experiment which is totally unique: the Turkish Revolution is the most just and progressive phenomenon on the post-war national and international scale' (Aydemir, 1990 [1932]: 36). First, with its political philosophy, unprecedented in the Islamic world, Kemalism provided a model of modernization for Muslim countries[3] – such a modern state was formed in a predominantly Islamic country for the first time. Secondly, the political philosophy of Kemalism can be seen to differ, to a considerable extent, from other Western political philosophies. Some argue that the Kemalist state took nationalism, republicanism and secularism from the French Revolution while taking statism, populism and revolutionism from the Russian Revolution (Kislali, 1997). And some go so far as to say that 'there is no reason why one should not regard the westernisation movements as the scientific basis of the Turkish revolution' (Karal, 1997: 12). So we may be forced to accept that the Kemalist principles were of Western origin, given that the idea of modernity was imported from the West. However, as has often been emphasized in this book, borrowings from the outside world are subject to reinterpretation. The basic principles of Kemalism had never been put together and interpreted in quite the same way in any previous context. For instance, unlike the Russian and Chinese models, the Kemalist model aimed, as much as possible, towards development in democracy.[4] The uniqueness of the Kemalist state was due to contextual features as well as to the specific interpretation of the meaning of modernity by Turkish modernizing actors. A particular version of secularity, for example, can be considered here. In contrast to the Christian view of secularity, in Turkey the state was seen as the provider of religious services. In other words, the state was not understood as an autonomous institution opposed to the autonomous institution of Islam; rather, it was viewed as compulsory that the state provide religious services, although not itself structured according to Islamic rules. This was continuous with the previous era. The Ottoman Empire saw Islam as its partner in governing over subjects.

The origins of the Kemalist state deserve to be paid close attention.[5] Most Kemalists were military men and this is the main reason why the Kemalist state is readily seen as a military state (Insel, 1995). The social source of Kemalism, however, was an alliance of different sectors of society: the military and civil elite, the merchant class, landowners and provincial notables occupied the seats of the Grand National Assembly and of the Republican People's Party (RPP). Although it cannot be denied that the Turkish army played a pivotal part in the emergence of Turkish modernity, one aim of Kemalism's political philosophy was to eliminate military features from the political arena. Unlike the Ottomans, Kemalism promised a society and polity that would not be managed by the military. In the 1920s, in a move unprecedented in Turkish political history, the connection between army and government was broken (Aydemir, 1998). For the first time, the military was asked not to act as a political agent. This was a signal that Kemalism did not aim for continuity with the past; the Turks should have a civilian government. Kemal, an ex-general and the first president of the republic as a civilian, forced generals to choose between the military or politics. This was not the only act of Kemal aimed at cutting connections with the army. More importantly, he entrusted the duty of defending national independence and the republic to the 'youth' and not to the army. As Ahmad (1993: 9) argues, 'Throughout the single-party period (1923–1945) the army was completely isolated from political life … The army was given a place of honour in the republic but it was also removed from the mainstream of the social and political life of the country.' However, the Turkish army could not easily be isolated from politics.[6] Despite revolutionary attempts to break with the historical military legacy, history emerged to play a powerful role.

By eliminating pashas from the political arena, Kemalism's republican principle seemed to be moving convincingly in the right direction. Kemalism aimed to establish a republican democracy as quickly as possible: one year after the foundation of the republic, oppositional groups were allowed to form political parties. The Progressive Republican Party was formed against the RPP in 1924. In a few months counter-revolutionary actors were seen to be occupying the opposition party. Their ultimate goal was to bring back the caliphate, which would have meant the dissolution of the new regime and the democratic republic. A dilemma unsurprisingly appeared: were the opposition to come to power, it would not maintain democracy. The Kemalists believed, however, that without developing a democratic, enlightened society, the road to 'civilization' would be destroyed. Thus, it was argued that, before reaching the 'good life', people have no choice but to trust state elites. Ambiguity necessarily haunts this process: 'liberty' is promised but, on the road, 'discipline' is seen as being legitimate. This was certainly the view of the leftist Kemalism that was powerful at the time. Particularly, in the 1930s, this leftist Kemalism became an advanced political centre for debates about the nature of the regime. A group of leftist Kemalist intellectuals argued that Turkey did not need a multi-party democracy, but a revolutionary party-state system (Aydemir, 1990 [1932]). According to this view, if Turkey had seen itself as a democracy without developing the conditions for it, the consequence would have been disaster. The 'drunkenness' of becoming a liberal democracy was seen as false consciousness in a country that provided the model of fighting against the 'liberal' West (Aydemir, 1990 [1932]).

A distinctive feature of the Turkish experience could be used to illustrate this theme. Before the rise of society, the state dominated over the collectivity. The Ottoman Empire was already a central authority and, thus, Kemalism did not encounter serious problems in this respect. The problem, however, was how to build a society. The state, unlike for example in the British experience, emerged as the teacher of society. The Kemalist state understood itself as the agent of civilization: things had to be done for the sake of people in spite of people. Historical continuity should be emphasized here: the first Kemalists grew up in an old patrimonial tradition which assumed the dominance of the state over society. This helps us to understand why, in the Turkish case, the main agent of modernization was the state elite. The agents of modernization, of course, differ from context to context, conflicts within societies being an important determining factor. For example, in Western Europe, civil conflicts gave rise to the bourgeoisie as an important agent of modernization. However, in the Turkish experience, the central conflict emerged regarding responses to the rise of the West, which produced a new state elite that became the central agent of modernization. But secondary modernizing actors also emerged in Turkey: in particular, women, teachers and lawyers were important actors in the promulgation of modern ideas.

Kemalism made great strides towards achieving its ambitions. Between 1923 and 1938, the industrialization of Turkey was achieved. A new generation was educated within a secular national system. It was aimed to centralize the country by means of a newly built railway network; the train took modernity with it wherever it went. Peasants were taught mechanical agriculture. However, the modernizing project was not easy: the aim was to reach a rational society on the basis of political action, but people are also cultural beings. In the next section, we shall briefly examine Turkish society at the time when Kemalism was making efforts to 'civilize' it.

The Rise of Society

In the early 1920s, the Empire was dead. The Turkish peasantry in Anatolia had squandered their energy and their blood in the struggle to conquer and defend alien lands and peoples. They had already seen the state as an evil that had sent them to distant lands to fight wars. In their local settings, they were facing the brutality of the local political leaders and armed forces of the state (Ahmad, 1993). It was this peasant collectivity that was the legacy of the Empire to the republic. Perhaps more important was the fact that the ruled community of the Empire failed to develop power independent of the state. There was no 'civil society' based on market forces and private ownership. In brief, autonomous cities, towns and estates were absent from the Empire (Mardin, 1969).

In 1927, the population of Turkey was recorded at around thirteen million. Only 18 per cent of this population was living in cities. The Kemalists aimed to alter this predominantly agrarian country into a modern one in a very short period. How to make this 'immature' society side with the revolutionary project was the crucial question of the time. The Kemalists needed to ask what sort of structure held this collectivity together in order to find social partners. It was definitely not the bourgeoisie, nor was it the industrial working class: in 1915 a report showed that there were only 182 industrial enterprises and 14,046 workers (Aydemir, 1998: 351). Nor were the Turkish peasants inclined to revolution, perhaps because there was no powerful landed aristocracy in Turkey. Unlike the Russian and Chinese models, then, the Turkish revolution did not mobilize the peasantry. The emergence of the strong modernizing state as the main agent of change in Turkey must be understood in relation to its historical context.

The Anatolian peasantry witnessed the increasing power of *agas* (landlords) and *esraf* (notables) in the last period of the Empire. The state was too distant from peasants, especially in times of crisis, but the *agas* and *esraf* were always near, although they exploited the peasants (Ahmad, 1993). It was this characteristic that led peasants to distrust the state. The new Kemalist state had struggled to reach this peasantry in order to emancipate it; the problem was the lack of autonomous social actors who could play a crucial part between the state and the individual. History haunted again: there were not many autonomous agents between the Ottoman state and its subjects. Rather, the relation of the state to the people was much more direct. Only in the last period of the Empire had a sort of landowner class emerged. Kemalism thus proposed that only by means of *esraf* and the sheikhs, the religious leaders, could the peasants be reached. Hence the Kemalists were forced to take as their allies the notables who held an important place in the People's Party.

Kemalism opened up a space of opportunity for people in society to enter into the political arena. In this respect, well-educated and self-aware men, influenced particularly by Russia, were regarded as the moulders of public opinion, with the ability to change society (Ahmad, 1993). The Kemalists saw that they could not bring about social revolution either through the peasantry or through the *esraf*; the state required a core of educated people to take decisions and put them into practice. Modern society, in one respect, means a 'reading public'. However, 'immature' Turkish society lacked education: only 8 per cent of the population was literate. Kemalism brought about two reforms: the unification of the educational system and the replacement of the Arabic script by the Roman alphabet. Overnight, an educated minority of 8 per cent was made illiterate as part of the process aiming to bring about universal literacy. In common with other revolutionaries, the Kemalists believed that the emancipation of the population could be achieved by education. Although important efforts were made, an immediate problem emerged: where were the peasants to be educated? This was an important question, given that the peasantry was the largest sector of society. Local notables hindered the education of the peasantry, although the Kemalists at first hoped to enter the villages by means of these men. Under difficult conditions, a unique educational system was to be produced. Educating young people from the villages and teaching them about Kemalism was regarded as a better solution. The Kemalists aimed to reach the peasants by means of educational institutions. By educating the daughters and sons of peasants to be teachers, the Kemalists aimed to bring about dispute and opposition in villages; those teachers went back to their own villages to teach children, but also to guide villagers towards a 'rational world'. Village institutes were short-lived, being shut down by the right-wing government in the 1950s, who saw them as breeding-grounds for communism among the youth. Nonetheless, to a considerable extent, over a very brief period they did give rise to 'enlightened' groups; differentiation was achieved as a duality between teacher and imam.

It seemed urgently necessary, to the Kemalists, to dissolve the hegemony of sheikhs and religious leaders in Anatolia. The crucial tensions between the modernizing state and conservative society were particularly apparent in terms of secularizing reforms. Self-management of social institutions, which required rationality, was thought to be difficult as long as sheikhs remained in society. The emancipation of individuality also depended on secularization, because in order to see themselves as self-reliant masters of their own development, human beings have to escape from the belief in divine forces. It could also be argued that a secular worldview is important for economic development and hence for the autonomy of society – people must be concerned with this world rather than thinking of the world to come. It is clear that Kemalism emphasized secularism precisely because, without it, the key significations of modernity – freedom, rationality, autonomy – could not make sense. In the Ottoman Empire, the common factor linking the state and the people was Islam, the Islamic community and the Islamic state (Mahçupyan, 1997). Kemalism aimed to replace this commonality with the process of secularization. Therefore, when Kemalism abolished the caliphate, some religious men saw the fact that a Muslim collectivity was forced to live under a non-Muslim polity as a serious situation. There were bitter reprisals, such as the Sheikh Sait revolt and the Menemen faction. It was only afterwards that the Kemalist state recognized that a liberal policy towards counter-revolutionary movements could not succeed. In contrast, Islam had to be considered as a state policy, a public service provided by the state. This control of religion was later to be exploited by right-wing parties against Kemalism (see Aydemir, 1999).

The collectivity in Anatolia was not a coherent whole. Life was maintained in small local communities and differences between them were significant. The Kemalists tried hard to eliminate differences, to standardize practices and identities, with the aim of creating society as a coherent whole. For example, it was possible to recognize *tarikat* people from by their style of dress, so the Kemalists introduced dress reforms aimed at dissolving the differences between local ethnic and religious communities. In this attempt, Kemalism faced strong resistance: many people, for example, did not want to replace the fez with the hat, so wearing the fez was made illegal. To an important extent, this reform played a part in bringing about change: for example, in the 1920s, female students wore shorts in what was a predominantly Muslim society (Göle, 1996). Using the power of law, the state is able to some extent to change social reality in order to fulfil its ambitions. However, formal, legal methods cannot completely succeed in controlling society. For example, the Kemalist state brought about a reading public which, in turn, could not be completely controlled.

As we have seen, the Kemalist era (1923–45) presented a radicalization of differences, oppositions and dualities, with the aim of creating a new society. The public was confronted with the challenge of 'development': for example, the daughters of conservative parents were put in classrooms with boys and without veils, so that some parents were unwilling to send their daughters to schools. However, Kemal's adopted daughters were exemplars of modern women: one of them had become a professor of history and the other a pilot. The radicalization of oppositions marked the rise of society; this must tell us that modern society can never represent a totality. This can be seen particularly if we consider the rise of the Turkish economy, which, as we shall see in the next section, created disputes, conflicts and clashes which, in turn, played an important part in shaping modern Turkish society and the modern Turkish state.

The Rise of the Economy

It is possible to regard modernity as the rise of the economic sphere. In other words, in modernizing periods, economic activity comes to the fore, viewed as the motor of 'civilization'. Economic development has generally been taken to be a most important criterion in terms of the power of modernity. Therefore, within modernity, a prominent distinguishing feature of human beings – work – develops. And this characteristic becomes a driving force for reaching modernity. In other words, modernity is a disciplining phenomenon of economic activity: the basic material achievements of human beings are achieved within modernity by the systemization of economic activity.

However, the systemization of economic activity necessarily requires 'efficiency', which becomes an element in the search for the 'good life'. In other words, economic modernization implies instrumentality: a means-ends calculation. Therefore, rationality emerges as an unavoidable principle for building modernity. This is because economic modernization requires some basic processes that have been understood to be organized on the basis of the efficiency of calculation. Human reason is viewed as achieving 'civilization' by altering standards of living. It needs to be stressed here that in the rise of economic action there is always a risk of erosion of the ultimate values of a socio-cultural world. However, this potential danger cannot obstruct the economic modernization without which modernity cannot be achieved. Thus, the rise of economic action, like the rise of a rational state and a national society, is unavoidable for building modernity.

The Kemalist project gave central importance to economic development from the very beginning, viewing economic development as a vital process for reaching modernity. The conditions of life could be altered by improving standards of living, and this emerges first in the economic sphere. However, saying that economic development is an unavoidable process for reaching modernity does not mean that there is one universal model of the modern economy. The characteristics of a particular national economy are affected by historical and civilizational context. The Turkish experience, although it is often thought of as a Westernizing model, cannot be reduced to a European model of economic development. We shall briefly examine how the Kemalist model of economic development differed from other models and show why Turkey is currently finding it difficult to become fully compatible with Western liberal economic policies.

The new Turkey inherited a struggling and inadequate economy from the ruins of the Ottoman Empire (Avcioglu, 1973). A project of modernity had to take this situation seriously in order to avoid half-measures. Before attempting to analyse the Kemalist view of the economy, I shall briefly consider why the legacy of the Ottoman Empire hindered economic modernization. The institutional shape of the Ottoman Empire included elements that were blocking possible economic developments coming from the societal sphere. The Empire organized the socio-economic world, which included three main categories: the rulers, the sultan and his military and civilian bureaucrats, including the *ulema*; the ruled, *reaya*, both Muslims and non-Muslims; and local leaders, *esraf*. In this system, the most prominent feature was the autonomy of the state. The state was the sole locus of power in the Ottoman system. Between the state and society there were no local estates, as there were in European feudalism; this was the case, particularly, because private property was not guaranteed by the Ottoman system (Mardin, 1994). That is, there was no landed upper class able to challenge the state's power, which, in turn, would have led to the free economic development of society. The Ottoman Empire possessed an agrarian economy and society and an imperial state. This imperial state was exploiting all sectors of the collectivity without favouring any of them. A crucial point here is the lack of autonomous structures and actors that could play a role between the sultanate and the subjects. It could be said that civil society was absent from the Empire. Thus, an important point to consider is what defined domination and authority in the Empire. Domination in the

Ottoman Empire was not based on economic position. Rather, power was connected to political and military organization, a historical fact that could explain why, in present-day Turkey, power relations cannot be analysed purely by considering the economy. In brief, the central dynamic was the political authority which controlled most of the land; status was the first factor determining wealth but a bureaucrat's wealth remained the property of the state on his death. Within this sort of socio-economic system, the state could best be described as a 'financial' state; that is, the Ottoman state's political economy was designed to maximize the tax collected from the agricultural sector.

During the eighteenth century, the Empire began to be transformed into a 'capitalist economy' of the time. This was achieved on the basis of free trade which was allowed by the *tanzimat* era (1839–76). As a result, the Ottoman economy was unable to defend itself against European competition. Due to the economic capitulations made to foreign capital, the Ottoman Empire was reduced to being at the mercy of Western capital, and became a semi-colony of the West (Çavdar, 1970). Western states lent money to the sultanate, and the sultanate, in its attempts to Westernize itself, increased consumption, but without any corresponding increase in production. This also played a part in the semi-colonization of the Empire. From the beginning of the nineteenth century until the 1920s, the position of the Empire as a semi-colony of Western powers, particularly Britain and France, led to two developments in the Ottoman economy. First, a commercial bourgeoisie arose, most of whose members were of non-Turkish origin – Greeks, Christians and Jews. Secondly, Turkish agriculture in Anatolia was, to some extent, opened to the Western market (see Avcioglu, 1973). However, these two developments were not radical factors in the renewal of society and state. As a semi-colony, the Ottoman Empire became the 'sick man' of Europe, to be divided into many parts and subject to colonizing attempts by Western powers, particularly Britain and France. As has been mentioned, these attempts to colonize Turkey resulted in Turkish victory. And it was after gaining political independence that Turkey was to establish a new, Kemalist, political economy.

The Kemalist political economy was a product of the experience of the first ten years of the Turkish republic. In other words, the Kemalists did not develop a clearly defined political economy alongside the foundation of the republic; rather, a view of the economy was developed from practice. Nevertheless, as early as 1923, a new economic policy, based on the centrality of industry, was introduced by the Kemalists. Kemalist political economy was capitalist yet, at the same time, anti-imperialist. This may seem contradictory, in that the Kemalists were making concessions to foreign capital while working against it at the same time (Kongar, 1985). In fact, there is no contradiction in a political economy being both capitalist and anti-imperialist at the same time. That is, foreign capital was welcome as long as it did not damage the nation's economic development (Ahmad, 1997). However, this sort of political economy was very difficult to establish, particularly since the Kemalists faced a challenge from the new Turkish bourgeoisie.

The Kemalists saw no distinction between political and economic independence, arguing that without an independent national economy, political independence would not survive. Thus, the Kemalists opposed the economic views of the rising commercial bourgeoisie and landowners. Both groups had seen national independence primarily as important for political sovereignty. Economic sovereignty was not significant because both groups believed that they had much to gain from economic subservience to Europe (Kongar, 1985). Therefore, it becomes clear that Kemalism was not simply a bourgeois project. Had this been so, Turkey would have fallen under the mandate of either Britain or France. The Kemalists refused to accept the role ascribed to the new Turkey by both imperialist Western nations and the internal commercial bourgeoisie, that of commercial middleman between East and West. Against the bourgeois view of a commercial political economy, the Kemalists without doubt regarded industry as an essential component of the new Turkey. The question remained, what model of industrialization was to be followed?

The first answer was an open economic model based not just on liberalism but on active state support for private accumulation. This policy was practised between 1923 and 1929. The Kemalist state was not an instrument used by the dominant social class, it was a political body that aimed to develop a Turkish bourgeois class. What was the primary goal of Kemalism in supporting private capital? The answer is that it was thought possible to produce a 'national bourgeoisie' on the basis of active state support for private accumulation. However, there were conditions for supporting private capital, whether local or foreign. Since anti-imperialism was a founding principle of the republic, in an open economy supported by the state some crucial measures were taken to protect that economy. For example, the first private national bank was established by the Kemalist leadership in order to end the dominance of foreigners in the banking system. Thus, the actual goal of the first economic policy was to create a national bourgeoisie through state support and resources. However, this economic nationalism did not yield desirable results; foreign investments could not be nationalized. Although the growth rate reached 8.5 per cent in the 1920s, this disappointed the Kemalists, who expected more development. This disappointment created a period of self-questioning in the late 1920s.

The Kemalist model of development was to come about in the period from 1930 to 1939. The protectionist economy, between 1930 and 1932, as a reaction against the open economy, yielded positive results: the growth rate of industry rose to 14.8 per cent, the highest since the foundation of the republic. At the same time, however, the leadership of the Kemalist party was not satisfied with economic growth. This gave rise to self-questioning, not only because of unsatisfactory development, but also because of the problem in the redistribution of development. The consequences of economic development increased the living standards of bureaucrats and the bourgeoisie, while larger sectors of society did not benefit from it, especially the largest sector, that of the peasantry. The villages were not modernized economically and the 1929 depression brought about deterioration in prices for the peasants' produce; the peasants became dependent on moneylenders and economic collapse hit the villages. State support for private accumulation also had the negative conse- quence that corruption became rife in the new Turkey. Under these pressures, the Kemalist leadership realized that a new economic policy was needed, starting with the critique of liberalism, which was regarded as an undesirable method for the modernization of Turkey. The new political economy was to be a statist one: in 1931 Mustafa Kemal proclaimed: 'In the economic area ... the programme of the party is statism' (Boratav, 1997: 174). What was Kemalism's hope with the introduction of the statist economy?

In a statist economy, the state can be interpreted as the owner of the industrial sector and the controller of agricultural commodities. In such an economy, the state can increase prices of industrial goods, while paying low prices for agricultural goods as their main purchaser. Therefore, investment for further industrial accumulation can be provided. Alternatively, invested capital can be used for social and welfare purposes, with a low rate of economic development (Boratav, 1997). In this kind of political economy, the state normally opposes the dominant social class in order to increase the autonomy of the polity to become an agent of transformation. However, Kemalist statism did not fully adhere to this model.

The Kemalist statist economy came about as a synthesis of the two eras, 1923–29 and 1930–32.[7] In other words, an open economy based on state support for private accumulation and then a protectionist economy evolved into a semi-statist economy. With this model of development, the Kemalists realized some crucial ambitions. Perhaps the most important success was the nationalization of foreign investment, given the anti-imperialist nature of Kemalism. The state was regarded as the major productive and investing agent. In the industrialization process, the state was the decisive force and it was seen to support agricultural commodities. This was achieved by planning the economy. In the post-First World War era, Turkey was the first country after the Soviet Union to have central five-year economic plans. The key feature of these plans was the establishment of state enterprises that changed the environment wherever they were built. These policies harmed the interests of the foreign-oriented commercial bourgeoisie, but a small industrial bourgeoisie benefited from this era (Boratav, 1974). This era as a whole can be seen as a period of capitalist accumulation, in which the state was the dynamic force; and the achievements were remarkable.

By 1939, Turkey was no longer the Turkey of the 1920s that had imported flour, sugar and cloth. Basic consumer goods, as well as a quantity of capital goods, were being produced in state factories. This success could be related to three effective measures. First, foreign trade was controlled by the state. This provided a positive import–export balance. Secondly, the internal market was controlled by the state to an important degree, and this enabled further industrialization. Finally, in contrast to the original policy of an open economy, the state now used the invested capital directly for industrialization rather than for supporting the private sector. This prevented economic corruption. Between 1932 and 1939, economic growth was running at around 10 per cent, a higher rate than that between 1923 and 1930 (Avcioglu, 1973).

This development altered the socio-economic features of society. The Kemalists hoped that all sectors of society would gain from economic development, but in fact it created serious conflicts. A bureaucratic elite assumed itself to be the agent of civilization, with the task of achieving modernization, particularly in the economic sphere. The task claimed by the bureaucrats was deemed incomplete in the early 1940s. Despite the replacement of the open economy by a semi-statist economy in the 1930s, a Turkish bourgeoisie, albeit a weak one, did emerge. In these developments, local leaders, with whom the RPP could not break completely, came to be important merchants and 'capitalist farmers'. This group's ambition was to reduce state control over trade and to open the Turkish economy more widely to the Western market. Conditions in the villages, however, did not improve to a satisfactory degree. Because some of its main social partners were landowners, land reform was not achieved by the RPP. The prices of agricultural goods did not increase, especially because state investment for industrialization was regarded as more important. As noted above, the Kemalist revolution did not succeed in mobilizing the peasantry, partly because of the historical lack of an exploitative landed aristocracy in Turkey; the Turkish peasantry did not find the Kemalist ambition of altering the old regime desirable. More importantly, in later modernities, politics is privileged over economy. The Kemalist state was not based on a dominant social class, but regarded itself as the representative of the whole nation. The Kemalist view of society was developed in relation to this political economy: the Kemalists argued that Turkish society was not composed of opposing social classes but, for the sake of development, the division of labour was seen as unavoidable. For this reason, the RPP was regarded as the party of the whole nation because it promised not to favour any particular social sector. However, a classless society is the utopian fantasy of revolutionary regimes. The Kemalist economic modernization brought about new dualities rather than resolving contradictions in society.

Although industrialization was successfully achieved in comparison with conditions in 1923, Turkey did have a long way to go. In 1938, Mustafa Kemal died, his legacy living on as Kemal Atatürk, the father of the Turks. From then until 1946, the RPP governed society and economy according to the old one-party system. Those years, between 1939 and 1946, could be seen as unproductive for the Turkish economy for two basic reasons: the outbreak of the Second World War and the difficulty in putting the five-year economic plans into practice. The RPP government did alter the Turkish economy, but further alterations were needed for developing a powerful economy. Furthermore, economic problems played a central role in the transition to democracy. Thus, in the next section, we shall analyse historically the relations of economy, society and state to democracy in Turkey.

The Relations of State, Society and Economy to Democracy

The Kemalist regime, between 1923 and 1946, was an authoritarian one, but it included the potential for democratization, and this enabled, in 1950, a peaceful transition from an authoritarian to a democratic polity. It might be thought that a one-party system would more easily lead to a totalitarian regime, while transition to democracy generally requires the mobilization of society in civil war or bloody revolts.[8] However, the authoritarian Kemalist polity forcefully aimed to transform itself into a democracy. This can be seen by emphasizing two characteristics of Kemalism. First, Kemalism was not intended as a closed, monolithic polity; rather it could be seen as a general foundation for a modern polity, which then was subject to political actors' perspectives on it. Secondly, the Kemalist Party, the RPP, from the beginning included a plurality, albeit a limited one.

The Republican People's Party, founded in 1923, was originally based on the Defence of Right Societies, which were founded by local groups during the liberation war to resist the imperialist invasion of Anatolia. These societies were united in a single organization – the Society for the Defence of Anatolia and Rumelia – at the Sivas congress in 1919. When the Grand National Assembly was established, its main members were the leading cadre of the liberation movement, military and civilian intelligentsia, and those people who had established the defence societies (see Aydemir, 1999). This structure naturally included potential opposition to the Kemalist group, which was known as the 'first group', with the 'second group' emerging as the opposition. This could be called a limited plurality within an authoritarian polity. Because the Kemalists planned to found a democratic regime, this limited opposition was encouraged by Mustafa Kemal to establish a political party in 1924, just one year after the foundation of the republic. The opposition formed the Progressive Republican Party, which, however, dissolved itself after the Sheikh Sait revolt in 1925. Again, in 1930, Mustafa Kemal encouraged some of the representatives in the assembly to form another political party, the Liberal Party, which was also dissolved by the state because it was dominated by reactionary groups. In his lifetime, then, Mustafa Kemal failed to institution-alize a multi-party democracy. This, however, did not put an end to the ultimate ambition of the Kemalist project. The later leader of the RPP, Inönü, the second man of the republic, dedicated himself to completing the unfinished task of founding a democratic polity.

Thus, until 1950, the newly emerging Turkish society was governed by the RPP, which, through commitment to Kemalism, allowed the transition to democracy. In 1946, a party emerged from within the RPP called the Demo-crat Party (DP). Announcing itself to be the voice of the nation, the DP reflected the unavoidable opposition that was to come about as a result of the modernizing years. The party was formed by an alliance of different sectors of society: its founder members were Celal Bayar, a businessman and banker, Adnan Menderes, a cotton-growing landlord, and Fuat Köprülü, a historian. Although the leaders of the DP could be seen as products of the RPP regime, the rise of the 'new men' in and by means of the DP should be considered.

The DP was, in the first place, a movement from below. Most of the members of the Grand National Assembly were 'new men'; they did not come from the bureaucracy, but were mostly local leaders, coming from local settings. In this alliance, landlords had a very important place and, in fact, the polar-ization in the RPP was partly due to its attempts towards land reform in the 1940s. It seemed that the DP was a symptom of the maturation of 'civil society'. 'Enough, the word is the nation's' was the symbolic slogan of the DP, emphasizing the importance of society against bureaucracy. Society had already been polarized during the Kemalist era. Two cultures were already at stake in the 1930s: the secular culture of an influential minority and the Islamic culture of the majority. A commercial bourgeoisie had arisen; bureaucrats had enjoyed possession of the mission of 'civilization' in the name of economic develop-ment; peasants were already being influenced by Kemalist teachers to ask whether the sheikhs were right; the industrial enterprises gave rise to a Turkish working class, albeit a weak one.

The Democrats came to power in 1950 by means of free elections. This marked a beginning and an end; there were losers and winners. The year of 1950 could indeed be viewed as marking the beginning of the second phase of the Turkish republic. An authoritarian model of development was replaced by a democratic regime.[9] Whether or not the new regime was to be based on democratic principles was directly dependent on the 'new men'. The Kemalist era aimed to develop a foundation of republican democracy for the country and, in 1946, the transition to democracy was both permitted and supported by the RPP. The 'new men' who came to power by means of free elections could have maintained and developed the new parliamentary democratic regime. However, although these Democrat governors were new, a number of them were members of the RPP until they formed their own party. The question was, therefore: could they rid the country of the mentality of a one-party government? The founding figures of the republic did not only overcome the mentality of the one-party system, they also lost the elections and their position as the sole authority, precisely because of their own decision to allow multi-party democracy. The RPP accepted this result, regarding itself as the opposition party in the assembly and allowing the DP to form a government. The future of Turkish democracy was to be based on the ideas and actions of the 'new men'. Thus, we need to consider the DP in terms of its perspectives on the economy, society and polity.

Any critique of modernity perhaps starts with critique of the economy. Aydemir (1999), however, believes that the DP did not completely differ from the RPP in terms of economic policy, arguing that both parties' economic perspectives were based on the attempt to reach a capitalist economy on the basis of state support for private accumulation. However, as he also adds, the DP was a party that necessarily responded to the demands of the people. Since the DP was elected by the people, not as a party that assumed power by revolution as the RPP did, it had to consider the people's needs, wishes and interests. To a considerable extent, the village votes brought the DP to power. An important reason for this was that the Kemalist era did not succeed in bringing about change in the countryside to any great extent. The DP, however, did not achieve power only with the votes of the peasantry; it also emerged as the representative of landlords and the commercial bourgeoisie, giving it a social basis across different and opposing sectors of society. Although the peasants were being exploited by both landlords and the commercial bourgeoisie, the RPP had not convinced them that the state offered better conditions. The Kemalists promised that the peasants would be the real masters of the new republic. However, the RPP could neither fully achieve its Enlightenment in the villages nor could it provide the peasantry with enough economic opportunities.

The DP relied on votes in the villages because it knew that the Kemalist era had disappointed the peasantry. But equally important was the fact that the language spoken by the 'new men' was different from that of the men of Enlightenment, the Kemalists. The language of the new men was familiar to the peasantry.

According to the new prime minister, Adnan Menderes, the RPP government practised bureaucratic interventionist capitalism (Aydemir, 1999: 188). For the DP, an alternative economy ran on a liberal model. It could be argued that, within a liberal economy, it is difficult for the government to see itself as dealing with the art of resolving contradictions in society on the basis of justice; rather, political authority may leave societal contradictions untouched. This may be why some regard the DP era as a period of freedom for civil society. For example, some see the Democrats as opening opportunities for civil society by liberalizing the economy (Göle, 1994). Where the DP differed from the Kemalists was in the former's emphasis on opening up the economy to competition, as opposed to the Kemalists' focus on development as the objective of the whole nation. According to the Democrats, society consists of different sectors and competition between them should be allowed. However, a law-based government could not provide the conditions for such a liberal model. Rather, the government was to assign itself the role of opening up new opportunities for the groups in society that had brought the DP to power. But this kind of liberalism was to oppress other groups, such as workers, and, in turn, it was to mean a deterioration of the democratic regime founded by the Kemalists.

The basic developments that took place in the 1950s need to be considered for seeing the DP in practice. Although the villages were prepared for development by the RPP era, the DP achieved change by putting an end to a long discussion over whether schools or roads were the priority for modernization. Motorways were built in the early 1950s and this succeeded in integrating the villages into the national market, bringing Turkish agriculture into the capitalist system (see Ahmad, 1993). Under the DP, then, the major changes in the Turkish experience resulted from the emphasis on agriculture; heavy industrialization was not a priority for the Democrats as it had been for the Kemalists. This was related to the social coalitions supporting the DP – the commercial bourgeoisie and the landlords.

In societies, forces that are undermined in one way or another come to the fore as decisive dynamics at a later period. The commercial bourgeoisie and the landlords in Turkey, not permitted to achieve their ambitions during the Kemalist era, found democracy at a time when they were to begin to play a determining role in the country. The DP era, between 1950 and 1960, spelt freedom for these groups. Since the Kemalist insistence on heavy industrialization was in their interests, they emphasized that Turkey could gain more from commerce with the West than from the 'difficult' attempts to industrialize the country. It was now time for them to achieve their goals. Turkey was to experience another change: the power of the existing commercial bourgeoisie increased while new economic actors joined this group. The merchants that emerged from the countryside became important politico-economic actors on whom the DP depended. These merchants were either landowners or owners of small businesses before becoming important economic figures. They demanded two changes: the mechanizing of agriculture and the unconditional opening up of the economy to the Western market for the sake of the national economy. Both of these demands were responded to positively by the political authority. This was a crucial move that did not sit well with the anti-imperialist characteristic of the Turkish republic, and was to create problems in later years.

According to the Democrats, Kemalist Turkey had hoped to realize a utopian fantasy in terms of the political economy. That is, autonomous development was seen as isolating Turkey from international capitalism. To overcome this, the Democrats set about the integration of Turkey into the Western world as quickly as possible. This move, first of all, provided the DP with foreign capital. American aid for modernizing agriculture brought hope to the villages but, in particular, to the landlords. For example, the number of tractors in Turkey rose to 44,000 between 1950 and 1960 from 4000 in 1949 (Aydemir, 1999: 218). This mechanization increased agricultural production, which provided more opportunities for the commercial bourgeoisie in terms of trade. But it also resulted in millions of landless peasants moving to the cities, which were unable to accommodate them. In short, economic policy during the 1950s did not take account of what could happen when agriculture is mechanized in a capitalist economy while industrialization is neglected in the cities. Not only did unemployment emerge as a central problem, but military and civil officers and workers in state enterprises also failed to benefit from the new era. Workers' and officials' standards of living dropped, especially because the government spent all investments and external loans on the mechanization of agriculture and on the increasing prices of agricultural goods. This situation was to produce reactions against the DP from the very people who had once supported them.

The rise of opposition to the DP was not only due to economic policy, but also to the fact that the Democrats were not democratic in the true sense of the word. Rather, they thought in terms of absolute power: elections were seen as the only criterion of legitimacy, and democracy was understood as hegemonic rule by the party gaining the most votes (Aydemir, 1999). Multi-party democracy could be interpreted in terms of each social sector forming a political party that works to achieve its own objectives. However, no political party could claim to be the sole 'owner' of the country because democracy does not mean – or should not mean – domination by the party gaining the highest amount of votes. If a political party in power does understand democracy in this way, the regime can no longer be legitimated as a genuine democracy. The DP assumed that since it came to power by democratic election, it had absolute authority.[10] This was to play a dominant role in 'legitimizing' the 1960 military coup.

Two groups in particular reacted against the economic and political perspective of the DP: the university and the military. Protest emerged from the university in the form of an alternative politico-economic perspective and was transformed into action by the military. However, the reactions of the university and the military against the DP could be seen as the final stage of the dissatisfaction of the larger part of society. Workers' right to strike was denied; the press was censured; the republicans were harassed by the government in all possible ways. Rising inflation and a stagnant economy forced the Democrats to exploit Islam for political ends. These were indications that the 'autonomous society' was not yet mature. Had it been so, the Democrats would have been required to be democratic in the true sense of the word. Anti-imperialism, secularism, republicanism and democracy were all negatively affected during the DP era. The urgent question of the late 1950s was this: how can a government that does not obey the constitution be overcome? Or, in other words, how can an illegitimate government be forced to give up authority? History provided a possible answer. In 1908, the sultanate had been oppressing the people to the greatest extent in history and the military intervened to establish a constitutional regime; again, at the end of the First World War, the imperialist Western states aimed to divide and rule Turkey and resistance to this came from the young military officers who were to found the Turkish republic.

There were fights against the government at universities and industrial enterprises but none other than the military could act powerfully against political authority. Aydemir (1999) tries to explain this with reference to the nature of the military men. These men were educated to believe in action and had the means to act more easily than any other sector of society. But this view disregards a central feature of the Turkish military: the fact that the Turkish military regards itself as the guardian of democracy, assumed to be the only desirable regime. The Turkish military was given the task of defending democracy by the constitution and, in the late 1950s, democracy had already deteriorated.

On 27 May 1960 a military coup broke out. Some were to call it 'the second institutional revolution'. The military intervened to restore democracy. In stark contrast to other military coups (for instance, that of Franco in Spain [1936–75], Abdul Nasser in Egypt [1954–70], or the colonels in Greece [1967–75]), the Turkish military assumed power for a strictly limited period, relinquishing it as soon as law and order were restored.[11] This coup was unique in Turkish history; as Ahmad (1993: 121) notes, 'it was the first and the last successful military intervention made from outside the hierarchical structure of Turkey's armed forces'. It was not a generals' coup. It was, in contrast, young officers who achieved a coup for the firm establishment of 'true' democracy. It should be called an institutional reform. The military called on republican professors to elaborate a new constitution, to be the most democratic Turkey had ever had. The important innovations of this constitution were the constitutional court, whose function was to check the constitutionality of legislation, and the state planning organization, whose objectives were to provide socially just economic development and to achieve full employment.

The 1961 constitution should be seen as a Kemalist attempt to complete an unfinished task: the institutionalization of a democratic polity and an industrialized economy. The constrained workers were granted freedom by the new constitution: they were given the right to form unions and political parties and the right to strike. The destroyed autonomy of the universities was renewed in 1961. The constitution also provided the guarantee of freedom of the press. Socialists were, for the first time, given the right to form political parties and to express their critique of Turkish society and the Turkish state. In the constitution, socially just economic development and full employment were also emphasized; the state was redescribed as a 'social state', meaning a welfare state. Later years would tell a different story.

This new move was very important in terms of the legalization of opposition. The 'radicalization' of opposition bore fruit. The Kemalists in the 1930s had insisted that Turkish society was a classless society, but it was now announced that society included opposing classes and that, without granting freedom and rights to the working class, democracy could not be founded. We see here how a project of modernity can transform itself in response to changes in society. This particular project of modernity, Kemalism, assumed responsibility when the country experienced difficulties, especially in terms of the democratic regime. But this characteristic was not always understood to be power for the sake of real democracy; rather, over time it was reinterpreted as a means of disciplining. I shall return to this later.

In the atmosphere following the new constitution, there was a further polarization of society and politics. Workers established DISK, the confederation of revolutionary workers. The opposition did not remain indifferent; businessmen formed TUSIAD, the association of Turkish industrialists and businessmen. From then on, these two associations were to play important parts in the lives of Turks. Ideological polarization was mainly between the anti-American left (the Kemalists, the Workers' Party, universities) and the pro-American right (the rising bourgeoisie, landowners, liberal intellectuals). The 1960s were a period of democratization and the development of civil society. Some autonomous organizations were formed by the people without the support or influence of the bureaucracy. For example, it was no longer only Kemalism that opposed imperialism: autonomous leftist student unions were protesting against the imperialist attempts of the USA and the Soviet Union.

In terms of the economy, the 1960s could be called a second era of nationally organized capitalism. With the 1963–67 economic plan, it seemed that Turkey experienced the second industrial revolution. The growth rate reached 8 per cent in the 1960s. New economic actors also emerged in this era. Salaried managers played important roles in both state enterprises and private business. The national bourgeoisie began to transform small firm-based production into big business. Growing industry also increased the percentage of workers in the country. The same years witnessed workers' movements and strikes, with the workers becoming increasingly difficult to control. The Workers' Party had seats in the parliament and was the most powerful opposition in the assembly. The freedom at universities allowed students to form their own autonomous unions, which played an important part in the development of democracy but, also, in the legitimation of the 1971 military coup.

The decade from 1961 to 1971 was the first in which liberty was enjoyed, but it was to give rise to further disciplinization. The right came to power in 1965, and Süleyman Demirel, the prime minister, announced immediately that it was impossible to govern society with the existing constitution. The 1961 constitution was providing 'liberty' more than 'discipline', which the Turkish right did not appreciate. The police were prohibited from using physical force against workers and students, which led the right to believe that 'communism was on the way'. Certainly, this was an invitation to the army to intervene. Here, we necessarily return to the theme of the military.

As has been said, in 1960 the Turkish military for the first and last time achieved a coup from outside the hierarchical structure of Turkey's armed forces. Generals had somehow become the tools of young military officers. The reverse became the case after 1961. The high command assigned itself to transform the Turkish army. The generals entered the sphere of business and industry; OYAK, the Army Mutual Assistance Association, was created. In a decade, OYAK became an important partner in the automotive industry; it also owned 20 per cent of the petrochemicals company Petkim and the food-canning company Tukas (Ahmad, 1993). The high command controlled the army fully; opposition was suppressed. As a consequence of these developments, the army defended the system by shelving its Kemalist ambitions.

Rather than change and development, the high command's concern this time was with 'stability'. This army looked very different from the army of 1960. The military had sided with republicans in creating the democratic constitution of 1961; but, by 1971, the military looked on the RPP with suspicion because of its slogan 'This order must change'. Atatürk's party was, this time, blamed by the generals.

The 1960s revealed that Turkish society included a plurality of viewpoints, and the democratic 1961 constitution provided ways of expressing this plurality openly. However, such plurality, especially the ideas of leftist political ideologies, was assumed by the military high command to be dangerous and divisive of society. The 1971 generals' coup can be seen as the result of a phobia: fear of communism. The Workers' Party was dissolved and three student leaders of the 1968 movement executed despite efforts made by the leader of the RPP, Inönü. DISK was searched by the police; leftist teachers were targeted. An extraordinary move was made by the army to imprison two intellectuals, Çetin Altan, a socialist, and Ilhan Selçuk, a radical Kemalist (see Ahmad, 1993). Liberty was paid for with unbearable discipline. 'Revolution' and 'change' became the nemeses of the system and of the military. The atmosphere changed; radical rightists gained the upper hand; the state helped the youth organization of the Nationalist Action Party, which took vigilante action against leftists. Creating discipline was the objective of the new military coup, which replaced liberty-oriented constitutional laws with disciplining ones.

Having achieved its aim, as it thought, of 'disciplining' Turkish society, the military reinstated a multi-party system, and in protest against the disciplining regime of the military and right-wing politicians, the people brought the RPP to power in 1973. This act was another element in the radicalization of oppositions, this time leading to unwanted results. The RPP could not form a government alone in 1973, although the party won 44 per cent of the votes. Ecevit was not willing to make a coalition with the right; the only chance was to form a coalition with Erbakan's Islamist party. The former enemies came to form a government together. Even more astonishing was the fact that the two parties agreed on some issues; both were anti-imperialists and both believed in freedom of speech. However, the prime minister, Ecevit, resigned on the assumption that new elections would be held and that the RPP could get rid of the Islamists. Bitter years were to come: all the right-wing parties formed a coalition, named the Nationalist Front.

The Nationalist Front's aim was to fight against the left in any way possible. Its policies were based on utopian future-oriented ideologies. Marxist-Leninist workers and students were the main opposers of the radical nationalists. The radicalization of oppositions shocked Turkish society this time; it was no longer moving towards modernity but falling into anarchy, which was an invitation to the army to impose martial law. The Nationalist Front was a serious attempt to reconstruct Turkish society completely on the basis of ultra-nationalism. The Turkey of the second half of the 1970s seemed to be experiencing a civil war: the police supported the nationalists for the sake of discipline, while most intellectuals supported the leftists for the sake of liberty. Because society was not unified, the military high command believed that more discipline was needed to create stability. This internal factor was supported by an external one. The USA supported Turkey as an example of a 'moderate Islamic country': neither a radical one which would block American interests in the Middle East, nor the Turkey of before, which had allowed socialism to emerge. Therefore, the USA supported the Turkish high command in its attempt to impose Islam as a powerful factor in politics, believing that this would reduce the likelihood of socialist or communist movements gaining power in Turkey.[12]

On 12 September 1980, the military intervened in what was to be the most disciplining of the coups. With the 1971 coup, the generals had achieved the abandonment of most of the basic laws in the 1961 constitution. This, never-theless, was seen as insufficient because the country had not achieved stability. According to the totalizing perspective of the generals, conflict could be overcome by unifying society; a plurality of viewpoints could not be tolerated, because plurality usually leads to (some degree of) conflict. The 1980 military coup in Turkey could be seen as an attempt at reconstructing society by interpreting Islam as playing the role of keeping the Turks together. It was claimed that if young people were educated according to Islam, Turkey would be rid of communist youth. This was, therefore, a totalizing attempt to reconstruct Turkish society on the basis of a 'nationalist Islam'.

The 1980 generals' coup, therefore, opposed Kemalism particularly in its encouragement and support for 'Islamization'. In stark contrast to the Kemalist view, the generals saw Islam as the cement holding the Turks together. A lack of Islamic education was seen to be the essential reason for the rise of leftism. The generals included Islamic lessons in the school curriculum; it was, from then on, compulsory for every Turkish student to take religious courses in primary, secondary and high schools – a practice Kemal would have hated. During the three-year military regime, the *imam-hatip* schools (schools for training prayer leaders) increased from 258 to 350. The graduates from these schools were given the right to go on to study at universities. The number of Koranic schools increased from 2610 to 4715 and the number of students at these schools rose from 68,486 in 1980 to 155,403 in 1989. Without taking into account this state support it is impossible to analyse the rise of Islamism in con-temporary Turkey. The generals imposed a state programme of 'Islamization' for the sake of discipline; they thought of Islamic culture as the framework for making people live together harmoniously. But they were to fail: no longer could culture play such a role. This is why Islamic militants pose a danger to the military today.

After establishing this regime, the high command allowed a multi-party democracy to re-emerge in 1983. Of course, the generals were careful as to which parties to allow; for example, no socialist party could be formed. The coming years were to be known as the Özal years. The 1980s and the 1990s constituted a continuation of the military's ambitions, with an unlimited liberal economic policy as the driving force, Islam made the powerful force of political life, and the replacement of 'radicalization' with mutuality. The crucial point must be that the modernizing elite was replaced by a technocratic elite: central importance was accorded to specific policies and provision of services rather than to ideology. Depoliticization is the key word necessary for understanding the current era in the Turkish experience. Attempts were made to do away with future-oriented revolutionary politics and these succeeded, albeit only for a while: Islamism came to fill that place.

Recent problems in Turkey can clearly be seen as the results of this disciplining regime. When the state takes up a position on the side of a particular group in society, corruption becomes unavoidable. Particularly when the state views some groups as partners of the polity in the government of society, it can be interpreted as a resource to be exploited. In Turkey, during the 1970s and 1980s, the state included illegal organizations that, it was thought, were deployed against the 'enemies' who were assumed to be dividing Turkey. These illegal organizations were formed by the ultra-nationalists who saw no difference between themselves and the state. Both believed that they had to fight against the enemies of the nation. An organic connection between ultra-nationalist militants and the state was thus formed. A 1996 traffic accident made this fact quite clear: a nationalist terrorist was found in a minibus with an MP from a major right-wing party and a police chief. Therefore, radical disciplining can be argued to have institutionally corrupted the state. And this was, partly, for the sake of having an unlimited market economy.

The liberalization of the Turkish economy has created new winners and losers. If we describe liberalism in terms of freedom and duty, we must see modernity in terms of both liberty and discipline. In other words, individuals are allowed to act on their own interests, but must also recognize others' property. In the 'contract' between individuals, absolute freedom is impossible. All individuals are free, because they are rational, but that makes them subject to 'universal principles'. That is, a self-interested individual recognizes that his or her claims are acceptable to others who are also rational beings. So, in a liberal political economy, since self-interested individuals strive to maximize the satisfaction of their wants, they need to market their labour or capital and to buy goods produced by others. As a consequence they become 'socially productive beings'. However, this liberal economy, at least for the Turkish experience, could be seen as a utopian fantasy.

An economy that is legally unaccountable has gained a certain force in the country. Corruption has become a dominant feature of the current economy. Why did the promising economy of the 1930s result in the current disaster? I shall try to answer this question before considering some prominent characteristics of the current economy. The goal of creating a national bourgeoisie on the basis of state support for private accumulation should have included a proper answer to the following question: what would be the model for the redistribution of the state enterprises built by the people's effort? Should the state have continued to be a main producing agent or should it have returned – sold back – the invested economic institutions to the public for social and welfare purposes? The state, however, from the beginning of the republic had always supported private capital. It was when the bourgeoisie no longer required state support that the problem of privatizing state economic enterprises emerged. The state was always the powerful centre with which the bourgeoisie needed to have close relations but, particularly since the early 1980s, the supportive sometimes controlling state has been assumed to be no longer necessary. That is, the state's product, namely the bourgeoisie, no longer regards the state as its 'master'. And when this product became the master, it argued that it was capable of doing business better, and the state found it feasible to privatize state enterprises.

The corruption in the current economy is directly related to this privatization process. However, before corruption by means of privatization, in order to argue for privatization, governments in the 1980s had to corrupt the state economic enterprises. The Özal governments, during the period of unlimited liberalism between 1983 and 1989, corrupted the Public Economic Enterprises in order to prepare the argument that privatization was not merely a possible solution, but a scientific rule for escaping Turkey's economic problems (see Cangizbay, 1995). When a state enterprise becomes unproductive and does not yield profit, it becomes easier to argue that it should be sold to private capital. Privatization is simply insisted on as necessary due to 'objective criteria' and for the sake of 'democracy'. It is not asked whether privatization is a politico-economic choice of a particular social class; rather, the reduction of state power by means of the privatization of state enterprises is emphasized as a means of making way for democratization. Thus, privatization is insisted on as a prerequisite for democratization. At first sight, this argument seems plausible. That is, when the state becomes a 'technical' state with no economic task, its job being to govern society in order to resolve contradictions on the basis of law, it may not able to act as an agent of the population. Therefore, further democratization could be assumed to be necessary. However, this perspective has to consider an important sector of the country: the peasantry. The peasantry represents around 35 per cent of the Turkish population and is directly related to the state with regard to economic activity. Despite the fact that, today, 65 per cent of the population is urbanized, compared with only 18 per cent in 1927, peasants in the country still play a crucial role. Economic policies over the whole period of the republic could not 'proletarianize' the Turkish peasants: although rapid urbanization has taken place since the 1950s, the proportion of people working in the agricultural sector is much higher than in Western European societies. This situation could be considered in two ways. First, the peasantry in Turkey could not be changed because they were not involved in the Kemalist revolution. Secondly, the Kemalist interpretation of modernity does not understand urbanization to be a crucial component of modernization. Rather, modernization in the villages themselves was thought to be both possible and desirable – as we have seen, for example, in relation to the village institutions. However, this policy was open to challenge by counter-policies. The village institutions were closed down by the coalition of land-lords, the commercial bourgeoisie and the Democrat Party. It then became very important to gain village votes in elections, and, to this end, temporary solutions for peasants were implemented rather than long-term development. Nevertheless, the villages have changed and modernized. New economic actors from the villages participate in the wealth of the country, particularly by means of modern telecommunications technology. The villagers are no longer seen as uneducated and exploitable; they can no longer be controlled by the polity and the economy. Perhaps a more important consequence of the unproletarianized Turkish peasantry is that the government currently aims to found 'village-cities' as a commitment to Kemalism. Village-cities are groups of villages in the same region connected to one another around a 'central village'. If this project is achieved, a model of a different modernity in the villages could be genuinely fulfilled.

Politics have shifted from confrontation to tolerance; the extreme leftists and rightists, who had rejected existing orders, have been replaced by moderate liberal and social democratic parties. However, one response to this has been the emergence of the Islamist party as a new radical party. The 1980s and 1990s have witnessed the state's Islamization programme, but have also given rise to various organizations within civil society. Some have formed unions for human rights and others for animal rights. A care for nature has emerged on the part of some people, while others focus on women's rights. In other words, multiplicity and plurality have proved impossible to suppress. Neither the state nor culture nor economic criteria can hold the population of Turkey together and homogenize it. To illustrate this situation, we could consider the Kurdish question and the rise of Islamism. No matter how imaginative Kemalism was, the historical and civilizational context will always play a role in people's responses to cultural and political innovations and borrowings. The Kurdish question and the rise of Islamism could point to Kemalism's limits. 'Culture' plays a pivotal part in defining the situation in the country. However, there is no single culture that could be thought to hold the Turkish population together. A civilizational multiplicity, Turkey faces a potential war between its cultural worlds. In this situation, the disciplining programme of the state has been a most important factor. The militant nationalism of 1971 to the 1980s necessarily found that the Kurdish opposition and the Islamization programme of the 1980 military coup played an important part in the rise of Islamism. However, despite all the totalizing attempts, multiplicity could not be suppressed. Society emerged as an arena of conflict and, therefore, organizations within civil society began to play an important role in the country.

A Turkish civil society can therefore now be seen to exist. Although this may be seen as an achievement of the Kemalist project, the clashes between the Kemalists and their opponents also played an important role in the emergence of a civil society. Kemalism's openness can be seen to have influenced the establishment of social organizations. Many democratic and anti-fascist organizations are Kemalist. This may be seen as current Kemalism being in the hands of the people, an important goal of early Kemalism. Therefore, it could be an important opportunity for Turkey if Kemalism can be rescued from the hands of the state as a legitimizing element. The biggest organizations in society are Kemalist organizations that do not regard the present state as Kemalist. However, these organizations will only be able to wrest Kemalism away from the state if the majority of Kemalists come to understand that the defence of the state does no good for Kemalism either. Thus, a further democratization of Turkey indeed requires that Kemalism become the property of organizations within civil society, so that it cannot be used by a state regime as a legitimizing tool.

In conclusion, modernity cannot be analysed as a unity, but must be seen as a field of tensions: the radicalization of dualities must be seen as a constitutive element of modernity. In the Turkish experience, the radicalization of oppositions has played a dual role: certainly, it moved people towards modernity but the price was high. Modern Turkish society cannot be seen to represent a coherent whole; rather, there has been diversity within a limited unity. Of course, the pre-modern social world also included plural cultures. However, two distinctive features of modernity enable greater cultural plurality. First, cultural worlds are less isolated from one another in modernity, increasing the relations between different cultures. Secondly, moving from one cultural identity to another is easier than in pre-modern cultures in which changing cultural group was very hard, if not impossible. As a consequence of these characteristics, modern society becomes a field of tensions, because the oppositions between multiple cultures are recognized. The radicalization of dualities between different world-interpretations marks a distinctive feature of the Turkish experience of modernity.

In terms of the relations between the state and society, 'disciplining' and 'liberalization' must be taken as the two characteristic dynamics of modernity. The state assumes itself to be the integrating sphere of society, but this has led to bitter stories. The Kemalist state promised liberty by creating spaces of opportunity for people in the creation of an autonomous society. However, Kemalism could not predict what should be done if a polarized society becomes violent in searching for solutions. Certainly, the Kemalists believed that the army could no longer play a socio-political role, but the army in fact sided with one element of society in the 1970s and 1980s and took the place of politics in the integrating sphere. Discipline could not be achieved by the power of law; rather, physical violence was used.

Not only economic issues but also different interpretations of the world and people's relation to the world play a fundamental role in the creation of tensions. Society becomes polarized, not only through the institutionalization of social classes, but also, as the Turkish experience shows, because of cultural and civilizational oppositions. This has a special place in the Turkish experience, because the Turks have never definitively belonged to a clearly defined civilization. This, in the first place, provided an opportunity for moving the Turks towards modernity: when a civilizational framework cannot be clearly defined, it is easier to introduce innovation. However, it is for the same reason that a common culture cannot be invoked to hold the Turks together. This was the strategy of the 1980 coup and of the Özal era, but the consequences reveal its failure: Islam was invoked to eliminate ideological differences, but it radicalized the issue. Currently, Islamism occupies an obviously prominent place in the life of Turkish society. Relations between the state and the Islamists have given rise to interesting perspectives; for example, some view the emergence of Islamism as marking the end of Kemalist modernity (Gülalp, 1998). Thus, it is urgent to consider the question of Islam seriously. In the next chapter, I shall analyse the relations between Islam and modernity in the Turkish experience.

CHAPTER 5

Islam and Modernity: Radical Openness to Interpretation

Since the Iranian Islamic revolution, the voices of Islam have made some observers curious as to one question: was modernity accepted by 'different', non-Western cultures? Referring to the example of 'new Islam', Islamism, some critics argue that modernity has been refused by non-Western cultures (Mestrovic, 1998: 156). Others argue that the Islamist movement clearly indicates the arrival of the postmodern era (see, for instance, Ahmed, 1992; Sayyid, 1997). Turkey presents a particularly interesting case for observers who want to understand the nature of the relations between Islam and modernity. With its particular project of modernity, Kemalism, Turkey has often been seen as the model of modernity for the Muslim world. However, the Iranian Islamic revolution represented a serious challenge to Kemalism, because Iran had chosen the Turkish way of modernization, to an important extent, as its model for development.[1]

Turkey is often seen as representing a 'secular' Muslim society. Yet Turkey is also known for its tension-ridden relations between modernity and Islam. Recently, Islamic voices have been heard more strongly than ever before, yet, in turn, secularists speak out against Islamism. On the one hand, Turkey has been regarded as 'Western', but on the other hand, the Islamic face of Turkey is a constant presence in relation to political issues. For instance, Turkey is (at the time of writing) being considered for membership of the European Union, but it is also a member of the Islamic Union. This duality immediately divides observers of Turkey into two opposite camps. For instance, Lewis (1988: 4) states that '[in] almost all of the sovereign states with a clear Muslim majority, Islam is the state religion; many of them have clauses in their constitutions establishing the Holy law of Islam as either the basis of law or the major source of legislation. The outstanding exception is the Turkish republic, which under the guidance of its first president, Kemal Atatürk, adopted a series of [secularizing] laws in the 1920s'. But, on the other hand, Ahmed (1993: 98) argues that '[the] challenge to the notion of Turkey as a European nation, the strong, unmistakable signs of Turks rediscovering their Islamic identity are everywhere: the full mosques, the pride in the Ottoman past, the women with their hijab, even men wearing the fez'.

As these opposite perspectives clearly reveal, it is important to pay attention to the question of Islam on the basis of the Turkish experience in order to try to understand the nature of relations between Islam and modernity. In particular, both Islam and modernity can and should be conceptualized as open to interpretation. This has not been done so far: existing studies of the relations between Islam and modernity tend to see Islam as either completely incompatible or fully compatible with 'Western modernity'.[2] The main problem in these studies is that both 'Islam' and 'modernity' are taken to be coherent visions of life (see Gellner, 1992) – two different, equally totalizing world-interpretations which are therefore seen as incompatible (Watt, 1988; Nasr, 1987). There is, however, a radical openness to interpretation in both Islam and modernity. Therefore, they can both be lived according to various configurations. Just as the theme of varieties of modernity could open up plausible ways for social theory to review itself, so the theme of varieties of Islam could shed light on the understanding of the Muslim world.

As will be argued in this chapter, the Turkish experience clearly shows that neither Islam nor modernity can exist independently of historical and cultural context; there are multiple modernities and multiple Islams, inflected by the particular contexts within which they exist. What is significant about Turkey is that neither Islam nor modernity emerged first in the Turkish lands; but rather than becoming straightforwardly 'Islamized' or 'Westernized', the Turks reinterpreted both Islam and modernity. It must be argued that particular socio-historical experiences cannot be adequately analysed by means of standardizing, normative models: we cannot determine a society's level of modernity by using European Enlightenment as the standard model of modernity, nor can we explain a society's 'Muslimness' by using the Koran to provide an explicit model of Islamic life.

This chapter aims at problematizing understandings of relations between modernity and Islam by arguing that Turkish society indicates both the plurality of Islams and the possibility of different configurations of modernity. First, we must examine why and how Islam and modernity have so far been taken as opposing each other, to understand why some commentators insist on the necessity for Islam to resist modernity and why others argue that it is necessary to Westernize Islamic societies. I shall take a critical look at these understandings of Islam by arguing that realms of human life can be formed differently in different social contexts, both in traditional times and, especially, under conditions of modernity, rather than building arguments on references to idealized, 'original' versions of the projects of Islam and modernity. I shall then use the Turkish case to argue against the common views that modernity and Islam are incompatible, that there exists a 'pure' form of traditional Islam, and that the only way for Islamic societies to be modern is through Westernization. Thus, by analysing both modernity and Islam as projects open to interpretation, this chapter will question modernist, postmodernist and traditionalist views of Islam with illustrations from the Turkish experience.

Islam and Modernity as Projects

Critics invoke idealized versions of both modernity (understood as the project of European Enlightenment) and Islam (understood as the Islam of the Prophet's lifetime) in order to argue that the two are irreconcilable in terms of their understandings of life. Clearly, if we compare socialism and liberalism, for instance, it would have to be noted that there are incompatibilities rather than consensus between them. Nevertheless, we cannot therefore argue that liberalism represents modernity, while socialism is a rejection of it. On the contrary, liberalism and socialism express two different versions of modernity. Equally, I want to insist that by referring to Western liberal modernity as the standard model of modernity, and to the Koran as the provider of a 'closed' way of Islamic life, we cannot analyse the present conditions of Islamic societies. Rather, it must be stressed that the relation between Islam and modernity cannot be one of total exclusion.

Islamism's recent rise to the fore in Islamic societies has led to the development of two critical views. First, Islamism is seen as decentralizing the West; that is, it represents the postmodern era which is bringing modernity to an end (Ahmed, 1992; Sayyid, 1997). Secondly, Islamism is taken to be the manifestation of pre-modern traditional phenomena (see Watt, 1988; Lawrence, 1995). When these arguments are looked at closely, the centrality of the West is striking. Discussions of Islam's relations to modernity are centred on the perceived equivalence between modernity and the West. Hence, Islamic societies must either reject modernity – because it is the system of the Christian West – or be forced to accept the advance of another civilization. In these perspectives, an argument for or against Islam's compatibility with modernity cannot be maintained without considering the West.

However, there is a way of showing Islam and modernity to be compatible without centring the argument on the West. Viewing Islam as hostile to modernity has its roots in the definition of Islam as uniform and unchanging. In other words, it is argued that there has always been one Islam, ordered by the Koran and exemplified by the Prophet (see Nasr, 1987). This understanding does not allow for a plurality of Islams, nor does it credit modernity as acceptable in Islamic societies. This Islam is viewed as an anti-modern, traditionalist world-interpretation (see Watt, 1988; Gellner, 1992). However, the Islamic East should not be viewed as a totality; rather the plurality of cultures and forms of Islam in the region needs to be recognized.

Islam was a project of the 'good life' which emerged in the tribal society of Arabia in AD 611. The first practitioner, and so the exemplar, of this project was the Prophet Muhammad. Because of this, the *sunna* and *hadith*, the sayings and practices of Muhammad, represent one of the two sources of Islam, in addition to the Koran. Islam was defined by what the Prophet did, so that, under his authority, disputes could be resolved. The death of the Prophet, however, marked an important event: the dispute over the interpretation of Islam came to the fore, and the issue of succession gave rise to conflicts within Islam. The first major division, that between Shia and Sunni Islam, was born out of discussions as to who was able to interpret the law since the death of the lawgiver, the Prophet. For the Shia faction, the successor should be one of the first Muslims and close to Muhammad. But for the Sunni faction, the problem of succession could be solved by election. Since then, different interpretations of Islam have emerged and spread around the geographical space of the Islamic East. The multiple interpretations of Islam arose due to differences in cultures: Islam was not accepted without any revision or question in the many different cultures outside its birthplace.

Nevertheless, some critics argue that Islam was always the master signifier in all Islamic societies regardless of their particularities (see, for example, Gellner, 1992). This argument is maintained by viewing the caliphate as the centre around which global Muslim identity was structured (Sayyid, 1997). One wonders how it is possible to generalize the views of people who lived within the radical plurality of Islams. However, what history tells us is that the caliphate had lost its unifying capability, long before its abolishment by the Turks in 1924, precisely because none of the specific interpretations of Islam could assimilate its other multiple interpretations.[3] It should not be surprising, then, that the Ottoman sultans did not place importance on the caliphate, although it had been passed to the Ottomans in 1517 after the conquest of Egypt.

In short, the plurality of Islams must be considered in understanding the relations between modernity and Islam. Just as the equivalence between modernity and the West must be problematized, so too must the equivalence between Islam and the Arab world. So far, I have argued that both modernity and Islam must be understood as able to be lived in different configurations. However, what happens when Arabocentric Islam and Eurocentric modernity are compared needs to be considered. Thus, I shall now consider some of the crucial oppositions that have been understood to exist between 'Islam' and 'modernity'.

The principle of individual autonomy, understood as central to the liberal project of modernity, has been seen as a catalysing element in tensions between Islam and modernity (see Nasr, 1987). An idealized version of community-oriented Islam does not recognize the principle of individual autonomy, whereas in the liberal project of modernity, for the sake of decollectivization, the emancipation of the individual as the self-reliant master of his or her life is overemphasized. This means that, under conditions of liberal modernity, the ties between human beings are supposed to be thin, with rationality supposed to govern life.

Human beings, however, are by their very nature communal beings: 'all human activities are conditioned by the fact that men live together' (Arendt, 1958: 34). Without community or society, individuation cannot be conceptualized and thus modernity, as a human condition, has to be based on 'sociability' rather than on isolated individuals. In the cultural programme of 'original', Western modernity, individualism is based on the belief in a 'pure' identity as an individual that takes precedence over an identity as (for example) French, Russian, a worker or a Muslim. As Wagner (1994) notes, an essential ambiguity of Enlightenment lies in the relations between, on the one hand, individual autonomy and reason, and, on the other hand, notions of 'the common good' and 'human nature', which are not qualities of individuals. Furthermore – due not least to the fact that moral order and social control require that individual identity formation be related to social identities – every identity formation is necessarily a social process. Atomistic social philosophy seems to fail, because individual identity is not free from cultural contexts.

Equally, Islam cannot be generalized as strictly communitarian in all the socio-historical contexts in which it exists. Rather, Islam is open to interpretation in terms of the relations between the individual and society. First, the Koran, as the source of knowledge, is always open to interpretation. The unity of individuals under the divine intellect seems problematic. In other words, since the Koranic verses do not constitute a unity, most of them being solutions to given socio-historical problems during the Prophet's lifetime, Muslims take particular verses as guides to life, finding enough room for their own understandings of Islam. This could be argued as opening up an opportunity for a form of individuation. For instance, Ibn Rushd (known in the West as Averroes) could not be easily seen as a mere member of the Islamic *umma*, since he followed ancient Greek philosophy as well as Islamic teachings. Secondly, and perhaps more importantly, in Islam, in contrast to Christianity, there is no clergy through which individuals relate to God. When individuals are not guided by clerical authority, an individual perspective on religion should be a stronger possibility. Thus, it may be argued that this aspect of Islam opens up opportunities for a form of individualism.

What then must be stressed is that individual autonomy within modernity can exist in various forms and to various degrees depending on the social setting. Arnason (1997), in his scholarly work on Japanese modernity, does not give central importance to individual liberty as a distinguishing characteristic of modernity, but I think it is problematic to talk about modernity without considering the degree of individuation present in a particular context. However, I am not simply attempting to make Islamic views of the individual and the community appear compatible with Western understanding. On the contrary, I would insist that the 'liberation' of individuality cannot be seen as unique to the West, but that, in Islamic communities, there have been *different* processes of individualization.

In relation to understanding the world, the views of 'Islam' and 'modernity' are seen as opposed (see Nasr, 1987; Gellner, 1992). The holder of knowledge in Islam is ultimately the divine intellect; 'true science' is based on the supra-human level. That is, intelligence is a divine gift to human beings; the divine intellect is superimposed on the human intellect. So, the ultimate criterion of reality is God. The Koran is the only source of true knowledge and the basis for arriving at perfection. 'Modern' thought, in contrast, is anthropomorphic, recognizing no principle higher than the human. Modern thought can be seen as 'all that is merely human' and, therefore, it is essential for it to diverge from the divine source of knowledge. Thus, modernity's 'true science' is based on human reason. The ultimate criterion for reality is the individual human being. Perhaps this is best expressed in Descartes' well-known phrase: 'I think, therefore I am'.

Considered in this ahistorical perspective, then, Islamic sciences may appear incompatible with rational sciences.[4] However, historical reality does not bear this out. Islamic scholars were the main figures who taught advanced science and philosophy to Westerners. Ibn Sina, Ibn Rusd, Farabi and Ibn Khaldun were no less important than Newton, Descartes, Locke or Kant, and carried ancient Greek philosophy and an advanced science to the West in the thirteenth century.

In fact, in the Koran, *ilim*, 'knowledge', is the second most common word after 'Allah'. The emphasis on knowledge allowed Islamic scholars to emerge as important figures in world thought. Against the view of those Westerners who argue that Islam did not give rise to great men in human history, there are many exemplary figures.[5] Not only the Koran, but also the *sunna*, Muhammad's sayings and practices, provide the interpretation that science is central to life. For example, a phrase from Muhammad could be used to interpret Islam as placing essential importance on science: 'Search knowledge even if it is in China'. However, this should not be taken to mean that Muslims consider modern science in the same way as Westerners. This question depends on how modern science is interpreted: some social contexts might see it as the instrument for achieving mastery over nature, as Westerners generally have done, while other contexts might view modern science as the means by which to acquire knowledge of the world without mastering it completely.

Another crucial opposition is seen to lie in modernity's differentiation process as against Islam's integration. The separation of realms of human activity is overemphasized by modernist social theories (see, for instance, Parsons, 1971). The 'ideal' Islamic community, in stark contrast, is regarded as perfectly unified; that is, no fragmentation is allowed to take place (Ahmad, 1983). Islam is believed to achieve this unity through the framework of the 'final judgment'. In other words, Islamic morality governs all activities and is, thus, a unifying element. This is indeed questionable because differentiation and integration can take various forms in modern societies depending on context. Rather than readily accepting Islam's integration as incompatible with modernity's differentiation process, the degree of integration and differentiation could be taken to explain distinctions between Western modernity and Islamic modernities.

In fact, modernity can never be seen to provide autonomy for human realms to the same degree in all contexts. For example, it cannot be argued that 'civil society' means one and the same thing for all modernities. In the Japanese and Russian experiences, for instance, state and society have been much more closely integrated than in the Western experience (Arnason, 1997, 1993).[6] This observation supports the argument that, in terms of integration and differentiation, a modernity within an Islamic society would not resemble the modernity of a Christian society.

In relation to the debate about the (in)compatibility of Islam and modernity, the economy occupies a crucial place. As we have seen, economic activity comes to the fore in modernity as a driving force in the development of the conditions of life. Islam is assumed to resist the centrality of the economy in human life (Berkes, 1976). The economic model of Islam is often emphasized as an anti-modern economy. However, it can be shown that Islam is compatible with modernity in terms of economic activity, although Islamic societies do not necessarily accept the Western economic model. In Islamic countries, both liberal and socialist models of economy have found a place, although these countries have added their own characteristics to them. I shall briefly show that both liberal and socialist models have not met resistance from Islam. The practices of the Prophet Muhammad provide sources for liberals to conclude that Islam encourages competitive economic activity. Muhammad was a merchant himself and he proclaimed that 'commerce is the basic activity for the survival of the Islamic community'. Not only the life of the Prophet but also some verses in the Koran provide evidence that Islam is compatible with the liberal economic model. For example, the Koran grants the right of individual private property. Some liberal observers, such as Mehmet (1990: 77), go further: 'In terms of market relations Islamic economic doctrines are most compatible with perfect competition based on private property ownership and private enterprise'. Socialists, on the other hand, emphasize the communitarian characteristics of Islam. It seems that Islam promises equity, rejects profit and delegitimizes the charging of interest. Therefore, socialism seems, to some observers of Islam, to be a more compatible model. Moammar Kaddafi emerged as the political leader of Islamic socialism, or 'socialist Islam'. Perhaps more importantly, the most influential ideologue of the Iranian Islamic revolution, Ali Shariti, expressed socialist views in the lectures he gave across the country after completing his PhD in sociology in Paris. Thus, it is clear that Islam is open to interpretations in terms of economic models. It is not that the modern economy cannot be accepted by Islam, but that it could take a different shape in Islamic societies.

For some critics, the incompatibility between Islam and modernity is unavoidable, because secularization does not apply in Islamic contexts (Gellner, 1992). A strong adherent of Enlightenment rationalism, Ernest Gellner believes that 'to say that secularisation prevails in Islam is not contentious. It is simply false' (Gellner, 1992: 5). For Gellner, the main feature of Islam that is assumed to prevent secularization is the absence of clergy. In Islam, Gellner (1992: 8) writes, 'no distinct sacramental status separates the preacher or the leader of the ritual from the laity ... There is no clerical organisation.' What Gellner wants to say is that, since in Islam there is no clerical institution such as the church, it is not possible to see Islam and the state as two different institutions.

Secularization should allow the individual to relate directly to God and not through a priesthood and, I think, Gellner would agree with this. It is possible to argue that secularization is in fact much more compatible with Islam than with Christianity. Since, in Islam, believers are already 'free' in their relation to God because there is no clergy through which believers relate to God, it should be much easier for secularization to take place. A huge effort was required to separate the church from the state in Christian societies, whereas there is no need for such an effort to be made in Islamic societies. However, for Gellner, since there is no clergy, it is impossible to separate Islam from the socio-political sphere. Since Gellner does not take a historical approach, he does not paint an accurate picture of Islam's relation to secularization. In fact, it is difficult to find a theocratic state in Islamic history.[7] For example, as we shall see, the Ottoman Empire was not shaped by religious men but, in contrast, formed its own Islamic institutions. Thus, plurality existed in Islam from the beginning, whereas secularization has only existed in the West since the Renaissance and the Reformation. Apart from a lack of historical perspective, Gellner misses another crucial point: secularity may refer to something different in Islamic societies. Since Gellner believes in the coherence of modernity, secularization, for him, must follow the same process everywhere. It should be observed, however, that a version of secularization is possible in Islam. As Turkey shows, the state does not need to found a separate institution for religion; rather it needs to provide religious services without legitimizing itself with religious principles.

Up to this point, I have considered some of the aspects of human life that have been considered most difficult in terms of the reconciliation of Islam with modernity.[8] We have seen that neither modernity nor Islam can easily be seen as a standard world-interpretation. Rather, it is essential to emphasize the varieties of both modernity and Islam in exploring the relations between them. In the next section, we will see that the theme of varieties of modernity and Islam is fruitful in the light of the Turkish experience.

Different Islams and Different Modernities

It is important to consider the beginning of relations between Islam and the Turks. There are three main views on this issue (see Aydin, 1994): first, that the Turkish world of the time shared some basic features with emerging Islam, leading the Turks to commit themselves to becoming Muslim; secondly, that the Turks came into the Islamic world as conquerors, later becoming defenders of Islam; and thirdly, that the Turks were religiously colonized by challenges from the Arabs. I think that these three views taken together point to the truth. Islam, like any other religion, includes common conceptions of life; therefore, it might share similar features with the Turkish way of life of the time. It is evident from history that the Arabs aimed at turning the Turks into Muslims, but the Turks did not forget Arabic brutality when they came into the Muslim world as conquerors and gained power themselves.

This starting point indicates that it is possible to talk about the concept of 'Turkish Islam'. In other words, the Turks developed their own specific way of relating the self to Islam; they were not willing to abandon their existing cultural orientations for Islam's perceived universality. Since the Turks were both the conquerers of Islam and of the Islamic world, their relation to Islam differed from those of other Islamic societies. For instance, unlike the others, the Turks had a tradition of man-made law, the *kanun*, which they never allowed to diminish in importance in comparison with the *sharia*, the Islamic law. Thus, we have to recognize the existence of a specific form of Islam in Turkey, contrary to the assumptions of observers who have rejected the 'regionalization' of Islamic history (see Hodgson, 1960).

Here it is important to pay attention to the era preceding the 'secular' Turkish republic, the Ottoman Empire. Neglected by most observers, the Ottoman Empire needs rather to be conceptualized in terms of a complex and dialectical relation between the forces of Islam and the interpretation of the 'secular' world. Many see the Ottoman Empire as an Islamic theocracy (see Turner, 1999; Arsel, 1987). However, the Empire never fully met the conditions of such a theocracy. First, the caliphate, in a Sunni sect, must be the centre around which a 'global' Muslim identity is structured. Far from aiming at structuring a global Muslim identity, the Ottoman sultanate did not even put the status of caliph to use until the end of the eighteenth century. Secondly, Islamic *sharia* law was never prioritized over *kanun*, as many observers claim (see Watt, 1988; Ahmed, 1993). It is argued that two institutions were used to guarantee that the sultan obeyed Islamic rules (Mahçupyan, 1997). These were *seyhulislam* (the highest religious authority in the Empire) and the *ulema* (the Islamic scholars), which expressed the Islamic aspect of the Empire. However, neither of them could ever master the sultanate, because it was the sultan who governed the Empire with teams such as the *ulema*. Therefore, *ulema* and *seyhulislam* were built by, not formative of, the sultanate.

If we cannot place the Ottoman Empire in a purely Islamic context, how should we then understand it? In contrast to perspectives that assume that Islam controlled all aspects of everyday life in the Ottoman Empire, from law to gender relations, we need to understand that, in the formation of the Empire, various elements came from various civilizations – Islamic, Byzantine, Turkic and Persian.[9] The Central Asian background, for instance, gave the Ottoman mosques their unique forms, although some believe that Ottoman architecture was completely Islamic (see Nasr, 1987). Borrowing from 'different' civilizations has a much longer history than is often assumed. What is crucial for the present purposes is to see how 'Turkish culture' was already situated between the 'West' and Islam long before the start of Kemalist modernization. If we wish to talk about 'Westernization' in the Turkish world in Anatolia, we must at least start with the conquest of Istanbul, in 1453, rather than reducing

Western characteristics in Turkey to being the outcome of Kemalism. Perhaps more important is that in the Ottoman Empire, until the nineteenth century, 'Easternness' was never idealized (Berkes, 1976: 372). In brief, understanding Turkish history requires a different interpretation than merely placing it in a history of Islamic civilization.

Turkey never became a full member either of the 'centre' in the West, or of the Islamic East; rather, it always remained peripheral. This is not to say that the Turks were powerless, but that in terms of civilization they were peripheral both to the West and to the East. Turkey was never peripheral in the sense in which the term is used by dependency theorists – that is, it was never a colony of either the Islamic or the Western world. From 1914 until 1922, Britain, France and Italy made attempts to conquer Turkey, but this resulted in the Turkish victory over Western powers as the first success against 'modern' imperialism. However, the Turkish war of liberation was not waged only against the West, but also against the Islamic East. It could be seen as a revolt against the consequences of Turkey's peripheral position: Mustafa Kemal argued that the caliphate had been paid for in Turkish blood. Other Muslims had left the Turks to defend Islam and, in many cases, had fought against the Turks (Atatürk, 1983 [1927]).

Kemal was in fact pointing to the autonomization – the self-determination – of a culture that had already singularized itself both in Islamic civilization and in Europe. This is the main point raised by the critics of Kemalism: that Kemalism aimed to Westernize Turkish society (see Özel, 1992). Although it is possible to view Kemalism as a project strongly influenced by the European Enlightenment, Kemalist modernity cannot be argued to be a simple copy of European modernity. It is easy to contrast Kemalism and Arabocentric Islam but more difficult to understand why the Turkish experience is different from both the West and the East.

Kemalism did not just happen to come about in the Turkish society of the 1920s: it was continuous with the Ottoman modernizing reforms from the beginning of the *tanzimat* era in 1839. If Turkish society had been at a stage of 'Muhammadan' Islam, then neither the Ottoman reforms nor the Kemalist modernizing trends would have succeeded. Kemalism did however break with Ottoman modernization in the sense that, for the Kemalists, modernization had to be a thoroughgoing and revolutionary project, rather than a gradual reform of some sectors of society. Thus, a history that had already come to the point of breaking away from its peripheral situation was brought to the stage of a final break.

Kemalism, therefore, can best be understood as a possible solution to the problems of a specific social context at a specific time. Because of this, Kemalism

117

read Islam differently from other modernizing attempts in other Islamic contexts.[10] When Kemalism emerged in a society that was already partly Western, it did not find it problematic to Westernize this society to a greater extent. This can be understood in one of two ways: either we assume that the Kemalists aimed to shift Turkey from its peripheral position by moving it towards the Western 'centre', or we see Westernization as a means towards the autonomization of Turkish society. The current Turkish attempt to achieve full membership of the European Union supports the view that Turkey has attempted to gain a place in the centre of the West. However, there are a number of important reasons why we cannot simply view present-day Turkish society as the result of a historical move from East to West.

The crucial question in understanding the Turkish experience should not be whether Turkey could become a Western society. This is partly because the relation between Islam and modernity in Turkey was never one of total exclusion. In other words, the modernizers never aimed to exclude Islam from Turkish society; if they had, they would have encountered more severe opposition, which would in turn have made the project of modernizing Turkey far harder. Rather, something unique happened in Turkey in terms of Islam: historical experience – mainly the Anatolian life of the Turks – brought Mustafa Kemal to conclude in the 1920s that 'Turkish Islam' would not revolt against the secular republic.

Thus, it should not be surprising that Mustafa Kemal refused to become the caliph himself, as was proposed by the Khalifat movement in India (given his popularity as a Muslim hero, it is likely that he would have been accepted as caliph). While Mustafa Kemal was a heroic figure in the Muslim world for his stand against European imperialism, he nevertheless abolished the caliphate. 'The Khalifat committee in India was thunderstruck; their icon had been broken and their idol, Mustafa Kemal, had become the iconoclast' (Minault, 1982: 203).[11] This should indicate that Kemalist Turkey was not only moving further away from the Islamic centre, it was also refusing to take a position of leadership in the Islamic centre. Does this further indicate that Kemalist Turkey was moving to take up a position in the centre of the West? It is certain that the Kemalist project planned to advance Turkey to enter an era of 'high civilization' but this cannot prove that Kemalism was simply a Westernist ideology. We need to consider whether Westernizing processes are also connected with the 'autonomization' of a singularized culture. I shall briefly examine some of the most important processes of Westernization in the Turkish context.

In 1926, the Swiss civil code was adopted and assumed by the Islamists to be a replacement for Islam in the daily life of the Turks.[12] The Swiss civil code, however, was not simply copied, but adapted. This leads to two observations.

First, as we have seen, borrowing from 'alien' cultures was not unprecedented in Turkish life. Secondly, we need to consider whether the radical pluralism of Islams in Anatolia could have been maintained with only a secular civil law. We should also consider the extent to which the adoption of the Swiss civil code was continuous with Ottoman modernization. In the Ottoman Empire, two different sorts of law were already operating: *mecelle* (secular law) and *sharia* (Islamic law). Therefore, the emergence of a fully secular law may not be described simply as Westernization.

For the sake of nationalization, a reform in dress style was regarded as necessary by the Kemalists. The hat reform – the outlawing of the fez – was a key aspect of this. Again a borrowing is at stake here: if there had been a 'Turkish' style of dress, no doubt it would have been chosen over Western style. The Islamist opposition argued that the Kemalists saw Turkey from the Western point of view, as an 'Oriental' country, and that they therefore wanted to impose Westernization on Turkey by means of dress reform. In fact, however, the fez was another borrowing: it was Greek in origin and, thus, has nothing to do with Islam.[13] It is hard to argue that replacing Islamic dress was the business of Kemalism. Perhaps more important is the fact that nowhere in Islam is standard Islamic dress mentioned as compulsory. Hence, it is possible to practise Islam with the 'Western hat' just as it was with the 'Greek fez'.

When the caliphate was abolished, educational institutions were put under direct state control. However, this was also the case under the Ottoman state. In the Ottoman Empire, there were two separate educational systems: civilian and military bureaucrats of the Empire followed an education that, primarily, had nothing to do with Islam. A second education system produced the Islamic scholars of the Empire. Hence, Kemalist educational reform cannot simply be seen as a Westernizing process. In Kemalist Turkey, as in the Ottoman Empire, there was both an Islamic education system for *imams* and *muftis*, and a secular education system for other professions.

Kemalism should be taken to mean a radical change for Turkish society; it should not be taken to have been trying to achieve the impossible. Kemalism, in other words, did not force the Turks to live under a polity unimaginable for Anatolians. The state included Islam within its system; this was historical legacy. The Ottoman Empire did not leave Islam in Anatolia free; rather, the state was the most powerful interpreter of Islam. Therefore, the inclusion of an Islamic organization, *Diyanet Isleri Baskanligi*, in the state system was not a Kemalist invention: the state had to provide Islamic services. But what was new – extraordinary – was that Kemalism guaranteed a radical pluralism in interpretations of Islam, rather than forcing the population to understand Islam according to the state's interpretation as the Ottoman state did. By means of the education provided by Kemalism for the first time in Anatolia, many people came to interpret the Koran by reading the source directly, rather than receiving and obeying the sheikhs' perspectives. Under conditions of modernity, the already advanced radical plurality of Islams increased. Precisely by keeping this reality in mind, it is possible to understand why Mustafa Kemal thought that the Anatolian view of Islam would not revolt against the secular republic.

This may be why present-day Turkey experiences conflicts between Islamism and a radical plurality of world-interpretations. Conflicts between the Kemalists and the Sunni orthodox Islamists should be seen as conflicts about which type of modernity to adopt rather than as conflicts between modernity and Islam. Here, I understand 'Kemalists' to include not just the actively political followers of Kemalism, but the larger sectors of Turkish society. Therefore, different understandings and interpretations are found among this wide sector. Some, mostly liberals, view Islam as a religion of personal conviction, while some, largely Alevies, see Islam as a community-oriented religion but do not require an Islamic polity. Most groups read Islam as an important element of Turkish identity. However, a minority aims at making Islam the 'master signifier', and this is the ideology known as Islamism.

Islamism should not be viewed either as a manifestation of pre-modern 'traditional' phenomena or as a postmodern movement. Rather, Islamism can best be seen as a project of modernity, one that is entirely different from the Kemalist project. Islamist modernity would be totalitarian as well as an 'antagonistic' modernity. As Eisenstadt (1999) demonstrates, the ideological orientations of fundamentalist movements in general, and of Islamism in particular, share various features of the political programme of original Western modernity, especially Jacobin totalitarian ones. Islamism emphasizes the centrality of a total reconstruction of society by means of revolution. Islamism, in other words, does not tolerate any ambiguity, but aims at reconstructing the social world in a totalistic way. This shows that Islamism is not a traditionalist worldview;[14] it is, rather, a totalitarian response to problems of present-day modernity.

Thus, I disagree with those observers who view Islamism as a traditionalist world-interpretation opposed to modernity (see Tanilli, 1991). There are multiple interpretations of modernity and Islamism is one of them. In aiming to protect the majority of Turks from a unitary interpretation of Islam, present-day Kemalists must also realize that modernity cannot be long maintained by excluding some parts of society in the name of democracy. Kemalism itself provided the opportunity for people to interpret Islam in their own ways, so it might need to cope with 'difference'. In other words, there is no longer the possibility of living in a harmonious modernity, although neither is it desirable to see a uniform interpretation of Islam achieving power over the polity. It is important to stress that the conflicts between Islamism and a branch of Kemalism are conflicts between two coherent visions of life. Those Kemalists who see themselves as adherents of Mustafa Kemal Atatürk believe that a genuine modernity cannot include those Islamists who question the place of reason in society and politics. Islamists, on the other hand, do not tolerate any ambiguity, but aim to reconstruct society in a totalistic way by revolution. However, this is only one side of the picture, because there are other Kemalists and other Muslims who in fact hold power in present-day Turkey.

In contrast to those perspectives that see Islamism as a search for recognition for a particular identity, I would argue that as a consequence of the Islamization programme by the military, the Turkish lifeworld has been colonized by a nationalist Islam. Islamist groups are not seeking recognition as having a different, minority identity; rather, they seek hegemony. Since 1980, many Islamists in Turkey have found opportunities to further their ambitions. Many social scientists have assumed that the rise of Islamism in Turkey is linked to the state's radical secularism, against the religion of civil society (see for example Göle, 1996). However, this view does not take into account state support for Islamization. Islamist actors have not been prevented from achieving power; rather, since the early 1980s they have been at the centre of state activities. Having become, by means of state support, powerful actors in all spheres of Turkish society, they now argue that their values should shape the whole society. This must be understood as a serious attempt to colonize the cultural sphere of Turkish society.

Thus, the conditions of modernity in Turkey opened up a space for people previously outside modernity to participate in it. The consequences of this openness – a multiplicity of perspectives on Turkish modernity – are now being seen, and include the increase in Islamic politics. The openness of Kemalist modernity allowed people to interpret both Islam and, I think, modernity, according to their own views. Thus, the emergence of Islamism, at least in the Turkish case, cannot easily be seen as an outcome of authoritarian regimes.[15]

Nor should the emergence of Islamism be reduced to an outcome of economic problems (Gilsenan, 1990). In this view, the petty bourgeoisie felt it necessary to express itself through Islam to escape from the rule of a secular elite. This is an instrumentalist explanation which does not allow us to do justice to the self-understanding of a social group. Another common argument is that the problems caused by industrialization and urbanization are real factors in the emergence of Islamism (Fischer, 1982). Critics argue that urbanization created highly populated shanty towns whose inhabitants could not use the language of urban spaces but were also far enough advanced not to return to their previous position (Kongar, 2000). Therefore, these people find the language of Islamism feasible for the expression of their protests.[16]

This should not, however, lead us to argue that Islamism constitutes a break with modernity. In contrast, it is more convincing to see Islamism as a different project of modernity. If Islamism could achieve its ambitions, the social world would still be a modern one, but in a different configuration. Conflict between competing projects of modernity is unavoidable in a society that includes a radical pluralism of Islams. However, in this respect it is necessary to insist that a project to impose a single interpretation of Islam onto a radical plurality of Islams could never fully achieve its ambitions. It is this point that shows the conflict between the majority of Turkish society (despite the fact that it includes various different understandings of life) and the Islamist minority. This is not to recommend that the totalitarian project of Islamism should not be allowed to express itself in Turkey, but to note that this totalitarian project of modernity can never fully achieve its ambitions in Turkey. The emergence of Islamism as another project of modernity should not lead us to conclude that the adherents of two opposite projects cannot live together in the same society. In Turkish society, opposing projects of modernity – Turkist, socialist, and so on – have existed for a long time. And this is not an anomaly – unless we read modernity as a totality and as a coherent vision of life.

CHAPTER 6

Kemalism and Islamism on the 'Female Question'

In the previous chapter, my goal was to question the view that Islamic societies cannot be modern. Equally, however, we cannot see modernity in an Islamic society as simply a product of Islam. This is so precisely because modernity is a new phenomenon that requires an alteration of the existing socio-cultural world. The agency of modernity is important as well as the context. It is important to stress that, although Islam cannot be seen as incompatible with modernity, there is always conflict involved in the emergence and experience of modernity. And tensions between modernity and Islam have tended to be a central characteristic of twentieth-century Turkish history. More recently, the current socio-political system has faced an outright rejection on the part of political Islamism. Within these recent contestations, the 'female question' holds a prominent position, as can be seen not least in the fact that Islamist women appear as some of the most visible militants of the Islamist movement. In many respects, the 'female question' is indeed exemplary of the conflictual relations between Kemalist modernity and Islamism. This is so, as will be argued in this chapter, because some of Kemalist modernity's central trans-formations altered the role and position of women in society. In this light, it should not be surprising that Islamism, as a counter-project to Kemalism, also puts women in a central place in its movement.

Islamist women are fighting for an Islamist regime and, at the same time, against Kemalist modernity. However, in the Islamist women's rejection of modernity there are apparent contradictions which a simple opposition between traditional Islam and modernity is at a loss to explain. Their position can hardly be seen as a straightforward rejection of modernity grounded in their religious belief. Islamist women are mostly urbanized and educated. The opening of the universities to women was a major element of early Kemalism in order to provide equal educational opportunities and to let women enter the public forums of urban and professional life. Universities were, for the Kemalists, among the prototypical modern institutions and the entry of women into public university life was seen as a major step in the development of modernity. Today, then, we find women similarly using the opportunities provided by Kemalism in their role as spokespersons for opposite camps in current disputes. There are secular women, on the one hand, whose most important objective is to prevent the rise of the idea of an Islamic state and society, with Islamist women, on the other hand, working for the cause of Islamism. Although such dualism makes it difficult at first sight to read the contemporary shape of Turkish modernity, it is exactly such apparent contradictions that provide clues for a sociological theory of modernity, as insights into some of its unavoidably ambivalent features.

What is at stake? Do we have to conclude from these recent occurrences that Kemalism has failed in bringing 'enlightenment' into the Islamic 'darkness'? Does the emergence of Islamist women reveal that they are running away from the freedom provided by Kemalism? This context gives the analysis of Islamism in Turkey a particular sense of urgency. If Islamism's rise demonstrates the failure of Kemalism, then this is likely to have further repercussions for the understanding of contemporary varieties of modernity and the forms they may take. By trying to understand the actions and orientations of Islamist women in terms of relations between modernity and women – that is, by examining the relation of modernity to Islamist women – I am attempting to introduce a particular theme into the more general debate on modernity.

In the first place, it is true that views that women must not forget their 'natural' positions, that they must not let their roles and selves be reduced in discussions centred predominantly on equality, and that they should be first and foremost wives and mothers have been increasingly expressed in Turkey in recent years. Yet such statements are far from being confined to Islamic societies (Faludi, 1992). Such views obviously shake a feminism that has been aiming to achieve equality for women, but can be appreciated by another feminism that supports diversity rather than arguing for universality and equality.[1] In my view, it is important to set some of these arguments in the broader context of increasing critiques of modernity. Since, from the start of modern times, the 'female question' has been inseparable from the idea of modernity, any argument about the nature and role of women must also be seen as part of an argument about modernity. Equality-oriented feminism could be understood as part of a project of modernity that promised to liberate individuality and guarantee individual autonomy. The liberation of individuality necessarily includes the liberation of women since, otherwise, the project of modernity would fail in its commitment to universality. It could be argued that it is modernity that enabled women to share the public sphere and, by implication, to become self-determining subjects.[2] Thus, if women today oppose these forms of liberty, this should, it seems, be understood as a reaction against some experiences of modernity. By this, of course, I do not mean that the project of liberty has ever been completely achieved. As discussed earlier, the whole history of modernity could be read as a tension between liberty and discipline: modernity brought about individuals who are masters of themselves but, on the other hand, it disciplined forms of action and limited liberty for the sake of the sustainability of a social and moral order (Wagner, 1994). This observation, however, does not entail any doubt about liberty being an unavoidable feature of modernity. Any argument for the end of the individual, self-determining subject, then, must be understood as an argument for a transition away from modernity. Women criticizing the notion of the subject thus appear to be rejecting a key element of modernity, and to be supporting the idea that modernity has come – or should come – to an end.

This chapter will therefore look at Islamist women in Turkey in order to understand why some women appear to withdraw from a conception of freedom as part of modernity. We must analyse how Kemalist modernity views women and in what respect this perspective is opposed to Islam. As a background, the Islamic definition of women has to be considered to understand the tension between Kemalist modernity and Islamism on the 'female question'. The understanding of Islamism as a modern phenomenon enables us to perceive the contradictory elements in Islamist women's rejection of modernity.

Islam and Women

Islam is generally regarded as patriarchal and thus inimical to women's rights (Arsel, 1987). However, this feature could as well be seen as a characteristic of the conceptualization of gender differences in traditional ages in general. In other words, when Islam emerged, the social world was patriarchal and, thus, it would be unsurprising if Islamic conceptions were similarly patriarchal. Here we need to be more precise about the situation of women in so-called pre-modern times in general, and about the ways in which Islamic rules did – and, indeed, also did not – become historically implanted in Turkish society.

In discussing Islamic rules about women's lives, it should not be forgotten that Islam's view of women has always remained open to interpretation because of the contextual realities of the places where Islam has been present. Thus, we need to take lived socio-historical experiences into account as well as the Islamic rules explicitly defined in the Koran. Gender relations play a part in giving shape to the entire social world, and are generally assumed to present the most intractable difficulty in resolving oppositions between Islam and modernity (see Çalislar, 1991). In the Koran, it can be seen that for both physical and spiritual beauties and necessities, God created the two sexes in order for them to achieve perfection on earth. This perfection could be achieved with absoluteness and infinitude because God himself is both absolute and infinite. Absoluteness, thus authority, is manifested most directly in the masculine state, whereas the female body first reflects beauty and thus infinity. Therefore, it can be said that, for Islam, in order to reach unity, there is necessarily diversity. In Islam, it is this instrumentality that requires authority and obedience: man and woman.

In a male-dominated era the above understanding of man and woman was a temporary solution to the gender situation in a specific place: the Arab world. Gender relations always carry the possibility of causing problems in any social setting. Therefore, when Islam emerged, a solution was provided both for a specific time and for a specific place. The problem was not resolved, only extended. Since then, in different places and times, Islam's view of women has remained open to disputes. However, since the argument for the incompatibility of Islam with modernity has been grounded particularly in the explicitly defined Islamic rules about women's lives, we need to examine these rules briefly.

Since Islam was born as a state-religion (Tanilli, 1990), it aimed at defining all activities of life. Women's lives in both their public and private aspects were to be determined by Islamic rules. The Islamic definition of women is very much alive in the history of Turkish literature, because both its proponents and its opponents find it to be at the core of major disputes in society. Secularists mainly underline the patriarchal features of Islam by arguing that Islam actually sees women as second-class human beings (Arsel, 1987; Çalislar, 1991). From a contemporary point of view, it is hardly possible to argue against this opinion, because over long periods it was made impossible for women to share the public sphere and to play a full role in society. Since, however, the Turks were not originally Muslims, the particular relation of political Turkey to Islam must be understood against the background observation that Islam never determined the life of the Turks completely and that there was no 'reactionary Islam' until the emergence of modernity.

Islam aims to organize social life on the basis of the differences between the sexes (see Acar, 1991). While men are supposed to be active beings whose practices serve to secure the survival of the community, women are regarded as passive beings who should not have the right to make decisions on crucial matters of life. Islam aims to keep women exclusively within the private realm of life in which they cannot even develop a new identity or practice without the

126

permission of their husbands. Since women are taken to be essential to safe-guarding the moral order, they should not share life with men because this would quickly lead to moral corruption. Women are seen as natural creatures who could not develop civilization, whereas men, as cultural beings, have to operate and organize life. The important implication here is that it is part of the fulfilment of this male role to be responsible for the protection of women in every respect. In sum, tradition gives priority to men over women, and Islam, just like other religions, legitimizes this reality of traditional ages.

Islam gives particular importance to questions of sexual morality when discussing the rules of women's lives.[3] In Islam, women's behaviour is seen as the primary cause of infringements against the Islamic definition of morality. This is the major – and unavoidable – connection between veiling and morality in Muslim societies. Women have to be well veiled in order not to damage public morality. More generally, the case for women's passivity in an Islamic country is equally founded on this definition of women and their relation to morality. Since the female body always arouses men sexually and therefore endangers moral behaviour, women must not take part in the public sphere. It is widely known that a girl wearing a mini-skirt in public was raped in Iran before the Islamic revolution and that many observers believed that the girl had 'asked for it' by wearing the mini-skirt. It is no exaggeration to say that the concern over morality played a significant role in bringing about the Iranian revolution.

According to Islamic *sharia* law, women and men are not equal; different statuses are assigned to them (see Arsel, 1987). For instance, a single woman is an insufficient witness for a court case; there must be at least two women who witnessed the situation at the same time. Men can get married to more than one woman and can get divorced when they ask for it, whereas women can neither marry nor divorce according to their own will. The assumption of men's unquestionable authority over women made it possible to legitimize women's dependency on men in tradition by means of religion.

In the traditional reading of Islam, women were taken to be the creators and sustainers of the family, and the role of the mother as the creator of the family was, accordingly, mystically overemphasized.[4] The family as an institution was much more central to traditional societies than to modern societies, since, with the emergence of modernity, many functions of the family devolved onto the newly formed social institutions. Within the Islamic tradition, however, the family was also seen as the centre of a moral community based on the man's purity, which, in turn, is safeguarded by his wife's morality. For Islam, women who live their lives as moral beings within the family help to keep all members of their family morally pure. Women are the source and safeguard of social morality. Therefore, for Islam, the world should be divided into two parts, the public and the private: men's duties lie outside, in the public realm, and women's duties lie inside, in the private realm.

Men and women are created differently; that is why it is difficult for Islam to consider the equality of the sexes. Given this understanding, Islam, like Christianity, cannot theoretically be compatible with modernity, since one of the ambitions of Kemalist modernity, as we shall see, was to liberate women on the basis of equality. However, if socio-historical experiences had been exactly those of obedience to the explicitly stated rules of Islam, or of Christianity, modernity could never have emerged. The multiplicity in historical experiences must be held to show that Islamic rules have always been revised and reinterpreted and that, therefore, different developments have been witnessed. In this respect, the Turkish experience of modernity indicates that Islam is compatible with modernity, because explicit rules have never completely shaped actual practices. We shall see, in the next section, that Kemalist modernity prioritized women's liberation more than Western modernity did, and that Turkish modernity today differs from any other in terms of the importance of women in the public sphere.

Kemalism and Women

It should be noted that Kemalism, as a particular project of modernity, must be distinguished from 'original' Western modernity with regard to the 'female question'. Women were included from the beginning of the Kemalist project as essential actors in building a road to modernity, since it was believed that women would be agents in bringing about an actual break with previous history and in enlightening social life. Thus, the liberation of women has occupied a primary position in the history of Turkish modernity. Kemalism held that, in order to move towards modernity, liberation must start with that of women. This may be one of the features of Kemalism that still carries relevance for other Islamic societies. If a project of political reform succeeds in changing women and their situation, as the Kemalists argued, then the heart of traditional Islamic life is broken and a breakthrough achieved.

Turkish women were considered to be important actors in two basic processes in the Turkish experience of modernity: the nationalization process and the individuation process. The appearance of women who broke with the Islamic tradition was taken to be a major sign of a new form of social life. No longer defined and confined by their religious identity, many women embraced the national project and saw themselves first and foremost as Turks. And, since they demonstrated that being a modern woman was at the core of being a

Turkish woman, they showed, at the same time, that a Turk is a contemporary, modern human being, and that Turkey had embarked on the path to modernity. Symbolically, the secular, the national and the gender aspects combined in the early phase of the Turkish project of modernity. Women entering public life immediately played an important part in bringing about a national and secular society since, by means of that change, a radical break with former social practices could be demonstrated. The presence of educated and working women indeed meant an extraordinary change in a society that had an Islamic background.

As mentioned in Chapter 3, an important intellectual concomitant to this project of nationalization was the 'Turkish history thesis' that emerged in the 1930s. This thesis holds more specifically that, before the advent of Islam, Turkish women had already been equal to men. It is obvious that the aim here was to invent a history in order to accelerate modernization. However, it is indeed important to note that Islamic rules, including rules governing women's lives, were not completely implanted in Turkish society. In villages, as Berkes (1976) shows, women were not veiled according to Islamic rules. This relative diversity of cultural backgrounds may help to explain why it was easier for women to assume public roles in Turkey than in any other Islamic society, and in particular Arabic society. It may be a case of the effectiveness of the *longue durée* in history that, after centuries of formal Islamic rule, women in Anatolia turned out to support the Kemalist project.

In terms of the Turkish history thesis, pre-Islamic history is celebrated, especially for women's position in society. Mustafa Kemal's adoptive daughter, Afet Inan, for example, argued that when Islam was accepted, the status of women deteriorated (Inan, 1974). Or, for a contemporary view on the theme, we can consider the position of the political scientist, Ahmet Taner Kişlali who, in an interview on Turkish modernity, argues that 'before Islam the religion of the Turks was Shamanism and within it women were equal to men, but in the Arabic world at the same time women were less important than camels. Therefore, while Islam was progress for Arabic women, it abandoned the high importance given to women in the Turkish context. Those historical differences reasserted themselves during Kemalism, and Turkey has since provided the model of modernization for the Muslim world.'[5] The emerging hegemony of Islam was accordingly seen in terms of a loss of the society's Turkish origins. Thus, women were breaking connections with Islam by becoming models of modern life. In Kemalist Turkey, women came to be symbols of modernity, so that, for instance, as Göle (1996) shows, female university students wearing shorts demonstrated the degree of modernity in the Turkish society of the 1920s.

In Kemalist thinking the idea of modernity is necessarily related to the concept of individual autonomy. Liberation of individuality, for Kemalism, has to include the liberation of women because, otherwise, modernity would be only halfway accomplished and would fall short of its other basic tenet, namely universality. In the light of the aforementioned, we can see that the basic reason for this perspective was the particular condition of developing the project against an imagined Islamic past. In the transition to modernity, it is assumed that community has to be replaced by society. And the guarantee of individual autonomy is a necessary precondition for enabling people to escape from communitarian practices and identities. In this respect, again, women came to be seen as essential agents in furthering the societal project of bringing about individual autonomy. A move towards modernity entails that given rules are no longer unquestioningly accepted, but that attempts to change the conditions of life are made; and Turkish women were at the forefront of breaking dogmatic barriers. By this I mean that women started to believe that the world could be changed by human beings, if they refused to be the slaves of dogmatism, of established teaching or of the personal whims of the caliph or the sultan. That is why university attendance and scientific education were central; they gave women the opportunity to be more advanced than, rather than merely equal to, men. The important feature of women's liberation here is that Turkish women, to a considerable extent, liberated Turkish men. When women came to see themselves as subjects, the family began to change profoundly and, gradually, all of its members began to consider self-realization as more important than obedience to unquestioned norms.

If the view that women must be publicly visible, educated, working and on the side of modern life is a specific feature of Kemalism, it is obvious that this political project was indeed opposed to the traditional Islamic view of women. Women were active within Kemalist Turkey whereas, in the traditional view, they were passive. In Kemalist Turkey, women obtained equal rights and liberties much earlier than women in many other countries, including France, Italy and Switzerland. The Kemalists believed that, after Turkey had liberated women, they would support the Kemalist project whenever it was in danger. Does the emergence of Islamist women show that this hope was misplaced?

Islamist Women's Rejection of Modernity

In contrast to prevailing conceptualizations that tend to see Islamism as a reaction of tradition against modernity (Watt, 1988; Gellner, 1992), I understand Islamism as itself a political project in, and under conditions of, modernity. In order to develop this notion, I shall focus on Islamist women's rejection of modernity, trying to understand their motivations.

The main change Kemalism effected in the position of women was to liberate them from the fate of being merely mothers and wives. This means that women were taken to be equal citizens of the republic – in stark contrast, for instance, to the Islamist understanding prevailing in post-1979 Iran. The emphasis Kemalism put on changing the status of women is indeed remarkable, even in international comparison. For instance, female suffrage was granted in Kemalist Turkey in 1934, ten years earlier than in France, a country often regarded as the historical forerunner of modernity. Today, 30 per cent of university academic staff in Turkey are female, a situation that would be unthinkable in any other Islamic country (Kislali, 1997). Tansu Çiller, the leader of the Dogru Yol party, proclaimed herself to be 'a product of Kemalism' when she was elected Turkey's first female prime minister in 1993. However, these observations seem to make the emergence of Islamist women all the more astonishing. Why is it that such women appear to be fighting for a regime that would not allow them to share the public sphere? Is their emergence a strong indication of Kemalism's failure?

While women gained opportunities through Kemalism to share more fully in social life, they were also given responsibilities to enter into the social contract of the modern polity directly rather than through the mediation of men. The freedom of modern citizens goes along with commitments to state and society. Thus, the move towards the status of full subjects was not without ambivalence for women. It is possible to argue that fear – the loss of ontological security – may play a part in Islamist women's rejection of modernity: within the 'traditional' world women are protected and shielded by men, but within modernity, women must take responsibility for their own lives.

The views of Islamist women seem, in all important respects, to be opposed to the views a 'modern woman' would hold. Islamist women accept that which normally cannot be accepted by modern women – the belief in the superiority of men – so that we can conclude that, really, they reject modernity. In these Islamist women's view, women have to do what their husbands tell them, a view modern women normally cannot accept. Women have to be primarily good wives to Muslim husbands whereas, in the modern conception, both women and men are simply human beings. In the Islamist polity, in particular, women cannot have the right to participate in decision-making or even to vote, whereas in modernity's view, women are equal citizens in all respects, from choosing the government to becoming governors themselves.

Islamist women see modernity's women as corrupt creatures, particularly in terms of morality. In their rejection of the West, they even appeal to figures of the anti-imperialist argument.[6] According to the Islamists, modernity represented the superiority of the West, so that their project needs to show that the East is able to compete with the West, that the East provides an alternative to Western modernity. They find, in religion, a powerful element that can serve to demarcate the East from the West; or Islam from Christianity.

In order to show to what extent Islam differs from the West, Islamists emphasize the position of women at the core of Western societies. In their view, it is the women who are super-consumers of imperialist goods. It was the imperialist powers' access to women that first created moral corruption and, as a consequence, destroyed the Islamic community. Thus, it is possible for Islamists to argue, affirmatively, that the Koran provides a closed order and that women's position was 'opened' by modernists to destroy Islam. Women who do not wear veils cannot be seen as anything other than corrupt creatures whose actions opened society to immoral domination. Islamist women believe that they, by contrast, represent moral people and that society's moral decay could be prevented by veiling women, because the female body has to be out of the reach of men in order to make a moral order sustainable. The journal *Kadin ve Aile* describes the ideal woman as follows: '[She] completely devotes herself to her husband, she does not show herself to strange men, does not look at them. She does not go out without her husband's permission, and does not receive any male and female guests at home' (trans. in Acar, 1991). In all respects, this position seems to be so implicitly and explicitly opposed to modernity that we can assert that Islamist women reject modernity.

However, the analysis cannot stop at this point. The contradictory elements in this rejection must be examined for a social theory of modernity. That is, within Islamism, there is almost nothing 'pure' or 'authentic', since the escape from modernity seems impossible in any respect. We can begin to point out contradictions by noting that Islamism is historically situated within modern history; it did not exist prior to the emergence of modernity. The most important observation underpinning this insight is the fact that present-day Islamism takes its distance from historic Islamic societies. Traditional Islam, before Kemalism, is understood as a false Islam. Islamists refer to the time of the Prophet Muhammad and the four classical caliphs as the era in which Islam achieved perfection (see Gunes-Ayata, 1991). Since this is a reference to a long-gone era, whose social forms cannot be clearly identified, present-day Islamism becomes a kind of utopianism. It is important to note that this sort of utopianism never existed prior to the emergence of Kemalist modernity. But if Islamism derives its doctrine from the origins of Islam, we have to ask why it has only recently emerged as a political project.

There is clear evidence of the contradictions in the Islamist women's position. In traditional Islam, a woman cannot be a political actor herself, but Islamist women are highly militant political actors. This observation already tells us that Islamism is a political project within modernity. With regard to political regimes, Islamist women take a position that cannot be seen as compatible with their ideal Islamist regime. While Islamist women accept gender inequality, they argue at the same time that the Turkish polity is not a democracy and they demand the establishment of full democracy. Democracy, however, is a product of modernity and is based on equal rights, free elections and multiple political parties, whereas, in an Islamist regime, there can be no political parties, no elections, and no equality between the members of a community. Thus, it is unclear how an Islamist can argue the case for having more democracy. Nevertheless, many Islamists today argue that Turkey is not a democracy by comparing it with Western democracies. While such comparison may be justified on a number of grounds, it should not be overlooked that Kemalism always aimed at founding a democratic regime, even if its starting point was very remote from democracy. If today that aim appears not to have been reached, then there are only two directions the argument can take. Either we see the Kemalist project as unfinished and as needing to be carried further towards modernity, or we see it as unfeasible or undesirable as a project of modernity and as needing to be replaced by an alternative project. In either case, though, unavoidable reference is made to modernity, putting the Islamists – avowedly opposed to modernity – in a paradoxical position.

Related to this argument on a more general level, the issue of representation provides us with further unavoidable contradictions. Islamist women argue that they have to be represented, but political representation is precisely a characteristic of the modern polity. In traditional societies there is no issue of representation, since rulers do not need legitimation. For instance, in an Islamic community, a religious leader cannot be challenged on the grounds that he does not represent the group's interests or culture, because he is assumed to be chosen by God.

Another contradiction of Islamism is the conversion of God's messages into political slogans. Political slogans, like political contestations, must be regarded as characteristics of modern polities, in which a particular group or party needs to solicit support, or of modern revolutions, during which slogans are used to mobilize the population. The politicization of the masses is a modern condition; thus, in the case of Islamism, key forms of modern political action are being used in the name of a project that claims to reject modernity.

Perhaps the most striking contradiction resides in the fact that Islamist women aim at transforming social life by means of revolutionary change, which is a characteristically modern strategy. In religious understanding, life proceeds according to God's will and knowledge, so that any attempt at a

133

planned change of that direction would be both futile and meaningless. In contrast, modernity thinks in terms of the future rather than in terms of past or present times and, in doing so, it necessarily uses its own properties, namely rationality, science, technology and revolution, to shape the social world (see Koselleck, 1985). Thus, when we consider Islamist women's rejection of modernity, we definitely see it as making use of the means and forms of modernity. They need to argue rationally; they use modern technology; they receive their education at science departments; and, most of all, in common with the Kemalist modernizers, they aim at revolution.

As mentioned above, most Islamist women pursue higher education at universities. I now want to consider three examples of female Islamist university students in order to demonstrate the contradictions in their positions.[7] A particularly revealing example is that of a student who questions her father, who has always lived as a Muslim man. She says, 'I sometimes talk about the verses and hadits of our prophet to my father: "Father, when it was necessary, our prophet undertook his own tasks and helped his wife; he swept the house" – "Where," he asks, "where is it written?" That is, they don't know such things, and they don't accept them' (Göle, 1996: 104). In arguing in this way, the student explicitly avails herself, first, of the educational opportunities provided to her by modernity and, secondly, of the transformation of social behaviour that allows her to argue at all with her father in an Islamic family. In this and many other examples, the Islamist utopia is evidently ridden with contradictions. Islamists propose that it is necessary for human beings to live in peace with nature but, in fact, they often live in extremely modern buildings that do not even have a quasi-natural environment such as a garden. Or, to take another example, Islamists also argue for an ideal of equality in terms of economic life that seems to be influenced by socialism, a modern political ideal. Again, the reference must be utopian since historic Islamic societies never rendered equality possible, not least because Islam did not emerge on the side of the powerless. If we go one step further to assert that it is within modernity that projects of contestation for a better life emerged (see Eisenstadt, 1966), then current Islamism must be understood as essentially modern.

In an Islamic family, the parents unquestioningly make decisions for the children and, in particular, for the female children, whereas modern family ideals demand at least a gradual emancipation of children from parental oversight. While this feature, then, appears to mark another important opposition of Islam to modernity, female Islamist university students often argue for the right to make their own choices. For instance, one student says, 'My family in Eskisehir allows me to stay here because of my education. Or I can delay my marriage. But, in case I was enrolled in a Koran course, this would not stop them at all, and they could ask me to come back. Perhaps I don't want to be involved in family affairs before I feel I am a mature person. I don't know – maybe this is why I like studying' (Göle, 1996: 114). This example clearly demonstrates that Islamist women produce a new identity under conditions of modernity rather than merely accepting the traditional status of women. If they did not live under broad conditions of modernity, they would not be able to break with the traditional status quo. A new identity formation takes place which, in contradictory form, includes both tradition (the women's veiling and physical appearance) and modernity (women's education and participation in the public sphere).

Since education, particularly higher education, is generally seen as undesirable for women in Islam, it is important to understand the position female Islamist university students take on this question. In Turkey, people find it difficult to understand the position of female Islamist university students precisely because of the widespread belief that, according to Islam, women should not be educated. Reading philosophy or medicine as an Islamist is a difficult position to understand. Since university life is extremely public, a strict Islamist ought to believe that women should not be present there. Yet one of the female Islamist students says, 'we are studying to widen our horizons, not to be confined to a limited world' (Göle, 1996: 114). As mentioned earlier, one of the basic contradictions in the Islamist women's rejection of modernity is that they argue for a 'pure' Islam by means of an education provided by Kemalism. While Islamist women normally insist that Kemalism intended to eradicate Islamic belief, they should see it as a contradiction that, in Turkish history, it was only by means of Kemalism that they could come to know what the Koran actually says. Islamist women fight in public and together with men for a new form of social life, an Islamist one. But it is only since the development of modernity that women have been able to emerge as public actors, forming a new world together with men. If, according to actual Islamic rules, only men may engage in changing the overall conditions of life, then, to be consistent, Islamist women would have to wait for the men's struggle to be won rather than engaging in the struggle themselves.

How, then, are we to understand the ambivalent relationship between Islamist women and Kemalist modernity? As we have seen, although Islamist women's beliefs appear to constitute a rejection of modernity, their very ability to argue for these beliefs is fundamentally dependent on the conditions of modernity. Educated and urbanized Islamist women are only able to agitate for an ideal Islamist society because of the education and social and political rights granted them by Kemalism.

A plausible reading of these Islamist women would emphasize that, under conditions of modernity, they have developed a particular identity which, among other things, asserts a need to be different from Western or Westernized women. Towards that end, a recourse to Islam appears, particularly in terms of sexual morality. By means of veiling, these women intend to demonstrate how to be part of a moral community, in contrast to modern, unveiled women who represent moral corruption in their eyes. At this point, the appropriateness of the initial reference to a feminism that supports the postmodernist critique of modernity should have become clear: Islamist women's rejection of modernity goes along with such a form of feminism, although in the very different context of Islamic society. They put the universal principle of modernity into jeopardy without recognizing how dangerous their own conceptualization of life is: insisting that one way of life, among many diverse ways of life, is the only right one is liable to radicalize opposition.

The most problematic finding is that, on the one hand, Islamist women argue for a strictly Islamist regime such as the Iranian one but, on the other hand, they make use of the opportunities provided by Kemalist modernity. They seem, for instance, to value education at modern universities and participation in the public sphere, but neither of the two would be possible for women in their ideally projected Islamist regime. Islamist women are public actors in the country today, but they could no longer be if their desired regime came about. It seems that veiled women should consider whether they would miss the existing form of modernity in Turkey if one day they succeeded in replacing it with an Islamist modernity.

CHAPTER 7

A Theory of Modernity in the Light of the Turkish Experience

On the basis of the Turkish experience of modernity, this book has thus far argued that, to a considerable extent, existing social theory is invalid for analysing 'later modernities'. Some explicit lessons from the Turkish experience now need to be drawn in order to strengthen the proposition that the concept of varieties of modernity should be used to explore 'other' experiences of modernity. In this concluding chapter, therefore, I consider what can be learned from the Turkish experience for a social theory of modernity.

The Concept of Later Modernities

Since a plurality of histories, civilizations, modernizing agents and their projects indicates the existence of multiple modernities, the problematization of the assumed equivalence between modernity and the West is unavoidable. When social science accepts the West as another civilization among many, it can be recognized that ambitions to 'totalize' the world on the basis of Western values have had imperialist ambitions. It is because of this that Western modernity necessarily faced legitimate resistance. However, Eastern civilizations entered into an era of self-questioning partly because of the challenge posed by the imperialist intentions of Western modernity. It is undeniable that the idea of modernity in Eastern societies is imported from the West. Nevertheless, the fact that modernity first emerged in Western Europe does not guarantee that Western European countries provide the only instances of genuine or successful modernities. For example, one could show that American modernity is more advanced than European modernity, although the idea of modernity in America was imported from Europe.[1]

In short, modernity should not be viewed as the equivalent of the West.

Once the West is seen as a civilization among many, it is necessary to submit to the truth: the West is not the only specific context in which modernity can exist; there are other modernities. The concept of *later* modernities refers to an important category in terms of multiple modernities. The history of modernity could, in one way, be read as a history of tensional relations between East and West. Since Eastern modernities emerged after Western modernity, they may justifiably be termed later modernities. Challenged and shaken, the East has responded to the rise of the West with the creation of distinct modernities: those of Russia, China, Japan and Turkey. This should indicate that both earlier and contemporary modernization theories fail because original, Western modernity did not become the model of modernity for the East. I have shown that Turkish modernity, as a later experience, imported the idea of modernity from the West and, indeed, Westernized to an extent. However, the Western element in the Turkish experience does not suffice for Turkish modernity to be seen simply as the result of Westernization.

An argument for the existence of later modernities should necessarily question the convergence thesis within mainstream modernization theories. Societies in modern times do not converge, but maintain their distinctions, existing as a plurality of cultures. It is precisely for this reason that we must reject the understanding of the globalization of modernity as a diffusion of Western civilization. Modernity is globalized, but this globalization does not refer to a Westernization of the world; rather, it reflects the multiplicity of modernity. This may show that the current era is no longer dominated by the West, but that possibly a post-Western era is emerging. The post-Western era should not, however, be viewed as the beginning of postmodernity, because, as I have shown, modernity is not equivalent to the West. Therefore, even if European modernity is being dissolved, or renewed, the current era reflects the existence of multiple modernities. It should become clear that the perspective of later modernities is incompatible with postmodernist positions. Since the perspective of later modernities does not read modernity as a desire to achieve a controlled, totalized world, the existence of plurality in ideas and practices is not taken to refer to the end of modernity. Rather than understanding modernization to mean the homogenizing of distinct cultures, we should view the plurality of cultures and civilizations as an indication of the existence of distinct modernities. The concept of later modernities refers to Eastern modernities, but it needs to be observed that these modernities came about without colonization by the West; so, for example, the Turkish experience cannot be viewed in the category of postcolonial experiences. A genuine later modernity will include elements distinctive enough to problematize Western understandings of modernity; for example, in the Turkish case, the role of women as key actors in the transition to modernity.

However, this is not an argument for antagonistic modernities. By understanding modernity as an actor between civilizations, I emphasized its capacity to change cultures. Thus, modernity is able to reduce oppositions between civilizations. However, this does not mean that modernity should be understood as undermining distinctions between civilizations and leading to a 'global world'. Neither universalism nor cultural relativism seems to be desirable: Western universalism ignores non-Western cultures and cultural relativism can be taken to legitimate any cultural practice. Our investigation shows that not only the perspectives of globalization, but also those of relativism, need to be questioned. It is important to insist that the distinctions between modernities do not necessarily mean that there are fundamentally incompatible modernities; rather, they mean that there are multiple formations of modernity and multiple answers to questions that arise during modern experiences.

From the above argument, it must be recognized that the world is not open to a unitary reading. Rather, in the current phase of modernity, the social world emerges as highly complex. Dualities and dialectical occurrences need to be looked at with a view that places multiplicity at the centre of analysis. No single process or realm could be considered to be the central determining, ordering or shaping feature of human practice and identity. In this respect, it must be argued that neither globalization nor localization should be taken to be the central characteristic that shapes our lives. Plurality is a condition for human action. I showed that the Turks can no longer hope to achieve a coherent society, nor can they hope to isolate themselves from the global world. Neither local cultures and practices nor global occurrences alone could be taken to define the situation.

From this observation we can conclude that neither the thesis of the clash of civilizations nor the belief in the end of history can be considered to be convincing. Fukuyama's thesis of the end of history seems particularly untenable, because in order for us to conclude that history has come to an end, there should no longer be civilizational or national conflicts. However, the world has faced and continues to face significant struggles between countries and between civilizations. The crisis of statism and the collapse of the communist bloc were the background against which Fukuyama believed that it was possible to talk about the end of history. Fukuyama's thesis therefore stems from a perspective that views the twentieth century in terms of the clash between communism and liberalism. This must refer to the idea that both liberalism and communism did settle all questions about the ultimate goals of human beings, and that when one of these modern ideals terminally fails, the other deserves to be called 'the optimum mode of political organization'. Thus, Fukuyama (1992: 287) writes as follows: 'If history leads us in one way or another to liberal democracy, this question then becomes one of the goodness of liberal democracy, and of the principles of liberty and equality on which it is based'. The collapse of communism gave Fukuyama the sense that 'liberal democracy may constitute the end point of mankind's ideological evolution and the final form of the human government and as such constituted the end of history' (Fukuyama, 1989: 4). What is most striking in this perspective for the present study is that Fukuyama can be considered as a radical Westernist since, in his view, human history is reduced to the Western path of development. He argues that 'there is a fundamental process at work that dictates a common evolutionary pattern for *all* human societies – in short something like a Universal History of mankind in the direction of liberal democracy' (Fukuyama, 1992: 48). And he goes on to claim that '[the] Universal History of mankind was nothing other than man's progressive rise to full rationality, and to a self-conscious awareness of how that rationality expresses itself in liberal self-government' (Fukuyama, 1992: 60). Fukuyama (1992: 143–80) takes his Westernism from Hegel by understanding him as the first philosopher who maintained that history would inevitably end and that this end would come when the liberal state satisfied mankind's desire for recognition. By comparing Hegel with another Western theorist, Marx, Fukuyama concludes that 'the end of history' was thought of either as liberal democracy or as communist society. Against the Marxist view of the end of history, Fukuyama believes with Hegel that liberal societies are free from contradictions because they form themselves on the principles of liberty and equality. This is radically open to question, but my interest here is not whether communism could re-emerge to provide an alternative to liberalism; rather, I want to show that Fukuyama's thesis fails because he reduces multiple histories to a single Western history. An analysis based on a concept of later modernities, such as the one provided in this book, makes it possible to challenge successfully the end-of-history thesis on socio-historical grounds.

Fukuyama understands history as a single, coherent, evolutionary process by homogenizing the experiences of all peoples at all times. He necessarily does so, because it becomes easier to talk about the end of history when a totalizing view of history is held as the starting point. The idea of one-directional universal history is both ethnocentric and Western in origin. From Hegel to Habermas, mainstream social theorists have emphasized history as one-directional in the sense that the Western way of life stands at its end. The idea of unilinear historical development in fact reached its high point in post-Second World War modernization theory, which, however, had almost disappeared by the end of the 1970s. The collapse of the communist bloc then gave rise to neo-modernization theories that have emphasized 'convergence' once again. Fukuyama should be seen in this light, but, even in this context, his belief that the end of history has been reached represents an extreme position. In Fukuyama's perspective, the Western liberal way of life has resolved all deep contradictions and therefore nothing is left to struggle for or to desire. This is again open to question, but even if liberal democracy had resolved all contradictions and if as a result Westerners were satisfied, could this be seen to be true for all societies in the world? Could it be said that liberalism had achieved universality? The concept of later modernities suggests that there have been multiple ways to modernity and that those multiple ways have given rise to multiple consequences. These consequences do not converge anywhere, neither under the label of liberal democracy nor under that of communist society. Both communism and liberalism are Western in their origin, and in later modernities neither liberalism nor communism emerged in precisely the way in which they did in Europe or North America. In Russia, for example, communism was not free from Russian history and that history has not come to an end, because it certainly has not found a solution to all contradictions yet. Or, for example, Turkish culture cannot be said to have the ultimate goal of achieving liberal democracy in the Western way. The multiple consequences of the multiple ways to modernity indicate that history is far from coming to an end. For instance, Ilhan (2001) argues that China, Russia and Iran aim to form a bloc whose ultimate goal may not be liberal democracy. Now, in addition, I want to pick up the case of Islamism to demonstrate that history is not at its end. Islamism is not only a reaction against the new world order, but an expression of a particular identity which, although it can be understood as modern, cannot be seen as liberal.

Fukuyama (1992: 45) argued that 'for a very large part of the world, there is now no ideology with pretensions to universality that is in a position to challenge liberal democracy, and no universal principle of legitimacy other than the sovereignty of the people'. He does see Islam as a universal ideology, one that could potentially include everyone, but concludes that it cannot challenge liberal democracy. So, Fukuyama understands that in order to counterbalance liberal democracy, there must be a universal ideology that is able to reach out to all human beings. Fukuyama fails to understand that current Islamism's ultimate goal is not to create a universal world on the basis of Islamic values. Islamism rather aims to keep its distance from the West and from liberal democracy. In doing so, it develops a modernity of its own, which does not agree with the principles of liberalism. Thus, even if it is the case that all big questions are settled in the West, that deep contradictions are resolved under liberal democracy and that Westerners are satisfied with that, this can only tell us about the end of a particular history, that of the West. In Islamic societies, the big questions are not answered yet, and this is why Islamism emerged in the final quarter of the twentieth century and continues to garner support. I would argue, therefore, that Fukuyama should consider the plurality of histories and limit his argument to Western history rather than reducing the experiences of all peoples to the Western one.

From the importance of the plurality of civilizations in shaping human identity and practice, we should not conclude, though, that the distinctions between people are purely cultural by eliminating political, economic and ideological differences, as Huntington (1997) does. In striking contrast to Fukuyama, Huntington (1997: 125) writes: 'Alignments defined by ideology and superpower relations are giving way to alignments defined by culture and civilization. Political boundaries increasingly are redrawn to coincide with cultural ones: ethnic, religious, and civilizational. Cultural communities are replacing Cold War blocs, and the fault lines between civilizations are becoming the central lines of conflict in global politics.' The importance of culture was certainly once neglected in social theories. To remedy that neglect, however, the discovery of the importance of culture in terms of our relations to the world should not give rise to the equally one-sided perspective that nothing but culture is the determining element of human practice. But Huntington (1997: 308) takes precisely this view: 'cultural identities are central and cultural affinities and differences shape the alliances, antagonisms, and policies of states'. This is a one-sided perspective that does not accept the insight that the conflicts that shape change should not be reduced to the purely economic, cultural or political; and that, rather, the multiplicity of factors needs to be recognized. Certainly, emphasizing the existence of multiple civilizations as an important factor in global politics sheds light on understanding the current world era. However, what is not acceptable in Huntington's perspective is the belief that the *distinctions* between civilizations inevitably demonstrate that the current era is shaped by the *clash* of civilizations.

In the light of the concept of later modernities, it is possible to show that Huntington's thesis fails. I shall demonstrate this by means of three arguments developed in the present book. First, 'distinction' does not necessarily mean 'clash'. I have shown that the concept of later modernities is not based on the idea that multiple modernities are antagonistic modernities. I have developed a perspective in which modernity plays a certain part in reducing oppositions between civilizations. Civilization or culture is important for the creation of different modernities, but, in turn, modernity does not produce overall societal or cultural stability. Modernity does not permit societies to maintain their traditional cultural values unaltered; that is, modernity is never purely the product of a civilization or culture. I shall now pick up the case of Islamism, which is seen by Huntington (1997: 209–18) to be the most powerful opposition to Western civilization. By viewing current Islamism as an anti-Western ideology, Huntington concludes that a growing civilizational clash is emerging between the Christian West and the Islamic East. It is undeniable that Islamism means in one respect a rejection of the new world order, but this is only half of the story. I have shown that modernity alters cultures and that Islamic societies are not free from this. The analysis of Islamist women has shown that they do not purely turn towards traditional Islam as a source of identity; rather, they have developed a new identity under conditions of modernity. This new identity does not oppose the West as much as traditional Islam would do. The participation of Islamist women in the public sphere, for example, shows that under conditions of modernity women in different societies in fact share more than they would have shared in traditional ages. That is, modernity alters cultures and as a consequence civilizational oppositions are being reduced.

Secondly, the cultural element is not the only important factor in shaping human beings' lives, although it is very important that culture is rescued from its earlier neglect in social theories. Not only the cultural element needs to be interpreted in terms of the distinctions and similarities between modernities; rather, multiple factors should be analysed. Because the social world is complex, it cannot be understood on the basis of one fundamental feature. I have demonstrated that an economic and a political analysis are also necessary to explore the Turkish version of modernity. If it were true that cultural identities define all other practices and identities, it would be difficult to explain the clashes between people who are members of the same clan, ethnic group, or nation.

Thirdly, some observations on Huntington's neglect of the distinction between civilization and culture can show that the idea of a clash of civilizations is untenable. Huntington talks about civilizations as if they are blocs pitted against one another. He groups many different cultures together in a particular totalized civilization. For example, when he analyses the Islamist opposition to the West, Huntington takes 'the West' and 'Islam' as two coherent civilizations without saying a word about different cultures both in the West and in the Islamic East: he says, for example, that 'following the 1979 Iranian revolution, an intercivilizational quasi war developed between Islam and the West' (Huntington, 1997: 216). He continues: 'The underlying problem for the West is not Islamic fundamentalism. It is Islam, a different civilization whose people are convinced of the superiority of their culture and are obsessed with the inferiority of their power. The problem for Islam is not the CIA or the U.S. Department of Defense. It is the west, a different civilization whose people are convinced of the universality of their culture and believe that their superior, if declining, power imposes on them the obligation to extend that culture throughout the world' (Huntington, 1997: 217–18). On the one hand, we see here 'the West' understood as a totality, including both Eastern and Western Europe and the USA, and on the other hand we see 'Islam', including Iran, Iraq, Turkey and so on, understood as another totality. What is lacking here is a distinction between civilization and culture.

I have argued that Turkey cannot be taken to be unequivocally a member of an Islamic civilization; rather, Turkish culture can best be viewed as a singularized one, which interprets both Islamic and Western civilizations in its own way. So if we agree with Huntington that an 'intercivilizational war' is developing between 'Islam' and 'the West', how do we place Turkey in relation to this? When the Islamic East is not understood as a totality, however, it becomes possible to show that there are distinct cultures in one civilizational zone. Huntington (1997: 312) seems to realize this, when he advises that the USA and European countries should 'achieve greater political, economic and military integration and coordinate their policies so as to preclude states from other civilizations exploiting differences among them'. Here he seems to consider the possibility that the West should not be seen as a totalized, homogeneous civilization. Rather, for example, the distinctions between the USA and Europe should be taken into account to show that there is no such civilization as a Western one that includes Eastern Europe, Western Europe and the USA (see Lipset, 1996). In general, however, Huntington neglects cultural distinctions within single civilizations. However, these distinctions can lead to clashes and indeed wars between nations within a single civilization. Both the First and the Second World War, for example, were fought between Western states, while the Iran–Iraq war was a conflict between two Islamic countries whose interpretations of Islam nonetheless differed greatly.

Our investigations show that the totalizing perspectives of social theory must be challenged. Adherents of both modernization theory and the dependency perspective believe that their methods for analysing the process of change are applicable to all societies. While for evolutionist modernization theory, the causes of modernizing processes in societies are mostly internal, according to the dependency perspective, the causes are fully external. While the dependency perspective is pessimistic, modernization theory is optimistic. However, we have seen that both external and internal factors are involved in the alteration of lately modernizing societies. In the course of the Turkish revolution, international pressure, the vulnerable Ottoman Empire and rising intellectuals played pivotal roles. In the alteration of societies, therefore, we should not overemphasize one factor while excluding others. In terms of the development of a later modernity, the dependency theorists are correct, to some extent, to argue that autonomous development is required. But this development does not necessarily imply a socialist revolution. The development of a lately modernizing society is also possible according to a capitalist model. We saw that the Kemalist model of economic development is strongly autonomous although also capitalist. However, it needs to be said that this sort of political economy – both capitalist and anti-imperialist – is very difficult to achieve completely. Modernization theory is evolutionist and, therefore, explains social change by viewing the dominant value system as the adjusting sphere of society (Nisbet, 1969). However, disputes over goals are particular dynamics in defining the direction of change. In general, classic social theory's main question – how a diversified society could be held together – should no longer represent the starting point of social analysis. I have shown that the Turkish experience has been shaped by conflictual and tensional relations between different actors. There have been violent collective actions that, in turn, brought about measures to end conflicts in society, aiming to hold the Turks together by imposing a value system. However, neither Islam nor nation as an integrating element could unify Turkish society. Thus, the integration of society should not be overemphasized as the theme to be explored, although contradictions in society cannot be simply ignored. Thus, for a reading of multiple modernities, neither the integration theory of society, which assumes a social structure as a functionally integrated system, nor the coercion theory of society, which understands social structure as a form of organization held together by force, should be taken as the basis for the analysis. In both perspectives, society is seen as a whole, held together by a functional value system or by force. But, as has been shown, a modern society can in no way be conceived of as a coherent whole or as a system.

Finally, world-systems theory should be critically observed. For Wallerstein (1979), the unit of analysis is the universal historical system, the capitalist world-economy. World-systems theory assumes classes and nations to be the central actors of modernity. Therefore, ideology is seen as universal. However, as I have shown, conflicts between social actors, not necessarily coming from opposing classes or nations, play a role in shaping human practice. Reading the world in terms of a dichotomy between metropolitan capitalism and the non-Western periphery or semiperiphery does not explain how later modernities emerged, nor the fact that some of them are no less advanced than metropolitan, capitalist Western states. Contrary to the assumption of world-systems theory, modernizing non-Western states found that the problems caused by Western imperialism could be resolved on the basis of different models. That is, neither capitalism nor socialism, as an option for the development of later modernities, can be seen as a fixed, unitary model. Rather, both are subject to civilizational contexts and modernizing agents. Therefore, multiple trajectories of modernization need to be observed, especially because self-questioning and self-problematization, rather than simply Western imperialism, are the basic dynamics for societies in the transition to modernity.

Thus, my argument for later modernities does not side with the convergence thesis, but nor does it understand multiple modernities as necessarily antagonistic modernities. This is because, as has been indicated in this book, modernity is neither the property of the West nor is it simply a dimension of Western, imperialist power. There are multiple relations of modernity to civilizations and interpretations of modernity by civilizations. Therefore, later modernities are different interpretations of the world and of the self, but they are not necessarily antagonistic.

The Lessons for Present-Day Turkey

Modernization is a political issue. To build a modernity is to control an entire population. This, in turn, implies a political programme such as nationalism. Thus, a project of modernity is necessarily a political project. Since a political project, in the first place, means a systematic attempt to alter the existing social reality, a project of modernity needs to be read as a disciplining phenomenon. The belief that society can be reshaped by a political project is grounded in a view of society as an autonomous entity regulated by internal laws, rather than by God or nature – laws that can be fully explored and grasped by human reason. As we have seen, Kemalism reflects this feature clearly. That is, Kemalism was an intervention into society in order to create Turkish modernity. The need to manage society, however, poses a challenge to political projects. The 'disciplining' of a population may be attempted through violent revolutionary movements or by means of formalization on the basis of law. Law is an essential carrier of discipline: by means of law, the state can reinterpret social reality to serve its own ambitions. Kemalism should be read in terms of both revolutionary and legal change. For radical social change, a break with the old regime on the basis of political revolution was required; formalization through law was then needed to ensure the legitimacy of the post-revolutionary regime. In these ways, modernizing agents reinterpret the social reality. However, as we have seen, there is no single answer to the problem of disciplining people; rather there are different projects for doing so.

As part of my argument for the varieties of modernity, I have analysed the specific characteristics of Kemalism as a disciplining project. Planning and controlling came to be the two basic tools used by Kemalist actors, because 'reasonable' agents thought of themselves as having the right to alter society. Kemalism distinguished itself by imposing discipline for the further goal of liberation. The Kemalist revolution was not a bloody revolution in the sense that it did not emerge as a socio-political movement of a particular social class, as in the case of the revolutions of France and Russia (Skocpol, 1979). Since the Kemalists regarded their revolution as an emancipating project of the whole nation, the regime that they founded after the revolution of 1923 became a unique form of authoritarian regime. From the beginning, a limited plurality was included in the Kemalist polity. It was precisely because of this characteristic of Kemalism that the alteration of social reality became a very difficult process, leading to clashes between the modernizing state and factions within society. Law was viewed as being able to alter social reality; reforms were legitimated by the power of the law. But this led to clashes between law and tradition. Thus, the Kemalist project reflects, first of all, that a project of modernity means the disciplining of the population.

However, Kemalism cannot be conceived simply as a disciplining project, because it was also a liberating movement. The tenets of secularism, republicanism, populism, revolutionism and nationalism were important for the sake of liberty. Secularism, for example, provided opportunities for women to enjoy participation in the public sphere, while nationwide education allowed Islamic actors to reinterpret Islam as a political religion. Thus, even if a project of modernity aims to modernize the socio-cultural world on the basis of a specific conception of modernity, its own reforms provide opportunities for the people to interpret the world and themselves in different, perhaps conflicting ways. And the tensions between liberty and discipline were to give rise to new events; that is, the Kemalist project, like any conception of modernity, was open to different interpretations. Kemalism could be conceived of as an outlook, it did not intend to impose a closed system of thought on the polity and society in the long run. Although Kemalism is still interpreted differently by different political actors, bureaucratic elites converted Kemalist thought into a state ideology. It is basically for this reason that the Kemalist project has enabled both disciplining and liberation. We have seen this particularly through examining the relations between state, society and economy in Turkey.

In analysing the specific configuration of state, society and economy in the Turkish experience, we saw the importance of the radicalization of oppositions in society. I showed that the rise of Turkish society, the Turkish economy and the Kemalist state indeed depended on the creation of dualities. For the sake of radical social change, Kemalism aimed to create oppositions, because revolution was assumed to require radical disputes over the system. This feature is specific to the history of Turkish modernity. For instance, emphasizing science as the only true guide to life radicalized some existing dualities between Islamic scholars, the *ulema*, and the rising modernist intellectuals in the 1930s. This duality did not disappear but, on the contrary, has played a fundamental role in the history of the Turkish republic. Therefore, it is difficult to analyse the Turkish experience without considering the radicalization of dualities. It becomes clear that relations between state and society can be summarized in terms of the tension between liberty and discipline. The analysis of twentieth-century Turkish history shows that the whole century was a struggle between liberty and discipline.

In the analysis of the relations between the state, society and the economy, we noted that the realms of the social world are not separable from one another, although they possess a degree of autonomy. Rather, the state and society have the power to shape each other, while the economy crucially shapes relations between people in society as well as those between the state and society. In particular, Turkish society and the Turkish state cannot be viewed as independent of the economy, which has played a constitutive part in shaping twentieth-century Turkish history. Both administration (the polity) and production (the economy) are dominated by instrumental rationality, so that the 'system' to a great extent dominates the actors. That is, economic power, in terms of labour, exchange and consumption, and political power, in terms of the regulation of society, the maintenance of boundaries and geo-political activity, have partly shaped modern Turkey. Therefore, it is important to insist that to be modern is to face a paradoxical situation. Human beings are overpowered by the rule of law or formal rationality, yet they have the opportunity to fight to change their world in order to make it their own. On the one hand, the 'system' – administration and production – aims to standardize practices and identities on the basis of formal rationality, but, on the other hand, it is also under conditions of modernity that human beings have the opportunity to create their own identities without being completely deter-mined by the system. It is for this reason that the masses once excluded from the modern system can now participate in the modernity of Turkey. People who were once outside modern discourse – Kurds, Islamists, leftists and so on – now express an irrevocable plurality. The best example of the current configuration could be the existence of multiple television channels. Until the late 1980s, there was only state television, but now there are several private channels that reflect this irrevocable plurality. This is to say that, under conditions of modernity, plural world-interpretations cannot be eradicated, even if totalizing attempts are made using physical power.

For a reading of multiple modernities, the various possible configurations of state, society and economy are important indicators. The relations between liberty and discipline can provide clues as to the characteristics of the modernity under investigation, as can analysis of how the state in question conceives of itself and how the society in question presents itself. For instance, the Leninist state regarded itself as proletarian, yet a very distinct Russian experience has been written in world history. Turkish society, to take another example, was unable to present itself as either fully Islamic or fully Western, leading to a unique experience among Islamic and Western countries. The formation of the economic sphere also needs to be examined carefully to point out some of the distinctions between modernities. For instance, the Turkish bourgeoisie cannot be seen as similar to Western ones. In this, of course, the forces that define power relations in a society are an important factor. Since power was not purely determined by socio-economic criteria in the Turkish experience, the Turkish capitalist class could be conceived of as a product of a state-centred political project, and this feature distinguishes present-day Turkey from Western countries.

History showed its power, particularly in terms of the actors of Turkish modernity. In the history of the Turks, autonomous intellectuals, such as the *ulema*, had already acted as carriers of models of cultural and social orders, and thus their emergence from the Kemalist elite as modernizers should not be surprising. I argued that the emergence of Kemalist actors as the main agents of modernization was directly related to the historical background of Turkey. History provides possible options for human action and, therefore, it is an inescapable power that plays a pivotal role in shaping the modern experience. Without considering the power of history, it is impossible to analyse present-day Turkish society. As has been shown, for example, the role of the military cannot be explored by looking simply at power relations: the historical mission to protect democracy, assumed by the military as its duty, has also been an important factor. The importance of history in the shape of Turkish modernity, however, cannot be taken to mean that no break occurred in the Turkish experience. Without such moments of rupture, modernity cannot emerge. Although history played a part in the emergence of the Turkish project of modernity, new ideas – such as that of a democratic republic – were introduced by the Kemalist actors playing another constitutive part. Thus, for a reading of multiple modernities, both continuity – the power of history – and discontinuity – the creativity of social actors must be emphasized. In the Turkish context, it can be seen that Kemalism did not achieve an absolute break with previous history; it did not bring about a completely new Turkey – a Western nation.[2] Equally, Kemalism cannot be understood as aiming to change the natural evolution of Turkish society by bringing about a revolution for the sake of Westernization.[3] Rather, both continuity – the power of history – and discontinuity – the power of the project – should be invoked to demonstrate the proposal that Turkish modernity is neither a Western modernity nor a product of Turkish tradition.

On this basis it can be argued that some of the main problems as well as the achievements of present-day Turkish society are connected to the two basic principles of Kemalism: secularism and nationalism. Of course, more recent actors and projects are also responsible, but the founding principles of Kemalism have been interpreted as important factors in the emergence of the Kurdish question and the problem with Islamism, as well as in providing opportunities that have been enjoyed by the Turkish people. Kemalism, on the one hand, aimed to dissolve the social ties between people for the sake of delocalization. On the other hand, it aimed to bring people together on the basis of nationalism and secularism. Although the Kemalist regime cannot be seen to have aimed at institutionalizing secularism and nationalism as closed ways of thinking about society and the polity, both secularism and nationalism came to be subject to different interpretations by political actors. Secularism has been viewed as the most important principle of the Turkish republic by neo-Kemalist actors. This has not only brought about some serious clashes between secularists and Islamists, it has also been exploited by right-wing political parties for political ends. When a political project uses secularism as an overemphasized guide to life, an opposing project may turn Islam into a political religion, attempting to use the religion to 'colonize' the polity for its own ends.

It may seem that there is a contradiction between my argument in Chapter 5 for the compatibility of Islam with modernity and my discussion in Chapter 6 of the tension-ridden relations between Islam and modernity. Since modernity is never simply a product of tradition, but always requires modernizing agents, it should be clear that conflict will always accompany the emergence of modernity. In the Turkish case, the conflict between Kemalism and some parts of Islamic society should not be understood in terms of Islamic actors, from the beginning, rejecting modernity. In contrast, as I have shown, Islamism, as against Kemalist modernity, proposes a different sort of modernity. It could be conceived of as follows. First, Islam should not be understood as a civilization that rejects modernity; rather, the possibility of a different interpretation of modernity in Islamic societies should be considered. Secondly, insisting on the compatibility of Islam with modernity does not mean that modernity can be conceived of as a necessary result of the evolution of societies. Rather, the agency of modernization needs to be emphasized. On the one hand, I have shown that Islam cannot easily be regarded as an anti-modern civilization, but, on the other hand, I have emphasized that there are high tensions between Islamist and modern actors. This means that an analysis of Islam and Islamism should question perspectives of Islam as anti-modern, postmodern or traditionalist. The Turkish experience indicates that Islam, or rather the Islamic East, cannot be regarded as a coherent whole; rather, there are distinct cultures within Islamic civilization, such as the Iranian Shia culture. However, I have insisted that the Turkish case cannot be conceived of as simply an Islamic culture. Rather, the singularization of Turkish culture must be emphasized. Turkey should no longer be understood as a border country between Christianity and Islam; rather, it represents a culture that has always borrowed from the outside without being colonized or assimilated.

Nationalism provided the means for the militant nationalists to attain power. Nationalist ideology was not viewed as one option among many ideologies, but was, rather, interpreted as guaranteeing the legitimacy of the governments of Turkey. Nationalism was not only emphasized as a principle, but was written into the constitution as inseparable from the nature of the Turkish republic – which relates directly, for instance, to the current problem of the Kurdish question. The Turkish-Islamic synthesis has been overemphasized as a guiding principle for Turkish governments over the last two decades. This is the main reason why oppression and corruption are currently rife: a sort of 'legitimizing nationalism' has been corrupting the state and oppressing the people. It seems that nationalism is inseparable from the desire for power. The Turkish state has been colonized by nationalist sentiments and by a particular Turkish-Islamic culture, resulting in the 'true republic' remaining merely a distant possibility. How, then, can the people in Turkey live together peacefully?

Against the nationalists, whose primary values are the spiritual and cultural unity of the people, patriotic values – the republic and a free way of life –should be emphasized. Patriots may ascribe importance to Turkey as a particular country, but they should not attempt to force one way of life on its entire population. The republic could be interpreted as guaranteeing freedom for living different ways of life. For the nationalists, freedom does not matter, because their ultimate goal is to unite the people under the label of the Turkish-Islamic synthesis. Thus, solving some of the main problems of Turkey may require a patriotic perspective that emphasizes the right of all the people in the country to live their lives as citizens without being oppressed by a denial of political, social and civil rights. Cultural oneness does not make a republic stronger, particularly because it does not privilege freedom. In other words, it may be considered that the republic does not need cultural but *political* unity, which guarantees each cultural or ideological world the right to express itself. However, the republic needs to defend itself from internal enemies because a particular culture might try to colonize the state, in turn leading to the elimination of plurality by 'state terror'.

The perspectives that celebrate 'difference', division and incompatibility also need to be problematized. Humanism is currently about the right to 'difference', but why difference has to be privileged needs an answer. Clashes could easily emerge in vulnerable countries like Turkey if arguments for the rights of difference become exaggerated. Neither without solving the Kurdish question nor by insisting on separation can Turkish democracy be developed. Further democratization indeed implies the resolution of the conflict between the Kurds and the ultra-nationalists of Turkey.

The perspective that emphasized that the Turkish nation had to adapt itself to Western civilization is challenged by the fact that Turkish society retains peculiarly Turkish characteristics. This book has shown that the modernization of Turkey cannot be seen merely as Westernization. This is not only because the Kemalist interpretation of modernity was different from that of the West, but also because the features of Turkish society were not undermined by Western values; rather, dialectically, the West has been interpreted in two ways. On the one hand, the West has always provided a criterion for Turkey to check itself against in terms of whether its goals have been achieved. Yet, on the other hand, the West is interpreted as the negative external power to which reactions have emerged. Today, many Turks, from politicians to people on the street, claim that Turkey should be accepted by the European Union, while, at the same time, the West is seen as taking a negative attitude towards the Turks. This may be so because Europe has played an important part in the shaping of twentieth-century Turkish history and identity. It is assumed by some that Turkey is Westernized, while other observers argue that Turkey is far from being a European country. However, an alternative argument would insist that Turkey does not correspond to these two views because it is not a member of a clearly defined civilization. Thus, for a reading of multiple modernities, external forces should neither be excluded nor should they simply be insisted on as negative. In modern history, relations between societies and between civilizations have increased. It is easier for societies to know one another by means of modern telecommunications technologies and, therefore, in a society's identity-formation, its relations with other societies, positive or negative, play an important part in modern history.

Military and political power played the principal reordering role in the Ottoman Empire, but the Kemalists aimed to create a multiplicity of social actors. As we have seen, this Kemalist ambition has to some extent been achieved. No longer can the military and the polity alone be viewed as defining the situation; there are other players involved. However, in Turkey, power cannot be merely defined by socio-economic criteria, but is still directly related to politics and the military. Currently, the generals still have their voices heard, while some civilian politicians aim to break the power of the military in terms of the nature of the regime. In considering multiple modernities, the forces that determine the configuration of power relations in a particular society should be analysed, since they provide valuable information about the form of modernity in that society.

Three types of collective action have taken place in the Turkish experience: the competitive (the Turks competed with Western economies in the 1930s); the proactive (most movements aiming to extend modernity to the masses have been proactive); and the reactive (reactionary movements against modernization have emerged from within traditionalist groups). Most social movements concentrate on the possibility of extending modernity towards groups and classes that were once excluded from the system. And modernity as a tension between liberty and discipline emerges particularly when social actors who aim at extending liberty and opportunity face the brutality of the polity or of the army. Particularly, leftist movements for liberty were countered by the militant nationalism of the Turkish state in the 1970s and 1980s. Social movements in modernity can be viewed, in general, as being of two kinds. One is future-oriented, critical of the existing social order and proposing an alternative order to be attained in the future. This sort of movement employs arguments against both the present-day social order and the past in order to propose a better order for the future. Such movements are necessarily utopian, but it is this utopian characteristic that has played an important part in the transformation of society, although the idealized future has not been fully attained. The other type of social movement is past-oriented in that the past is idealized in comparison with problems faced in the present. In its aim of returning to a lost 'golden age', this type of movement is also utopian. A past is *invented* because of the problems that emerge under conditions of modernity. However, precisely because the idealized past is privileged under conditions of modernity, these movements cannot be understood as anti-modern movements, any more than future-oriented movements can be. Both socialists and Islamists operate within the institutions of modernity (for example, the universities).

It is also important to note that present-day Turkish social movements are not nationwide as before; rather, regional movements appear to be more important. For example, the people of a small city in the Aegean region, Bergama, have been protesting against the pollution in the region caused by a foreign-oriented gold-mining company. Or, for example, in Zonguldak, another small city, workers have been striking for their rights in order to prevent the state from closing the state firms in their region. But at the same time there are global social movements that Turks are involved in. For example, green movements in Istanbul are organized by Europeans and Turks together. It is clear, then, that neither localization nor globalization alone could be taken to define the situation. In analysing a later modernity, the critic needs to consider the specific characteristics of social movements and what they reveal about the society in question. For example, the Turkish Islamist women's movement seems to show that, in Turkey, a consensus about the meaning of modernity has not and cannot be achieved.

Finally, we can describe Turkey as civilizationally dual, but this should not be taken to mean that Turkey is simply a border country between Western and Islamic civilizations. Rather, as has been indicated, these dual characteristics in Turkey should be understood in terms of a singularization of culture. That is, the division between the West and the East cannot be used as a vantage-point for analysing Turkish modernity. Turkey includes features from both Islamic and Western civilizations, but these features take on new forms: the Turks in Anatolia interpret both Western and Islamic values in their own ways and, therefore, they are neither fully Islamized nor are they Westernized. From this point we can go further, to say that civilizational particularity can play an important role in defining the power of a modernity. Compared with other Islamic societies in the Middle East, Turkey experienced an easier process of modernization, and its singularized culture played a great part in this process. However, this is not to say that Turkish culture did not resist Kemalist innovations at all. Rather, for a reading of multiple modernities, the clash between modernizing agents and contextual realities must be viewed as important. As the Turkish experience indicates, the idea of modernity is imported from the West by modernizing agents in later modernities, but this cannot be assumed to mean that later modernities undergo a straightforward process of Westernization. The dialectical relations between modernizing agents and contextual realities lead to the fact that modernities differ from one another.

There still remains the difficulty of defining the place of a singularized culture such as Turkey within the global arena. The European Union is widely assumed to be the final door through which the Turks will pass. However, at the same time, it is said that it is almost impossible for the Turks to become members of the Union. One may argue that an alternative exists: turning back to the 1930s. Many non-Western societies were forcibly Westernized, while Kemalism acknowledged the Western way of life without becoming a colony of the West. That is, autonomous development was the driving force of the Kemalist project. It was in these terms that the Kemalist revolution was a worldwide revolution: liberation movements in the East, such as that in India, took the Kemalist victory over Western imperialism as their model. After gaining its political independence, Turkey practised a foreign policy that opposed the imperialism of the West, close, to some extent, to the Soviet Union. During the period between 1923 and 1938, Turkey was an autonomous country that was not controlled by the Western bloc. One might argue, then, that it is still possible for Turkey to be neutral and independent as it was in the early phase of the republic: Turkey may leave Europe and move, as the early republic did, closer to the Russian Federation, playing a crucial role in economic co-operation in the Black Sea region. Moreover, the new Turkish-speaking republics take Turkey seriously as their model for their own reconstruction. A neutral Turkey could also become a creative country in the Middle East (Ahmad, 1993).

Nonetheless, it is generally believed that Turkey's future will be shaped in and by the European Union. Both arguments, in fact, constitute parts of the truth: as has been indicated in this book, Turkey must be conceived of as a singularized culture rather than as a border country between Islam and the West. For example, it should not be surprising that Turkey is seen as the model of modernity for other Islamic countries while at the same time Turkish membership of the European Union seems very difficult, if not impossible, to achieve. I would argue that Turkey can neither become a completely Western nation nor can it isolate itself from the West.

Notes

Notes to Introduction

1. It cannot be denied that postmodernism, in the last few decades, has played a great part in the development of social theories of modernity, critical or advocative.

2. Perhaps it needs to be mentioned that observations of American modernity as a distinct 'other' modernity have been enlightening the field. See, for example, Wagner, 1999b; Lipset, 1996.

3. 'Imaginary significations of modernity' in this text refers to Castoriadis's understanding of the dual imaginary of autonomy and mastery. See Castoriadis, 1987.

4. Observations of distinctive characteristics of the non-Western world have played a crucial part in the rise of theorizations of 'postmodernity'. For example, the Iranian Islamic revolution has been understood to mark a beginning of postmodernity in its complete rejection of the West. See Sayyid, 1997.

5. Arnason (1997) does not explicitly distinguish between civilization and culture. See Delanty, 1998.

6. Distinguishing between original and later versions of modernity, in the first place, may seem to run parallel to modernization theory. However, this book does not start from the premise that original Western modernity provided a model for the rest of the world.

7. Colonial and/or postcolonial experiences could be categorized as another version of modernity, unlike the group of later modernities which precisely includes experiences instigated by indigenous actors. Three cases of later modernities are particularly important: Russia, Japan and Turkey.

8. For example, Eisenstadt (1997, 1978) tends to view the Turkish revolution as an outcome of the civilizational context, assumed to be Islamic, of the axial variety.

9. Without exception, theorists of nation and nationalism understand previous history and traditions as the basic elements in the formation of nations. See, for example, Smith, 1986; Gellner, 1983.

Notes to Chapter 1

1. Both modernism and postmodernism could be read as coherent visions of modernity.

2. Both modernist and postmodernist perspectives have viewed modernity as programmed by Enlightenment philosophers. See Yack, 1997; Kolb, 1986.

3. The idea of modernity as an endless trial was proposed by Kolakowski (1990).

4. Eisenstadt (1999) demonstrates that, in axial civilizations, there have always been tension-ridden relations between mundane and transcendental visions of human societies.

5. In this book, 'the West' refers to Western Europe rather than to Europe and the USA.

6. Modernization theory could be taken to show that modernity and tradition are contrasted by understanding the West as modern against the rest as traditional. See, for example, Eisenstadt, 1973.

7. Although it is undeniable that modernity emerged first in Western Europe, modernity cannot be seen as a purely Western creation. In the emergence of modernity, different elements coming from different civilizations played central roles. For instance, the West began to learn ancient Greek philosophy from the Islamic scholars, such as Farabi, in the thirteenth and fourteenth centuries. On the emergence of modernity, see the special issue of *Daedalus*, 127.3 (1998). However, some contemporary social theorists still insist on modernity as being a Western project. See, for example, Giddens, 1991; Habermas, 1994.

Notes to Chapter 2

1. In sociological theory, the best representative of the convergence thesis is modernization theory, whose birth was, as Eisenstadt (1973: 11) claims, 'very closely connected with the great upsurge of interest in "development" of underdeveloped societies'.

2. One theorist even described Westernization as a 'world revolution' (Laue, 1987). In this perspective it is an ongoing and irresistible process.

3. The idea of 'civilization' (in the singular) was developed, in the eighteenth century, as the opposite of 'barbarism'. Civilized society differed from primitive societies because it was urban, literate and settled, and it was seen as identical with modernity and with the West. It could be argued that this new definition of civilization was part of the West's search for an identity (Arnason, 2000a), although some argue that the West already had such an identity prior to the emergence of modernity (see Huntington, 1997).

4. Modernization theory conceptualized both modern and traditional societies as stable and integrated, whereas in modernizing societies conflicts between tradition and modernity often create inescapable instability. See, for example, Huntington, 1968.

5. For example, one could consider Eisenstadt's move from modernization theory, based on structural-functionalism, to a civilizational perspective as showing that modernization theory had failed.

6. Some Western authors, such as Turner (1999), claim that women were excluded from the nation-building process, but in the Turkish case this view does not stand up.

7. Among few analyses see Giddens, 1985; Mann, 1986.

8. For modernization theory's understanding of modernity as a universal order, see Parsons (1971), the most influential theorist in this area.

9. Huntington (1997: 139–48) sees Russia and Turkey as 'torn' countries in terms of civilizational zone.

10. For a world-systems perspective, see, necessarily, Wallerstein, 1979.

11. It is in this context that the civilizational perspective must be considered in social analyses. The increase of relations between civilizations, as an outcome of modernity, does not necessarily bring about global peace; rather, one question comes to the fore: who are we? The civilizational context is an important provider of answers. For example, during the conflict between the Serbs and the Albanians in the late 1990s, Turkey supported the Albanians and Russia the Serbs, not for reasons of ideology or

power politics but because of cultural kinship.

12. Here I use the term 'creativity of action' in the sense in which it is used by Castoriadis (1987): the ability of agents to help remake the institutional structure of the social world.

13. Relevant here is Lenin's argument that, for radical social change to come about, it is necessary that the hegemonic classes should find themselves unable to continue living in the old way (Lenin, 1992).

Notes to Chapter 3

1. For these three views, see Berkes, 1976.

2. See the Turkish newspaper *Cumhuriyet*, 10 April 2000. It was reported that some Kurds in the south-east are complaining that 'since terrorism is over now, we have been forgotten again'. A social democrat author and musician, Zulfu Livaneli, has also argued that the state should care more about the south-east now that the bloody clashes have ended (in the Turkish newspaper *Sabah*, 13 April 2000).

3. Outside observers are contradictory and do not agree as to the proportion of Kurds in Turkey. According to the CIA, it is 10 per cent, for Barkey 20 per cent, while it is 17 per cent according to Rouleaue. Quoted in Turkish Democracy Foundation, 1996.

4. Some authors (see, for example, Nezan, 1993) try to convince the public that the Kurds have a right to establish their nation-state inside Turkey, because there is no difference between the Kurds and the Central Asian peoples who were able to found their own states after the collapse of the Soviet Union. However, a crucial point is missed in this sort of argument: Soviet Russia had invaded Central Asia and aimed to Sovietize the peoples of Central Asia, whereas, in Turkish history, there was no similar event concerning the Kurds. Nevertheless, some observers try to rewrite history for the sake of creating a Kurdish nation. See Nezan, 1993.

5. The prime minister of the time, Turgut Özal, himself of Kurdish origin, frequently stated on television programmes that the PKK could not pose a serious problem for the Turkish state.

6. Republics grant rights and liberties for individuals and do not normally recognize minority or majority cultures. The nature of a republic would not permit politicians to grant differential status to cultural, social and economic groups. In Turkey, only Christians and Jews were recognized as minorities in 1924 because of the Lozan contract, but the Jews refused minority rights because they found no problem in being Turkish citizens.

7. *Milliyet*, 27, 28 February and 1, 2, 3 March 1993.

8. *Milliyet*, 6 September 1992.

Notes to Chapter 4

1. Divisions in social science, as Wallerstein (1987: 312) put it, came from 'the dominant liberal ideology of the nineteenth century which argued that state and market, politics and economics, were analytically separate (and largely self-contained) domains, each with their particular rules ("logics")'.

2. In fact, if one takes Kemalism as aiming to found a modern polity – and not as a power wishing to institutionalize itself as the ultimate order –then its populist approach could be interpreted as a principle of Turkish democracy: governance of people, with the people, for the people.

3. For the impact of the Kemalist project on the entire Islamic world, see Sahinler, 1991.

4. Some go too far and argue that Kemalism projected a 'new' civilization. See

Ozankaya, 1996.

5. On the social origins of Kemalism, see Ozbudun, 1997.

6. On the crucial place of the military in the Turkish experience, see Hale, 1994.

7. Kemalist statism was not simply a response to the Great Depression of 1929; see especially Boratav, 1974.

8. It is generally argued that a one-party system cannot be transformed into a democratic regime unless a violent civil conflict is involved. See, for example, Sartori, 1976.

9. The leader of the RPP, the second man of the republic, Inönü, declared in 1946 that he was Kemal's successor, and Kemal's ultimate ambition was believed to be democracy. Therefore, Inönü allowed multi-party democracy even by allowing oppositions within his own party. See Aydemir, 1999.

10. The DP's understanding of democracy could be seen as a 'tyranny of the majority'. This risk in democracy is in fact discussed by de Tocqueville (1956).

11. The Turkish military coup of 1960 may be compared to that of the Portuguese officers in 1974, who brought down the authoritarian regime and then withdrew from power having installed democracy.

12. On American approval of the coup, see Birand, 1987.

Notes to Chapter 5

1. Sayyid (1997: 70) aimed 'to demonstrate the wide significance that Kemal's ideas and policies have beyond Turkey ... Kemalism could not be treated as simply a local phenomenon peculiar to Turkey.' He also noted that '[u]ntil the Iranian revolution, the hegemony of Kemalism had not suffered any serious setback' (1997: 89).

2. A third option has recently emerged: Islamism is viewed as an indicator of the postmodern condition. This is not because Islamic societies are seen as having reached the highest point of modernity and therefore as having moved into postmodernity, but because Islamism is viewed as decentralizing the West, and therefore as postmodern (Sayyid, 1997).

3. In Eisenstadt's (1999: 20) opinion, Islam's basic drive to create a civilization by unifying the political and religious communities was never fully attained, although there have always been some who promulgate this ideal.

4. Islamic sciences can briefly be divided into five categories: *hadith* aims to fill gaps in the Koran by the prophet's sayings; *tafsir* is the study of understanding the Koran; *fikih* is the study of Islamic law; *tasavvuf* aims to interpret the secret meanings of the Koran and Muhammad's sayings; and *kelam* are discussions on the Koran held by the *ulema*.

5. For instance, an emeritus professor of Islamic studies, William Watt, believes that the *ulema* were never able to understand the superiority of the West (Watt, 1988). In response, we might ask whether the Renaissance could have emerged without Farabi, Ibn Rusd or Ibn Sina, just as we can ask whether we would be able to talk about socio-political modernity if the world had not had Kant, Hegel or Marx.

6. See also Shin, 2000 for an important observation in terms of how civil society is understood differently in South Korea.

7. Some might argue that post-revolution Iran is precisely an Islamic theocracy (see, for example, Abrahamian, 1993). However, although the Iranian regime is based on Islamic law, it also includes aspects, such as the women's movement and the university students' movement, that are characteristic of modern political regimes.

8. I have not considered one of the most crucial issues, that of the role of women, because the next chapter will deal precisely with a distinctive trait of Turkish modernity: Turkish women were essential agents in the transformation to modernity.

9. According to the Kemalist interpretation, Turkish civilization has encountered

three civilizations: the Chinese, under whose influence the Turks used the Altai alphabet; the Arabic-Persian, under whose influence the Turks used the Arabic alphabet; and the Western civilization, under whose influence the Turks have used the Roman alphabet. See Aydemir, 1998. This is important to show that the Turks have always borrowed from and been influenced by the civilizations with which they have met.

10. In this respect, it needs to be noted that Kemalism emerged in a socio-cultural world that had already distinguished itself from the Islamic centre. Therefore, it may not be convincing to use Kemalism as a general metaphor for describing the various Muslim regimes. Some critics, however, follow Sayyid (1997: 53), who argues that Kemalism can be used 'as a means of reading a wider Muslim political context'.

11. It is interesting to note that, while reactions against the abolition of the caliphate came from outside observers, inside Turkey, the abolishment of the caliphate was approved by the religious men in the Grand National Assembly. During the discussions in the Assembly about the caliphate in 1924, Sheikh Saffet Efendi and his supporters stated that the only legitimate authority was the Grand National Assembly and that this was entirely compatible with Islam (Aydemir, 1998). So it seems important to observe that, in the 1920s, the Turkish world in Anatolia had brought about religious scholars who had nothing against the abolition of the caliphate.

12. It is interesting that the Swiss civil code was also adopted by two other later modernities, Japan and China (Aydemir, 1998).

13. The hat was introduced to the people by Mustafa Kemal himself in Kastamonu, where he had the following conversation with the *mufti* of the city: Kemal: 'What is the form of the dress in Islam?' The *mufti*: 'There is no standard form of the dress in Islam. The form of dress depends on interest and need' (Aydemir, 1998: 244). In his talk to the public, Kemal asked: 'Is our dress style national?' The public answered 'No'. He then asked the further question: 'Wearing the Greek fez has been accepted as legitimate, then, why should the hat not be legitimate?' (Aydemir, 1998: 247). It is also important that when Kemal returned to Ankara from Kastamonu, the number of people wearing hats was almost as many as the number of people wearing the fez. Hence it is difficult to argue that the hat reform was a Westernizing process against Islam.

14. For traditionalist accounts of Islamism, see Abrahamian, 1993. I also find Eisenstadt's view of modern fundamentalist movements useful in order to see that Islamism is, in fact, far from being a manifestation of Islamic tradition. 'Although seemingly traditional, these movements are, in fact, paradoxically, anti-traditional. They are anti-traditional in that they negate the living traditions, in their complexity and heterogeneity, of their respective societies or religions and, instead, uphold a highly ideological and essentialist conception of tradition as an overarching principle of cognitive and social organization' (Eisenstadt, 1999: 98).

15. Some argue that the basic reason for the emergence of Islamism was that the authoritarian regime did not allow large sectors of society to participate in the political arena. Therefore, the mosque emerged as an arena of public discourse that the state could not monopolize. See, for example, Skocpol, 1982.

16. Some of the people who face problems due to urbanization no doubt support the Islamist party, but Islamism's emergence cannot be understood by emphasizing the problems of these people as a central reason; it is not predominantly a movement of urban working-class people, but rather a movement linked to the rise of a new middle class. It is, however, difficult to guage the number of genuine Islamists in Turkey because of 'protest voting': in the 1999 general election, the Islamist party, Fazilet, gained 17 per cent of the vote, but we would need to consider the amount of protest votes in this percentage.

Notes to Chapter 6

1. On 'feminisms' see Butler and Scott (eds), 1992. For equality-oriented feminism see, for instance, Phillips (ed.), 1987. For postmodern feminism, see Nicholson (ed.), 1990.

2. Modernity has been challenged by some feminist critics as a male-dominated project because of its emphasis on rationality and industry. It is argued that modernity focuses only on 'man' as a rational being, excluding other modes of being more associated with women, such as emotionality and nurturing. Again, industry requires powerful physical strength, so it is seen as an area confined to men. In this respect, modernity – once more – emerges as a many-sided phenomenon but, nevertheless, it cannot be argued that modernity is more male-dominated than other historical ages. Central to my argument is that the modern condition enables women to find space in which to become actors in history. For this argument, see, for instance, Felski, 1995.

3. For Islam's view of sexual morality, see, for example, Cosan, 1987. For a secularist view on the theme see, for instance, Çalislar, 1991.

4. See Arat, 1995. Arat discusses the journal *Kadin ve Aile* ('Women and Family') in order to analyse whether the Islamist women's movement could be compatible with feminism. Arat translated the following from the journal: '[We] know that it is the female bird that makes the nest and nurtures the ties of love among family members. You are the pillars of the nest and the foundation of society. Men become happy and successful because of you, when they come home, they forget the exhaustion of the day, the troubles and turmoil of life, and find consolation in you, sleep happily and contented' (*Kadin ve Aile*, 1995: 3).

5. I conducted interviews with intellectuals on Turkish modernity in Ankara and Izmir in October 1998.

6. It must be emphasized that, to Islamists, one of the valuable principles of Kemalism was anti-imperialism. Kemalism achieved the first success against imperialism in Asia and Africa.

7. The examples are taken from Göle, 1996, but are reinterpreted.

Notes to Chapter 7

1. It should be insisted again that, in this book, 'the West' primarily refers to Western Europe.

2. For a counter-argument, see Eren, 1963.

3. For a counter-argument, see Özel, 1992.

References

Abrahamian, Evrand (1993), *Khomeinism*. London: I.B. Tauris.

Abrams, Philip (1982), *Historical Sociology*. New York: Cornell University Press.

Acar, Feride (1991), 'Women in the Ideology of Islamic Revivalism in Turkey: Three Islamic Women's Journals', in Richard Tapper (ed.), *Islam in Modern Turkey*. London and New York: Tauris and Co.

Adorno, Theodor, and Max Horkheimer (1988), *The Dialectic of Enlightenment*. London: Verso.

Ahmad, Feroz (1997), 'The Political Economy of Kemalism', in Ali Kazancigil and Ergun Ozbudun (eds.), *Atatürk: Founder of a Modern State*. London: C. Hurst.

—— (1993), *The Making of Modern Turkey*. London and New York: Routledge.

—— (1977) *The Turkish Experiment in Democracy*. London: Routledge.

Ahmad, Khurshid (1983), 'The Nature of the Islamic Resurgence', in L. Esposito (ed.), *Voices of Resurgent Islam*. New York and Oxford: Oxford University Press.

Ahmed, S. Akbar (1993), *Living Islam: From Samarkand to Stornoway*. London: BBC Books.

—— (1992) *Postmodernism and Islam: Predicament and Promise*. London and New York: Routledge.

Akçura, Yusuf (1978), *Turkculuk*. Istanbul: Turk Kultur Yayinevi.

—— (ed.) (1928) *Turk Dili*. Istanbul: Yeni Matbaa.

Amin, Samir (1976), *Unequal Development: An Essay on the Social Formation of Peripheral Capitalism*. Hassocks: Harvester.

Anderson, Benedict (1991 [1983]), *Imagined Communities: Reflections on the Origins and Spread of Nationalism*. London: Verso.

Arat, Yesim (1995), 'Feminism and Islam: Considerations on the Journal *Kadin ve Aile*', in Sirin Tekeli (ed.), *Women in Modern Turkish Society*. London and New Jersey: Zed Books.

Arendt, Hannah (1958), *The Human Condition*. Chicago: University of Chicago Press.

Arnason, Johann P. (2000a), 'Civilizational Analysis'. Unpublished paper.

—— (2000b), 'The Multiplication of Modernity: Theoretical and Historical Perspectives'. Unpublished paper.

—— (1998), 'Multiple Modernities and Civilizational Contexts: Reflections on the Japanese Experience'. Unpublished paper.

—— (1997), *Social Theory and Japanese Experience: The Dual Civilization*. London: Kegan Paul International.

—— (1993), *The Future that Failed: Origins and Destinies of the Soviet Model*. London: Routledge.

Arsel, Ilhan (1987), *Seriat ve Kadin*. Istanbul: Orhanlar Matbaasi.

Atatürk, Mustapha Kemal (1983 [1927]), *A Speech Delivered by Mustapha Kemal Atatürk, 1927*. Ankara: Basbakanlik Basimevi.

Avcioglu, Dogan (1973), *Turkiye'nin Duzeni*. Istanbul: Cem Yayinevi.

Aydemir, Sevket Sureyya (1999), *Menderes'in Drami*. Istanbul: Remzi Kitabevi.

—— (1998) *Tek Adam: Mustafa Kemal*, III. Istanbul: Remzi Kitabevi.

—— (1990 [1932]), *Inkilap ve Kadro*. Istanbul: Remzi Kitabevi.

Aydin, Erdogan (1994), *Nasil Musluman Olduk?* Istanbul: Basak.

Bauman, Zgymunt (2000), *Liquid Modernity*. Cambridge: Polity Press.

—— (1992), *Intimations of Postmodernity*. London: Routledge.

—— (1991), *Modernity and Ambivalence*. Cambridge: Polity Press.

Beck, Ulrich (1994), 'The Reinvention of Politics: Towards a Theory of Reflexive Modernization', in Beck, Giddens and Lash, 1994.

—— (1992), *Risk Society: Towards a New Modernity*. London: Sage

Beck, Ulrich, Anthony Giddens and Scott Lash (1994), *Reflexive Modernization: Politics, Tradition and Aesthetics in the Modern Social Order*. Cambridge: Polity Press.

Berger, Peter (1977), *Facing Up to Modernity*. New York: Basic Books.

Berkes, Niyazi (1976), *Turkiye'de Cagdaslasma*. Ankara: Dogu-Bati Yayinlari.

Berman, Marshall (1983), *All that is Solid Melts into Air: The Experience of Modernity*. London and New York: Verso.

Birand, Mehmet Ali (1987), *The Generals' Coup in Turkey: An Inside Story of 12 September 1980*. London: Brassey.

Boratav, Korkut (1997), 'Kemalist Economic Policies and Etatism', in Ali Kazancigil and Ergun Ozbudun (eds.), *Atatürk: Founder of a Modern State*. London: C. Hurst.

—— (1974), *Turkiye'de Devletcilik*. Istanbul: Gercek Yayinevi.

Butler, Judith, and Joan W. Scott (eds.) (1992), *Feminists Theorize the Political*. London: Routledge.

Çakir, Rusen, and Levent Cinemre (eds.) (1991), *Sol Kemalizme Bakiyor*. Istanbul: Metis Yayinlari.

Çalislar, Oral (1991), *Islamda Kadin ve Cinsellik*. Istanbul: Say Yayinlari.

Cangizbay, Kadir (1995), 'Vatandassiz Turkiye ya da Molekulu Catlamis Devlet', *Birikim* 79 (November): 78–91.

Castoriadis, Cornelius (1987), *The Imaginary Institution of Society*. Cambridge: Polity Press.

Çavdar, Tevhik (1970), *Osmanlilarin yari sömürge olusu*. Istanbul: Ant Yayinlari.

Chaliand, Gerard (1994), *The Kurdish Tragedy*. London: Zed Books.

—— (ed.) (1993), *A People without a Country: The Kurds and Kurdistan*. London: Zed Books.

Cosan, Mehmet Emin (1987), 'Asil Kadin Yetistirelim', *Kadin ve Aile* (August).

Delanty, Gerard (1999), *Social Theory in a Changing World: Conceptions of Modernity*. Cambridge: Polity Press.

—— (1998), 'Social Theory between East and West: A Review Article', *European Journal of Social Theory* 1.2.

Deringil, Selim (1989), *Turkish Foreign Policy during the Second World War: An Active Neutrality*. Cambridge: Cambridge University Press.

Eisenstadt, S.N. (1999), *Fundamentalism, Sectarianism and Revolution: The Jacobin Dimension of Modernity*. Cambridge: Cambridge University Press.

—— (1997), 'The Kemalist Revolution in Comparative Perspective', in Ali Kazancigil and Ergun Ozbudun (eds.), *Atatürk: Founder of a Modern State*. London: C. Hurst.

—— (1996), *The Japanese Civilization: A Comparative View*. Chicago: Chicago University Press.

—— (1978), *Revolution and the Transformation of Societies: A Comparative Study of Civilizations*. New York: The Free Press.

—— (1973), *Tradition, Change and Modernity*. New York: John Wiley and Sons.

—— (1966), *Modernization, Protest and Change*. New York: John Wiley and Sons.

Elias, Norbert (1994 [1982]), *The Civilizing Process*. Oxford: Blackwell.

Eren, Nuri (1963), *Turkey Today and Tomorrow: An Experiment in Westernization*. London and New York: Frederick A. Praeger.

Faludi, Susan (1992), *Backlash: The Undeclared War against Women*. London: Vintage.

Felski, Rita (1995), *The Gender of Modernity*. Cambridge, MA: Harvard University Press.

Fischer, Michael M.J. (1982), 'Islam and the Revolt of the Petit Bourgeoisie', *Daedalus* 3.1: 101–25.

Friese, Heidrun, and Peter Wagner (2000), 'When "the Light of the Great Cultural Problems Moves On": On the Possibility of a Cultural Theory of Modernity', *Thesis Eleven* 61: 25–40.

Fromm, Erich (1941), *Escape from Freedom*. New York: Holt, Rinehart and Winston.

Fukuyama, Francis (1992), *The End of History and the Last Man*. Harmondsworth: Penguin.

—— (1989), 'The End of History?', *The National Interest* 16 (Summer): 3–18.

Gellner, Ernest (1995), 'The Importance of Being Modular', in John A. Hall (ed.), *Civil Society, Theory, History, Comparison*. Cambridge: Polity Press.

—— (1992), *Postmodernism, Reason and Religion*. London and New York: Routledge.

—— (1983), *Nations and Nationalism*. Oxford: Blackwell.

—— (1964), *Thought and Change*. London: Weidenfeld and Nicolson.

Giddens, Anthony (1991), *The Consequences of Modernity*. Cambridge: Polity Press.

—— (1985), *The Nation-State and Violence*. Cambridge: Polity Press.

Gilsenan, Michael (1990), *Recognizing Islam*. London: I.B. Tauris.

Giner, Salvador (1995), 'Civil Society and its Future', in John A. Hall (ed.), *Civil Society: Theory, History and Comparison*. Cambridge: Polity Press.

Gökalp, Ziya (1959), *Turkish Nationalism and Western Civilization*. Trans. Niyazi Berkes. London: George Allen and Unwin.

Göle, Nilüfer (1996), *The Forbidden Modern: Civilization and Veiling*. Ann Arbor: University of Michigan Press.

—— (1994), 'Toward an Autonomization of Politics and Society', in Metin Heper and Ahmet Evin (eds.), *Politics in the Third Turkish Republic*. Oxford: Westview Press.

Gramsci, Antonio (1971), *Selection from the Prison Notebooks*. New York: International Publishers.

Guibernau, Montserrat, and John Rex (eds.) (1997), *The Ethnicity Reader*. Cambridge: Polity Press.

Gülalp, Haldun (1998), 'The Eurocentrism of Dependency Theory and the Question of "Authenticity": A View from Turkey', *Third World Quarterly* 19.5: 951–61.

Gunes-Ayata, Aysc (1991), 'Pluralism versus Authoritarianism: Political Ideas in Two Publications', in Richard Tapper (ed.), *Islam in Modern Turkey*. London and New York: I.B. Tauris.

Gutierrez, Natividad (1997), 'Ethnic Revivals within Nation-State?', in Hans-Rudolf Wicker (ed.), *Rethinking Nationalism and Ethnicity*. Oxford and New York: Berg.

Habermas, Jürgen (1994), 'Europe's Second Chance', in M. Pensky (ed.), *The Past as Future*. Cambridge: Polity Press.

—— (1989), *The New Conservatism*. Cambridge, MA: MIT Press.

—— (1987), *The Theory of Communicative Action*, II. Cambridge: Polity Press.

Hale, William (1994), *Turkish Politics and the Military*. London: Routledge.

Hall, John A. (1995), 'In Search of Civil Society', in John A. Hall (ed.), *Civil Society, Theory, History, Comparison*. Cambridge: Polity Press.

Hall, Stuart, and Bram Gieben (eds.) (1992), *The Formation of Modernity*. Cambridge: Polity Press.

Harvey, David (1990), *The Condition of Postmodernity*. Cambridge and Oxford: Blackwell.

Heidegger, Martin (1977), *The Question Concerning Technology and Other Essays*. New York: Harper and Row.

Heller, Agnes, and Frenc Feher (1991), *The Postmodern Political Condition*. Cambridge: Polity Press.

Heper, Metin (1994), 'Transition to Democracy in Turkey: Toward a New Pattern', in Metin Heper and Ahmet Evin (eds.), *Politics in the Third Turkish Republic*. Oxford: Westview Press.

Hobsbawm, Eric (1990), *Nations and Nationalism since 1780*. Cambridge: Cambridge University Press.

Hobsbawm, Eric, and Terence Ranger (eds.) (1992), *The Invention of Tradition*. Cambridge: Cambridge University Press.

Hodgson, Marshal G.S. (1960), 'The Unity of Later Islamic History', *Journal* of *World History* 5: 879–914.

Huntington, Samuel P. (1997), *The Clash of Civilizations and the Remaking of World Order*. London: Touchstone Books.

—— (1968), *Political Order in Changing Societies*. New Haven: Yale University Press.

Ilhan, Attila (2001), 'Vatan ve Namus', *Ileri* 1.2.

Inan, Afet (1974), *Vatandas Icin Medeni Bilgiler ve Mustafa Kemal Ataturk'un El Yazilari*. Ankara: TTKY.

Insel, Ahmet (1995), *Turkiye Toplumunun Bunalimi*. Istanbul: Birikim Yayinlari.

Karal, Enver Ziya (1997), 'The Principles of Kemalism', in Ali Kazancigil and Ergun Ozbudun (eds.), *Atatürk: Founder of a Modern State*. London: C. Hurst.

Kili, Suna (1980), 'Kemalism in Contemporary Turkey', *International Political Science Review* 1.3: 381–404.

Kislali, Ahmet Taner (1997), *Bir Turk'un Olumu*. Ankara: Umit Yayincilik.

Kolakowski, Leszek (1990), *Modernity on Endless Trial*. Chicago and London: University of Chicago Press.

Kolb, David (1986), *The Critique of Pure Modernity: Hegel, Heidegger and After*. Chicago and London: University of Chicago Press.

Kongar, Emre (2000), *Ikibinli Yillarda Turkiye*. Istanbul: Remzi Kitabevi.

—— (1985), *Toplumsal Degisme Kuramlari ve Turkiye Gercegi*. Istanbul: Remzi Kitabevi.

Koselleck, Reinhart (1985), *Futures Past*. Cambridge, MA, and London: MIT Press.

Laue, V. Theodore (1987), *The World Revolution of Westernization*. Oxford and New York: Oxford University Press.

Lawrence, Bruce B. (1995), *Defenders of God: The Fundamentalist Revolt against the Modern Age*. London: I.B. Tauris.

Lenin, V.I. (1992), *The State and Revolution*. London: Penguin.

Lewis, Bernard (1996), *The Middle East*. London: Phoenix.

—— (1988), *The Political Language of Islam*. Chicago and London: University of Chicago Press.

—— (1961), *The Emergence of Modern Turkey*. London, New York and Toronto: Oxford University Press.

Lipset, S.M. (1996), *American Exceptionalism: A Double-Edged Sword*. New York: W.W. Norton.

Lyotard, Jean-François (1984), *The Postmodern Condition: A Report on Knowledge*. Manchester: Manchester University Press.

Mahçupyan, Etyen (1997), *Osmanlidan Postmoderniteye*. Istanbul: Patika.

Mann, Michael (1993), *The Sources of Social Power*, II. Cambridge: Cambridge University Press.

—— (1986), *The Sources of Social Power*, I. Cambridge: Cambridge University Press.

Marcuse, Herbert (1964), *One-Dimensional Man*. Boston: Beacon Press.

—— (1941), *Reason and Revolution*. New Jersey: Humanities Press.

Mardin, Serif (1994), *Turk Modernlesmesi*. Istanbul: Iletisim Yayinlari.

—— (1969), 'Power, Civil Society and Culture in the Ottoman Empire', *Comparative Studies in Society and History* 11.3 (June): 258–81.

Marx, Karl (1959), 'Eighteenth Brumaire of Louis Bonaparte', in Lewis Feurer (ed.), *Marx and Engels: Basic Writings on Politics and Philosophy*. New York: Doubleday.

Mehmet, Özay (1990), *Islamic Identity and Development: Studies of the Islamic Periphery*. London and New York: Routledge.

Mestrovic, G. Stjepan (1998), *Anthony Giddens: The Last Modernist*. London and New York: Routledge.

Minault, Gail (1982), *The Khalifat Movement*. Oxford: Oxford University Press.

Mumcu, Uğur (1998), *Kürd Dosyasi*. Ankara: um: ag yayinlari.

Nasr, S. Hossein (1987), *Traditional Islam in the Modern World*. London: KPI.

Nezan, Kendal (1993), 'Kurdistan in Turkey', in Chaliand (ed.), 1993.

Nicholson, Linda J. (ed.) (1990), *Feminism/Postmodernism*. London: Routledge.

Nisbet, Robert (1969), *Social Change and History: Aspects of the Western Theory of Development*. New York: Oxford University Press.

Offe, Claus (1987), 'The Utopia of Zero-Option: Modernity and Modernization as Normative Political Criteria', *Praxis International* 7.1: 1–24.

Ozankaya, Ozer (1996), *Cumhuriyet Cinari*. Ankara: Imge.

Ozbudun, Ergun (1997), 'Social Origins of Kemalism', in Ali Kazancigil and Ergun Ozbudun (eds.), *Atatürk: Founder of a Modern State*. London: C. Hurst.

Özel, Ismet (1992), *Uc Mesele: Teknik, Medeniyet ve Yabancilasma*. Istanbul: Cidam Yayinlari.

Parsons, Talcott (1971), *The System of Modern Societies*. Englewood Cliffs, NJ: Prentice–Hall.

—— (1951), *The Social System*. London: Routledge and Kegan Paul.

Phillips, Anne (ed.) (1987), *Feminism and Equality*. Oxford: Basil Blackwell.

Poulton, Hugh (1997), *Top Hat, Grey Wolf and Crescent: Turkish Nationalism and the Turkish Republic*. London: Hurst.

Rahman, Fazlur (1982), *Islam and Modernity: Transformation of an Intellectual Tradition*. Chicago and London: University of Chicago Press.

Roxborough, Ian (1979), *Theories of Underdevelopment*. London: Macmillan.

Rustow, Dankward (1994), 'Turkish Democracy in Historical and Comparative Perspective', in Metin Heper and Ahmet Evin (eds.), *Politics in the Third Turkish Republic*. Oxford: Westview Press.

Sahinler, Menter (1991), *Atatükçülüğün Kökeni, Etkisi ve Güncelliği*. Ankara: Çağdaş Yayınları.

Said, Edward (1994), *Culture and Imperialism*. London: Vintage.

—— (1978), *Orientalism*. London: Penguin Books.

Sartori, Giovanni (1976), *Parties and Party Systems*. Cambridge: Cambridge University Press.

Sayyid, S. Boby (1997), *Eurocentrism and the Emergence of Islamism*. London and New York: Zed Books.

Sheyegan, Daryush (1991), *Yarali Bilinc*. Istanbul: Metis Yayinlari.

Shils, Edward (1981), *Tradition*. Chicago: University of Chicago Press.

Shin, Jong Hwa (2000), 'The Limit of Civil Society: A Review Essay', *European Journal of Social Theory* 3.2: 249–59.

Skocpol, Theda (1982), 'Rentier State and Shi'a Islam in the Iranian Revolution', *Theory and Society* 2.3: 266–81.

—— (1979), *States and Social Revolutions*. Cambridge: Cambridge University Press.

Smart, Barry (1990), 'Modernity, Postmodernity and the Present', in Bryan S. Turner (ed.), *Theories of Modernity and Postmodernity*. London: Sage.

Smith, Anthony (1998), *A Critical Survey of Recent Theories of Nations and Nationalism*. London and New York: Routledge.

—— (1986), *The Ethnic Origins of Nations*. Oxford: Blackwell.

—— (1971), *Theories of Nationalism*. London: Duckworth.

Stokes, Martin (1994), 'Turkish Arabesk and the City: Urban Popular Culture as Spatial Practice', in Akbar S. Ahmed and Hastings Donnan (eds.), *Islam, Globalization and Postmodernity*. London and New York: Routledge.

Tanilli, Server (1991), *Islam Cagimiza Yanit Verebilir mi?* Istanbul: Say Yayinlari.

—— (1990), *Yuzyillarin gercegi ve Mirasi*. Istanbul: Say Yayinlari.

TOBB (1995), *Doğu Sorunu: Teşhisler ve Tespitler. Özel Araştırma Raporu*. Prepared by Doğu Ergil. Ankara: TOBB.

Tocqueville, Alexis de (1956), *Democracy in America*. London and New York: New American Library and New English Library.

Touraine, Alain (1995), *Critique of Modernity*. Oxford: Blackwell.

Turkish Democracy Foundation (1996), *Fact Book on Turkey, Kurds and the PKK Terrorism*. Ankara: Turkish Democracy Foundation.

Turner, Bryan S. (1999), 'Globalization, Religion and Cosmopolitan Virtue'. Unpublished paper.

—— (1989), 'From Orientalism to Global Sociology', *Sociology* 23.3.

Turner, Charles (1992), *Modernity and Politics in the Work of Max Weber*. London and New York: Routledge.

Vattimo, Gianni (1992), *The Transparent Society*. Baltimore: Johns Hopkins University Press.

Wagner, Peter (2000), 'Modernity – One or Many?', in Judith Blaue (ed.), *The Blackwell Companion to Sociology*. Oxford: Blackwell.

—— (1999a), 'An Entirely New Object of Consciousness, of Volition, of Thought', in Lorraine Daston (ed.), *The Coming into Being and Passing Away of Scientific Objects*. Chicago: University of Chicago Press.

—— (1999b), 'The Resistance that Modernity Constantly Provokes: Europe, America and Social Theory', *Thesis Eleven* 58 (August): 35–58.

—— (1994), *A Sociology of Modernity: Liberty and Discipline*. London: Routledge.

Wallerstein, Immanuel (1987), 'World-Systems Analysis', in A. Giddens and Jonathan H. Turner (eds.), *Social Theory Today*. Cambridge: Polity Press.

—— (1979), *The Capitalist World-Economy*. Cambridge: Cambridge University Press.

Watt, M. William (1988), *Islamic Fundamentalism and Modernity*. London and New York: Routledge.

Weber, Max (1968), *Economy and Society*, II. Ed. Guenther Roth and Claus Wittich. Berkeley: University of California Press.

—— (1958), *The Protestant Ethic and the Spirit of Capitalism*. New York: Scribner.

Wellmer, Albrecht (1991), *The Persistence of Modernity: Essays on Aesthetics, Ethics and Postmodernism*. Cambridge: Polity Press.

Wicker, Hans-Rudolf (1997), 'Theorising Ethnicity and Nationalism', in Hans-Rudolf Wicker (ed.), *Rethinking Nationalism and Ethnicity*. Oxford and New York: Berg.

Winfield, R. Dien (1991), *Freedom and Modernity*. Albany, NY: State University of New York Press.

Yack, Bernard (1997), *The Fetishism of Modernities: Epochal Self-Consciousness in Contemporary Social and Political Thought*. Notre Dame, IN: University of Notre Dame Press.

Index